Managing and marketing technology

David Ford and Michael Saren

THOMSON
LEARNING

Australia • Canada • Mexico • Singapore • Spain • United Kingdom • United States

THOMSON
LEARNING

Managing and marketing technology

Copyright © 2001 David Ford and Michael Saren

The Thomson Learning logo is a registered trademark used herein under licence.

For more information, contact Thomson Learning, Berkshire House, 168–173 High Holborn, London, WC1V 7AA or visit us on the World Wide Web at: http://www.thomsonlearning.co.uk

British Library Cataloguing-in-Publication Data
A catalogue record for this book is available from the British Library

ISBN 1–86152–594–X

First edition 1996 (Technology strategy for business)
This edition 2001

Typeset by J&L Composition Ltd, Filey, North Yorkshire

Printed in Croatia by Zrinski

Contents

Figures

Tables

Preface

There has been an explosive growth in interest in technology management and technology strategy amongst managers and business schools. This is reflected in an increasing number of courses in the area at the undergraduate and postgraduate level. More recently, a number of books have emerged and increasingly the more general business journals contain articles which relate to the issue of managing technology.

Much of the existing literature looks at technological issues from a restricted perspective. Some concentrate on the issue of technological innovation. Others are concerned with technology from the perspective of public policy, or with the management of R&D. There are others which deal with product policy in companies or examine technological issues as they relate to manufacturing strategy.

This book attempts to offer a comprehensive insight into how companies can develop a strategic approach to the management of their technology. This approach can be outlined as follows below.

The book initially provides a context for the development of technology strategy. It discusses the importance of technology to corporate and national success and relates this to the problems that managers have in understanding and articulating the dynamics of technology in their own company and those around them.

The book then introduces the idea of the *technology audit*. This is used to demonstrate how managers can assess their current technological assets and the competitive position which results from these assets.

Following from the analysis of the technological position of a company the book turns to the task of how companies can and should *acquire* new technology. As well as developing technology internally through research and development, the book looks at other methods of acquisition such as by licensing-in or by joint-venture and shows when these may be appropriate.

The book then deals with the choices open to companies in *exploiting* their technology. The format of this section is similar to that of the acquisition section: different methods of exploitation are described in addition to using technology in the company's own products, such as contract manufacture for others, licensing-out, etc. The problems which may arise are discussed and the situations examined when each may be appropriate.

The book examines how companies can set up the managerial approaches necessary to develop and implement a coherent approach to the management of their technology and how this can be integrated into overall business strategy. It then illustrates this with an example of technology analysis and assessment in practice.

The book is based on a series of research studies in Europe and in the United States. The writing style has deliberately been kept simple to appeal to an audience which does not have specialist technological knowledge, whether at the MBA or possibly senior undergraduate level or as practitioners. The book is illustrated throughout with case examples from our research and consultancy. Parts of the material in the book have been successfully used on a range of post-experience teaching assignments in a number of countries and on MBA courses at the Universities of Bath in the UK and the University of Texas.

AUDIENCE

A major audience for the book is MBA students. It could form the basis for courses in technology management or more widely as a supplementary text for courses in business policy or strategy or industrial marketing. The book should also be suitable for senior undergraduate courses in technology management or as a supplementary text on integrative courses in strategy, industrial marketing, purchasing or operations management.

The style of the book and the wide use of named examples is intended to make it suitable for the practitioner market. It offers a clear guide for the *non-technical manager* to the tasks in developing and implementing a strategy for technology.

THE AUTHORS

David Ford is Professor of Marketing at the University of Bath, School of Management. He specialises in industrial marketing and is a founder-member of the Industrial Marketing and Purchasing Group (IMP). The group consists of researchers from six countries and has carried out a number of large-scale studies into industrial marketing and purchasing. The group has published over a dozen books and numerous articles in the area. Each year, the IMP Conference attracts well over 150 researchers who work within the group's interaction paradigm for the study of business relationships and networks. David Ford edited a collection of some of the group's work in *Understanding Business Markets*, second edition (Thomson Learning, 1997). He is also joint author of *Managing Business Relationships* (John Wiley, 1998).

Michael Saren is Professor of Marketing at the University of Strathclyde and began working on technology forecasting in the offshore oil and gas and energy industries. He is currently conducting a number of research projects including an EC-funded investigation into new product development processes and innovative sustainable products. His other research interests cover the areas of the strategic marketing of technology, relationship marketing and marketing theory. His work has been published in books and academic management journals in the UK, Europe and the USA, including the *International Journal of Research in Marketing, Omega, R&D Strategy, International Journal of Technology Management, British Journal of Management* and *Industrial Marketing Management*. He is a member of the editorial boards of the *European Journal of Marketing, Journal of Consumer Marketing, Business Strategy and the Environment* and co-editor of *Marketing Theory*.

Acknowledgements

Particular thanks are due to those who have supported our research over the past fifteen years: the Economic and Social Research Council, the University of Texas at Austin, the University of Bath, Base International Ltd and the numerous companies who have sponsored students or allowed us access. Thanks are also due to Richard Thomas, now of Heriot Watt University, who was our research officer over the past three years and who made a major contribution to data collection and conceptual development. Thanks also to colleagues in the IMP group and to a number of graduate students here and in the USA, Lyn Grieb, George Haley, Casper Jongerius, Richard Brewer, Keith Lake, Alan Trayes, Ron Shields, Steve Woodcock and Sarah Hampton who worked on case examples and other data collection. Thanks are also due to Chris Dudgeon and Guy Woodall of Offshore Technology Management and Nikos Tzokas at the University of Strathclyde.

D.F.
M.S.

Chapter 1

The technology problem

INTRODUCTION

'Technology' is a term which is widely and loosely used. On TV, when faced with a seemingly insurmountable problem the Bionic Man simply said, 'We have the technology!' and everyone was reassured that everything was going to be alright.

Since then any mention of 'high' technology or a 'technological breakthrough' in company meetings has been sufficient to provoke knowing and thoughtful nods among those present, but effectively to close down informed discussion. Everyone knows that technology is somehow 'a good thing' – rather like having a reputation for being warm-hearted and friendly – but most people have little idea how to develop it or how to capitalise on it when they have it. Technology is rather like a grey mist which floats behind a company's products and the processes by which they are made: they are tangible, it is not; they are easy to describe, it is not. There is a parallel between the ways in which many companies think about and discuss technological issues and how individuals talk about politics. In both cases the discussion is likely to be based more on prejudice than knowledge, with self-consciousness rather than self-confidence and in both cases the parties are likely to substitute bluff for reason. Few people in a company will be indifferent to the issue of technology but many are technologically illiterate and hence will be scared by it. Some will seek to avoid facing up either to the implications of technology or its analysis – at least until the grey mist suddenly solidifies and comes crashing around their ears in the form of a whole range of their products which are suddenly obsolete!

TECHNOLOGY AS A PROBLEM FOR COUNTRIES

Technology is a problem at the national level by virtue of its major role as a determinant of a country's economic growth and competitiveness. Economists have attempted to calculate precisely what proportion of historical economic growth has been caused by technological improvements, as opposed to the amount which is due to investment, population increase, trading patterns and other factors. Estimates vary, but there appears to be a consensus that technological change is responsible for a large percentage of economic growth. For example, one study[1] calculated its contribution for several countries as follows:

- Germany 50 per cent;
- USA   47 per cent;
- Japan   44 per cent;
- Canada   30 per cent;
- UK   25 per cent.

Technology and long-term cycles

Some economists also argue that technology affects the long-term cycles of growth and recessions in the world economy, which span fifty to sixty years. Mensch[2] found that 'clusters' of new technological applications precede, and may account for, the upswings in these cycles. As the peak of the cycle is reached and a downturn begins, the economy's physical and technological infrastructure is committed to mature technologies in which there are few opportunities for further improvements, and there is little incentive to apply new technologies at that point.

As the trough of the cycle gives way to the start of an upswing, firms must re-invest in capital equipment, which is based on new technologies. At the point where many industries and technologies are mature or declining the only way out of this technological stalemate is the application of new technologies to new products, which in turn creates new industrial sectors and markets that lead the economy out of recession. Thus, it is the new technologies that lead the new growth sectors that regenerate the economy. The role of national governments in encouraging, directing or facilitating investment in these new technologies is an important political issue.

Technology and comparative advantage

A further indication of the importance of technology at the national level is the explanation that nations will export in industries where they not only have a comparative advantage but also where their firms have a technological lead. For example, the Korean shipbuilding industry became an international leader by expanding the size of its shipyards, adopting new building techniques that increased productivity and developing the technical capacity to produce more sophisticated vessels. A combination of superior organisation, skills and technology secured their competitive leadership, not simply more abundant or cheaper resources.

The major asset of 'human capital' can compensate for a country's relative lack of material resources and energy, as the examples of Japan or Singapore illustrate. In advanced industries it is not necessarily the lowest cost producers which are the most competitive. Product development, quality and features are increasingly the key success factors in many markets. Even where price is still the key, low cost can be created by the application of computer-aided design and manufacturing as well as flexible manufacturing systems, thereby offsetting the competitive advantages of large-scale operations.

> The ability of a workforce to make the best of new technologies may be a country's best competitive advantage. Wealth in raw materials . . . barely matters – anyone can buy them. Proximity to rich markets matters less as transport costs fall relative to the value of goods . . . Only that intangible, vital quality, the environment of active brains and productive skills in which companies operate, is non-transferable.[3]

The home base

It is through the activities of individual companies that a nation's technological resources are transformed into commercial products, processes and services. From the company's viewpoint countries provide its supply of human capital and core technologies as well as its markets. Here, the concept of a firm's home base is relevant. 'The home base is the nation in which the essential competitive advantages of the enterprise are created and sustained.'[4]

Despite the advent of multinational and global enterprises, a firm will still retain a base in an area (which has often developed historically within a particular country) that provides its core process and product technologies. Other activities like manufacturing, assembly and supplies can be located elsewhere, perhaps nearer to markets, but the key assets of the home base are the availability at that location of its advanced skills and core technologies. Questions of how the home bases of significant companies may be retained and developed can only be fully addressed at the national as well as the company level.

Purchase and sale of technology and national competitiveness

Japanese market competitiveness was initially based on the adoption of foreign technologies, largely directed by the Ministry of International Trade (MITI). But to develop the technological lead on which long-term market advantage can be based Japanese firms, again with government intervention, developed their own, home-grown technology by investing more in research and development than their US rivals. Today Japan exports as much technology as it imports. Measured by the value of licence fees and royalties this ratio of technology exports to imports has risen from 39.4 per cent in 1975 to 99.8 per cent in 1989. A further indication of Japanese success in making the transition from purchased to its own technology is that in 1992 Japanese firms were granted more patents in America than German, French and British firms *together*.[5]

TECHNOLOGY AS A PROBLEM FOR MANAGERS

For managers, the technology problem is not restricted to the tasks of achieving productive research, developing good new products and modernising production methods. The manager's strategic technology problem is how the company can harness the technologies it has developed, together with those of its suppliers and others, and apply these to the strategic direction of the company. At a time when the cost of developing each new generation of technology is escalating, the company must strive to maximise its return on the technological investment it has made. Simultaneously, the company must direct its efforts to acquire for itself, or in alliance with others, those new technologies which are needed to maintain and enhance its competitive abilities.

It is easy to understand why some managers find it difficult to relate technological change to their ideas about developing strategy. Strategy formation is so often based on the supposed predictability of a company's markets and a set of carefully defined ambitions. Developments in technology do not fit comfortably within such a framework. Technological change is unpredictable. It can arrive with stunning speed and from areas far outside the manager's or the company's experience. Also, technology is often described and analysed from a purely technical viewpoint, which only specialists have the knowledge and language to understand. In many cases technology is seen as something which exists in laboratories and is the responsibility of research and development (R&D) specialists. The potential and implications of any change for managers and their companies is less easily described, understood or acted upon. Furthermore, for a company to make a technological leap into the future demands imagination, faith and levels of investment that are likely to defy the incremental logic of strategic management.

Nevertheless, it is widely accepted that technological change and its successful harmonisation with business capability and social acceptability is the key to the future competitiveness and growth of companies, industries and nations. All of the technological 'problems' we may isolate offer tremendous opportunities. Many senior managers do appreciate the role of technology in strategic management. Even in industries such as banking which spends $26 billion a year on technology in the USA alone it is recognised that: 'Technology now drives both improvements in customer service and new products.'[6] Firms' technology should not only be incorporated within their strategy, it should be a major element of their corporate vision. The development of that technological vision is the subject of this book.

We now turn to some of the problems in developing this technological vision in more detail.

The problem of a lack of innovation

We are frequently told that the rate of change of technology is increasing, but some industries may face a problem of a *lack* of innovation. A current problem is that several major industries, such as steel, fibres and petrochemicals have reached a point of market and technological maturity. Others which have enjoyed high growth in the past, such as consumer electronics, white goods, automobiles, now have low rates of market expansion or only replacement demand. This situation encourages firms to restrict innovation to incremental improvements in the same core technologies. Companies are unlikely to be able to justify or afford major developments unless they can see an opportunity for an application change such as a new market segment, another industry or another country. Alternatively, a technological advance outside their industry which they believe can be applied in it without high development costs can trigger investment and growth. The problems that managers face are being able to scan the technological environment widely enough to spot technological opportunities, being able to visualise the application of these technologies by their company and having the organisational skills to bring them to fruition.

A marketing solution to the problem of a lack of market and technical innovation would prescribe the development of new markets – such as in less developed countries – to regenerate growth. However there is another longer-term, 'technological' solution which managers must face. This solution looks to the creation of whole new industries, based on new technologies such as biotechnology or new energy sources which open up new investment opportunities and demand, thus generating a resurgence of economic growth.

Choice of types of technological development

Because technological applications in the economy tend to occur in 'clusters' at certain points in time, another problem for managers is that the type of technological development which is appropriate will vary at different stages of the economic cycle. The manager is faced with choices of investing in product or process technology and whether the technological change should be incremental or radical. The best methods of acquiring new technology and the opportunities for exploiting it will also vary at different stages in the economic cycle. This means that managers must develop a company strategy for technology that not only relates to the company's overall capabilities and intentions but fits with the timing of long-run economic fluctuations.

The problem of meta-technologies

Meta-technologies are those which have the capacity to radically transform many industrial sectors of the global economy. They provide managers with problems (and opportunities) as their potential application spreads through different industries and countries. These technologies can change companies' core products, production and business methods, bases of competition and patterns of supply and distribution. New firms and industries are created as mature ones are destroyed. Examples of meta-technologies and their potentially far-reaching effects include:

1 New biotechnologies, emanating from developments in microbiology, biochemistry and genetic engineering which will revolutionise the agriculture, chemicals, health and food industries.

2 Continued evolution and convergence involving electronics, telecommunications and information technologies, which will spread automation and new means of communication throughout the production and service sectors.

3 New energy sources and the technologies for their production and transmission which will affect the use of energy and its economics.

4 New synthetic materials which will be substituted for traditional natural materials in more applications as scarcity increases.

One problem for individual companies is how to assess the immediate impact of these meta-technologies on their operations as well as their long-term strategic implications. Despite the predictions of their widespread effects, the process and timing of the diffusion of meta-technologies within and across industrial sectors are by no means clear, except perhaps with hindsight. But these technologies are very likely to be applied in industries outside those in which they were developed. By the time this occurs, the techniques and methods which are involved in them largely will be complete, and so the problem for most firms in applying these technologies will be one of selection, not invention.

The problem of interdependence

The increased reliance on the application of new technology by business has produced several different forms of interdependence for companies. Examples include interdependence between:

1 Industry and scientific research establishments, such as universities, government research facilities and independent R&D laboratories. Companies rely more on external research specialists for the development of their core technologies of the future.

2 Production, service and support activities. The application of a new technology in one of these requires changes in the operations of others.

3 Products and processes. The focus of technological advance may shift periodically and interconnectedly between one and the other.[7]

4 Firms which supply products based on new technologies and the firms that use these products. These users are likely to be dependent on the suppliers for improvements in their technology base. The suppliers also depend on the users to define the type of developments for which they will be the market.

5 Firms jointly producing or financing technological developments through joint development, collaborative R&D, and co-operative technology agreements.

6 Different functions within the firm. It has been found that firms which are successful in realising the full returns from their technologies are able to match their technological developments with complimentary expertise in other areas of their business, such as manufacturing, distribution, human resources and marketing.[8]

7 Industries that use similar technologies so that they begin to overlap or converge. This interdependence can be seen in the computer industry, where boundaries now overlap those of the telecommunications, office equipment, entertainment and consumer electronics industries. This type of interdependence is illustrated in Figure 1.1. Technological interdependence between previously separate industries produces new competitors for the

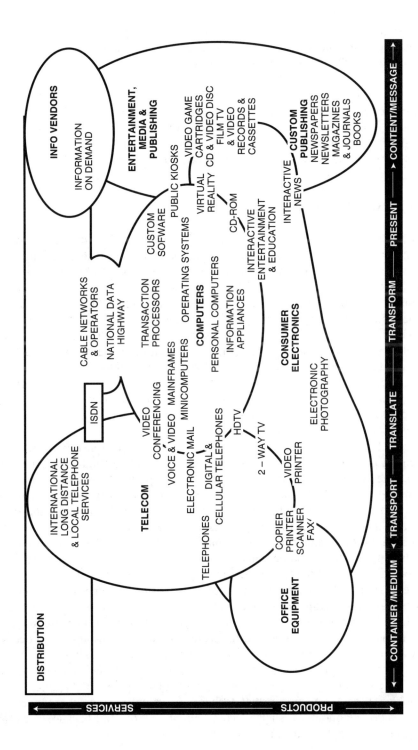

Figure 1.1 Overlapping and merging technologies
Source: The Economist, 27 February 1993.

firm from other industries – and new alliances and acquisitions. For example, the interdependence between the consumer electronics hardware and software industries led to the acquisition of Columbia Pictures by Sony.

These interdependencies in using technology add to the complexity of analysis and management. The practical reality is that one firm alone may be unable to retain total control of all the technologies that it uses.[9] Managers may find that control of technology must be shared in order to retain it: 'No company can survive as a technological island . . . Today the watchword is not "divide and conquer" but "co-operate to compete."'[10]

The problem of the speed of change

There is some evidence that technological change is increasingly discontinuous and that product and technology life cycles are shortening. In several industries, ranging from aerospace and microcomputers to cement, it has been found that technology develops through periods of continuous, incremental change interspersed by shorter periods of radical discontinuities. These changes can be 'competence-enhancing', which benefit existing firms, or 'competence-destroying', which undermine them.[11] For example, many of the developments in personal computer software have been incremental improvements of a fairly predictable type, such as the sequence of upgrades to a particular software package. These tend mainly to be carried out by and to benefit existing firms in the industry. But there have also been radical developments – so radical that they have created new software categories. These usually have more specialised applications and displace some uses of the existing general-purpose products, thus spawning new market segments in which smaller, younger firms are often the market leaders.[12]

Having acquired a technology-based lead in a market or segment, it also is possible for these firms to cement their leading position. Because their market advantage is technology based it means that they do not necessarily lose their market supremacy once the technology becomes more widely available to competitors. The rise of the microprocessor market illustrates this possibility. Of the leading semiconductor integrated circuit producers in the 1960s only one – Motorola – had much success with the microprocessor. Intel, which was only established in 1968 and had a very small market before they introduced the microprocessor, became leader in the new market segment. By the mid-1970s most major semiconductor companies had attempted to enter the microprocessor market, but most were unsuccessful. Intel maintained and extended its initial lead with a sequence of new product introductions, whereas most competitors 'overshot' with their early products and had to spend development time and money extending their range to fill gaps in their product line. The upshot was that whereas a large number of firms entered the initial 8-bit microprocessor market, many fewer entered the 16-bit market and even still less the 32-bit race.[13]

Once a company gets ahead of its competitors in price and quality based on technological leadership, it can get even further ahead by sound strategic development and application of their core technology base. This means that technology is unlike the other factors of production so beloved of economists, such as land, labour and capital, because it can be made subject to increasing, not diminishing returns.

The problem of the time to market

In the past it typically took many years for a basic technical invention to be commercially applied. More recently, however, the competitive pressure to minimise 'time to market' combined with such facilitators as 'simultaneous' engineering and design techniques has significantly reduced both development and commercialisation times. This reduction in development times seems to be accelerating. An example of this occurred in AEP.

In 1989 a UK automotive components company AEP took an average of twenty-six weeks from a customer's first enquiry to develop, make, test and deliver a new design of automotive engine piston. Within two years they had reduced this response time to twelve weeks. By the end of 1993 they aimed to half this again to six weeks. 'The main driver of our success has been technology', according to Managing Director, Alistair McWilliam. The most significant factor in reducing time-to-market has been RAPIER (Rapid Analysis of Products by Integrated Engineering Routines), their new computer-based design and analysis process, which among other things, allows engineers to predict problems in both manufacture and product performance before they occur. Because the big car manufacturers are all subcontracting more piston design and manufacture as they rush to shorten their own time-to-market, AEP's speed of response has given them a competitive advantage over other suppliers. Opel has recently awarded them a single source supplier agreement for their Astra and Vectra engine pistons, cutting off Opel's previous German supplier.[14]

In order that firms may cope with the fast speed of response to increasingly complex and potentially far-reaching developments in technology, firms' technology strategies must be flexible and firms must be quick to react.

The problem of consumer expectations

Consumer and industrial users' expectations of the performance of products, processes and services have placed more demands on managers. Customers increasingly require and stipulate greater reliability, 'total-quality' and even 'zero-defects' from their purchases. In more and more markets competition is based on high technical performance rather than price. While technology does of course contribute to the achievement of these customer expectations, it also means that the performance criteria for new technical developments are becoming more rigorous. Technology standards, testing and operating performance are more exacting and expensive to conduct. This produces another problem for managers who have to ensure that their technologies can meet these stricter requirements of customers.

The dominant design problem

Technical developments are cumulative and self-generating, following particular paths with their own momentum. Once a solution to a technological problem emerges the possible routes of future developments are limited by the nature of the new technology. For example, the development of the internal combustion engine excluded other notionally possible alternatives. Furthermore, once a particular design becomes dominant it then defines how progress within it is to be measured in technical terms. This can be seen in two examples. For illumination technology progress is defined by 'lighting efficiency', so developments have been aimed at improving this and the results are measured in terms of lumens per watt. In data processing, once the technology of optical character recognition (OCR) had been developed, R&D in this field was aimed at improving the 'reading rate', measured by characters per second.

The dominant design is eventually incorporated in the accepted technical standard which is adopted by firms – either by choice, competitive pressure or legislation. This means that those managers involved with new technologies may often have to fight major battles if they are to achieve the wider market which may come with standardisation. This may involve using a variety of means of exploiting their technology including licensing and joint ventures with potential competitors.

The computer and consumer electronics industries have been riven with battles over standards as they have developed. Microsoft's operating software for personal computers (PCs), MS-DOS, quickly became the standard operating system for the industry after they licensed it to IBM on a non-exclusive basis in the 1980s. To date Microsoft have sold over 100 million copies, making it the best-selling software of all time and taking the company's capital value close to that of IBM itself. This was a particularly impressive performance in exploiting a technology that Microsoft bought the rights to for only $100,000. By encour-aging other software companies to develop applications programs for use with their system – together with the success of IBM's machines – Microsoft's MS-DOS rapidly became the dominant system. Together with its more user-friendly, pictorial successor, Windows, Microsoft now have nearly 90 per cent of the world market for PC operating software. In contrast, Apple's refusal to license the operating system for the Macintosh gave them an exclusive in the user-friendliness of their system. However, this also brought a considerable disadvantage because software writers have been unwilling to develop new applications for a system with such a restricted hardware base.[15] Rivals have been heard to suggest that the MS-DOS acronym should stand for 'Microsoft Seeks Domination Over Society'!

The problem of technology standards

A technology will eventually reach its limits with respect to accepted measures of progress. This is called the 'technological threshold' and can be defined as the highest level that can be reached in terms of the relevant technical dimensions by which progress is measured. When the technological threshold is being approached and progress within it has ceased to advance, there is a strong incentive for new technologies to be developed and applied to provide new and better 'solutions' – unless there is no need for it to advance further along that dimension. This is one way in which mature technologies are superseded by new ones. For example, in metrology the threshold of existing mechanical measurement technology is now being reached. The speed and efficiency of mechanical measurement has ceased to advance and now managers must explore new technological possibilities such as elec-tronics, ultrasonics, optics and laser technologies.

The widespread acceptance of a technical standard can present a problem to a company.

Once entrenched, standards can constitute a barrier to anything but incremental and compatible improvements. In personal computers and video recorders where standard formats have wiped out the alternatives which existed earlier, millions of consumers are committed to the dominant design technologies. It will be a difficult task to persuade them to abandon their products, together with the videos and software, even for a technically much better system – be it CDs, videos or disks. Mass consumer commitment to a technology builds-in future resistance to change. This is precisely why the now technically obsolete QWERTY keyboard has lasted so long.

But standards can also drive technological change. Ford, Chrysler and GM are all conducting research on the electric car of the future. The combustion-engined vehicle is judged to have reached its technological threshold and new environmental concerns have stimulated the search for a 'clean' technology alternative. Even once the existing problems such as battery weight are overcome, there are likely to still be problems of consumer acceptance. The key factor which justifies this development in the eyes of the motor companies is the looming imposition of technical standards by governments. As so often, California is leading the way: 'Were it not for legislation requiring that by, 2003, 10% of the cars sold in California produce zero emissions, there would be much less interest in electric cars.'[16]

Problems with the direction of technology

Another way in which the search for new technologies can be stimulated is through the emergence of a new problem which existing technologies cannot solve – even if they have not reached their 'normal' thresholds. We do not intend to attempt to explain here all of the causes of technological change, but it is important to recognise that the problems to which technological solutions are addressed are *not* supplied only by market demand. Market signals are an unsatisfactory explanation of technological progress because they imply a passive and mechanical reactiveness of technological change to market demand. The range of potential market 'needs' is in reality so large that it is effectively infinite. Market signals alone cannot explain why and when some developments occur rather than others. The market-needs explanation also neglects changes in technological capabilities which do not have any direct relationship with changes in the market.

Therefore, it is not enough for managers to identify customers' latent needs (even if they could) and then search for technologies to meet them. The problems to be solved (and thus the performance requirements of the technologies) may be generated by forces other than market needs, such as political, environmental and macro-economic pressures. For example, the development of American space technology in the 1960s through the agency of NASA was primarily motivated by political pressure from the Kennedy administration with the national objective for the USA of getting a man on the moon first. This programme led to far-reaching changes in technology in a number of areas, even extending as far as the introduction of heat-resistant Teflon coatings to pots and pans. Ecological considerations have exerted powerful pressure for developments in anti-pollution, recycling, nuclear and agribusiness technologies. Macro-economic conditions and consequent price/cost changes largely account for the drive to develop new sources of energy since the multiple escalation in the real price of oil in 1973 and 1979. Technological advances in wave power and wind power were stimulated by changes in the relative full-costs of other fuels. Indeed, the problems which lead to technological change can be caused by an existing technology, for example the air pollution problems generated by the internal combustion engine.

The possible paths of development of a technological capability are thus set by the direction, measures and standards which are inherent in the particular technology solution which is chosen – or found. Market signals or other needs can only affect the area of application and development within the limits set by the technology itself. Companies are thus limited and constrained in many ways in their future technological options by the technology solutions which they select, or have to adopt today. The processes by which managers can understand, interpret and manage these wide and major technological issues are encompassed within this book.

The problem of the social and environmental effects of technology

Since the first industrial revolution technology has been generally regarded by firms, consumers and governments as beneficial, progressive and something to be encouraged. However, in the last twenty years this attitude has changed. There is a new social awareness of the negative side-effects of technology and, consequently, more regulations are introduced to protect people's health, safety and the environment. Such regulation affects some industries more than others. Food-processing, pharmaceuticals, mining and automobiles are examples where the application of technology is strictly controlled.

Any company using new technologies must consider these wider social and political concerns, even if they are not explicitly covered by legislation. Accidents or disasters that are now heavily publicised and are attributed to a new technology, such as 'fly-by-wire' systems or automated oil recovery, can be enormously expensive and damaging to a company's reputation. Less obviously perhaps, companies are seen to be responsible for the effects of their application of technology on people and the environment. Today technology is a major element in firms' business ethics. Corporate responsibility must also be taken into account in firms' management of their technologies.

CONCLUSIONS

Technology presents a simultaneous problem and opportunity both for companies and countries. Our concern in this book is largely with the problems facing managers. However, it is important to emphasise that an understanding of the specific technological problems that a manager might face and the overall technological directions within which he or she works can only be achieved by understanding the wider social and political surroundings of his or her decisions.

For the manager, unanticipated technological change represents threats on a number of levels. At one level, technological change in a competitor can render a current product obsolescent. The impact of a new process technology can make a whole product range uncompetitive either because of the lower costs, enhanced performance or greater reliability which it allows. More profoundly, the impact of meta-technologies can render whole companies or even industries unviable. In contrast, the possession of technological 'assets' can lead to rewards through their exploitation in a company's traditional operations or more widely. Similarly, the strategic direction of a variety of methods of acquiring technology, whether through internal or external R&D, or licence or joint venture can provide the basis for strategic advancement. But, these processes of acquisition and exploitation will only be effective if the company has sound procedures for effectively assimilating and using the technologies it has acquired.

Finally, the scale, complexity and importance of technology problems and opportunities means that companies must take an approach to their technology which is comprehensive, integrated and strategic, rather than the more conventional idea of managing individual tasks of research, new-product development, process engineering, product marketing and licensing. This strategic approach to the acquisition, management and exploitation of technology is the subject of this book.

Example
Making technology a strategic issue

For many firms technology is a background issue which is confined to the R&D laboratories and the technical specialists who staff them. This example illustrates how a recognition of the close links between the management of technology and overall commercial success means bringing about change in planning, operations and organisational structure.

The example concerns the agricultural products division of a major multinational group. The division has two main activities: it sells animal feedstuffs to farmers; and it buys and sells-on cereal produce (which other divisions use in food production). The agriculture division is divided into around thirty profit centres serving local markets, each generally centred on a feed production or cereal processing plant. Many of these local operations were previously independent companies.

The farming industry (and hence its suppliers) has long been contracting, with subsidies and production levels under growing pressure from government and the international free trade lobby. For the division, the answer to this problem has been product differentiation and strong branding. They aim to supply the farmer's every need, putting together unique solutions for each

customer, such as 'customised' feed compounds. At the same time, costs need to be rigorously controlled to maintain margins. Therefore they need to maintain development of new feed crops, new feed additives and new processing methods. Technology is clearly important and in the late 1980s this was recognised and a number of actions taken.

The company was restructured. The central nutrition department which had been dedicated to feeds development was reorganised as 'Research and Technology' (R&T), with additional responsibilities for development, 'in any area that can bring us a competitive advantage', including production and information technology (IT). The company's nutritionists are now Development Managers, with combined responsibilities. For example, a manager may oversee both pig feed products and certain sources of generic feed ingredients. For the first time a Research and Technology Director was brought on to the division board. His remit is a broad one and including the following aims:

- to support local product management personnel;
- to identify external technical issues which may be of future value to the firm;
- to lead the development of new products, processes and basic techniques (using

company staff and through co-operation with universities and research consortia); and

- to identify, maintain and develop 'core competences'.

In order to reinforce technology–product–market links, R&T also took on a co-ordination role, gathering and forwarding technical information from and to functional departments and local businesses with the aim of ensuring that best practice is applied wherever appropriate.

Planning for technology became part of the strategy development process. Annual planning cycles now include explicit discussion of technological objectives, priorities and specific projects. 'Bottom-up' input is expected from all regions and managerial functions. The company strategic plan, redefined annually, formalises agreed conclusions.

Widening involvement in technology has been pursued through the development of 'R&T circles', formally bringing together internal developers, users and 'customers' of technologies. The results have been substantial. For example, administrative staff suggested improvements in computerised accounting systems which have been successfully implemented. More importantly, feedstuff formulation improvements are initiated more quickly as customer feedback is communicated, analysed and acted upon more efficiently.

The division has ensured that technology, like the market, is something that affects, and is dependent on, the whole company, not simply a specialist function.

REFERENCES

1   Freeman, C. (1981) 'Innovation as an engine of growth', paper presented at conference on Emerging Technology: Consequences for Economic Growth, Structural Change and Employment in Advanced Open Economies, University of Kiel, 24–26 June.
2   Mensch, G. (1979) *The Technological Stalemate*, Boston: Harvard University Press.
3   *The Economist*, 11 January 1992.
4   Porter, M. (1990) *The Competitive Advantage of Nations*, London: Macmillan, p. 19.
5   *The Economist*, 22 May 1993.
6   *The Economist*, 12 September 1992.
7   Abernathy, W. J. (1978) *The Productivity Dilemma: Roadblock to Innovation in the Automobile Industry*, Baltimore: Johns Hopkins Press.
8   Teece, D. J. (1986) 'Profiting from technical innovation: implications for integration, collaboration, licensing and public money' *Research Policy*, **15**: 285–305.
9   Pfeffer, J. and Salancik, G. R. (1978) *The External Control of Organisations: a Resource Dependence Perspective*, New York: Harper & Row.
10   Pierrino, C. A. and Tipping, J. W. (1989) 'Global management of technology', *Research and Technology Management*, May–June: 1–19.
11   Tushman, M. L. and Anderson, P. (1986) 'Technological discontinuities and organisational environments', *Administrative Science Quarterly*, **31**: 439–65.
12   Swann, G. M. P. (1990) 'The speed of technology change and the development of market structure, discussion paper, Brunel University.
13   Swann, G. M. P. and Shurmer, J. (1991) 'A simulation model of de facto in the PC spreadsheet software market', discussion paper, Brunel University.
14   *Financial Times*, 7 April 1993.
15   *The Economist*, 22 May 1993.
16   *The Economist*, 26 December 1992.

Chapter 2

What do companies do about technology?

INTRODUCTION

The aim of this chapter is to establish a starting-point for the development of technology strategy by seeing how companies currently deal with the technology issues they face. We first establish from where different types of firms are likely to obtain the technologies they need, whether from their own development, from suppliers of products or equipment or whether developing new processes are important to them. We then look at how companies organise themselves for the task of developing new technologies and this leads to a view of the ways in which they think about technology itself. Following this we look at some particular issues in technology management which companies face, such as licensing, joint ventures and other forms of co-operation, and questions of 'make-or-buy'. This in turn leads to an overview of the different approaches that companies take and to a categorisation of firms in terms of their overall organisation and sophistication in technology strategy.

WHERE COMPANIES OBTAIN THEIR TECHNOLOGIES

Different types of firms are likely to acquire the technologies they need for their operations through different mechanisms and from different sources.[1] These types of firms can be categorised as follows:

1 *Supplier-dominated firms*. These are found mainly in agriculture, housebuilding, profes- sional, financial and commercial services and in the traditional sectors of manufacturing. They tend to be small in size with little in-house R&D or engineering capability of their own. This category of firm has no product or process technology strengths of its own, and

so compete by buying technologies into the firm embodied in the form of products and matching these to customer needs.

2 *Scale-intensive firms*. These are found where manufacturing is highly mechanised, such as in large scale fabrication, assembly and processing. One important source of improved process technology for these firms is their own production engineering departments, through their activities aimed at improving productivity. Process technology is critical for these large-scale firms.

3 *Science-based firms*. These are found principally in the chemicals, electronics, electrical, telecommunications, computing, medical and biochemicals sectors. Their main source of technology for both new processes and products is their own R&D which is closely based on the development of the underlying sciences in universities and elsewhere. Most of these firms are large and would include companies such as IBM, ICI, Kodak, 3M and Glaxo. Firms in this category are mainly self-generating suppliers of new technology to other sectors.

4 *Specialised equipment suppliers*. Another important source of technology for scale-intensive and science-based firms is the relatively small and specialised firms that supply them with equipment and instrumentation. However, the technology transfer here is two-way. Large-scale and science-based companies provide these suppliers with operational experience, testing facilities and even design and development capabilities for new equipment and techniques. The equipment buyers in turn receive from the suppliers not only the technology which is embodied in the equipment purchased, but also technological know-how and the experience for improving production processes.

An individual firm can belong to two or even three of these categories, so that for example it can be both science based and scale intensive. The categorisation illustrates that technology links different types of firms rather than flows between firms in the same industry sectors. This means that it is important to understand the pattern of technological linkages which exist between firms independently from the industry in which they operate. Figure 2.1 shows this pattern of technology flows between types of firms. Supplier-dominated firms get most of their technology from production-intensive and science-based firms and there is another transfer of technology from science-based to scale-intensive firms. As we have seen there is also a two-way flow between these last two groups and their specialised suppliers of equipment.

ORGANISING FOR TECHNOLOGY DEVELOPMENT

For all but those supplier dominated companies that we have described above, the internal development of technology is likely to be central to corporate success. The organisation of this development activity and how it fits into the strategic direction of the company is thus a major element in technology strategy. For our initial discussion of the issues in organising the development of new technologies we will use General Motors (GM) as an example.[2]

When discussing how he managed technology, Dr Robert A. Frosch who was in charge of the GM Research Laboratories said that his laboratories occasionally had 'a terrible outbreak of systematic planning. In contrast, Donald Runkle, Vice-President of GM's

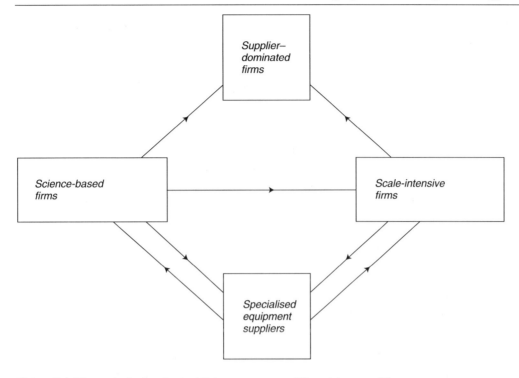

Figure 2.1 The main technological linkages among different types of firms
Source: Pavitt, K. (1994) 'Sectoral patterns of technical change: towards a taxonomy and a theory', *Research Policy*, **13.**

Advanced Engineering Staff suggested that 'planning for technology' took up a great deal of his time. These two divergent views are to an extent predictable because the management of technology involves a wide variety of different tasks, requiring different approaches. Again according to Frosch:

> The manufacturing engineer's approach to a process that makes thousands of identical components at high speed must be very systematic. It requires great planning and detailed record keeping. On the other hand, research cannot be dealt with systematically. That is not the way that people are stimulated to come up with innovative ideas.[2]

The two views also illustrate a central dilemma for companies when developing new technology. This dilemma concerns the balance which must be struck at the strategic level between control, direction and systemisation on the one hand and initiative and desystemisation on the other. Crudely stated, technology push (or R&D initiative) can take a company in wider directions than those it would choose, which may lead to, for example, product technologies which do not match its process skills or its abilities to reach the appropriate markets. In contrast, decisions based on narrowly defined market needs can fail to take account of the possible impact on products of developers' wider thinking or the actual impact on market requirements of customers' realisation of what *can* be done, let alone competitors actions.

The traditional approach to managing development

We can again use examples to contrast different approaches to decision-making in this area. General Motors illustrates a more traditional approach to managing development, where the specific task is to achieve lower production costs.

The first stage for the company involves analysis of both existing product and process technologies, and from this the overall technology strategies to achieve lower production costs are determined. The planners decide on which initiatives are likely to achieve these strategies and then a four-phase product development process comes into play:

- *Phase 1*   Technology and Concept Development;
- *Phase 2*   Product/Process Development
            Prototype Validation;
- *Phase 3*   Process Validation
            Product Confirmation;
- *Phase 4*   Production and Continuous Improvement.

Runkle's Advanced Engineering staff become involved during the first half of Phase 1, Concept Development, while the research function sees the completion of its work by about half-way through Phase 1. According to Frosch: 'I ought to be about done there – the concept is proven, shaken out, and selected'.

The main problems the company faces are at the hand-over points, such as those when Research hands over to Advanced Engineering, or when Advanced Engineering hands over to other areas for Phases 2, 3 and 4. According to Runkle: 'The corporation desperately wants to move toward more strategic co-ordination so that everyone is much more involved . . . It takes a long time right now to get a conversation communicated through the organisation.'

A Japanese approach to managing development

This sequential way of introducing new technology and its associated problems is not unique to General Motors. It has been characterised by the Japanese authors Takeuchi and Nonaka as the 'relay race' approach[3], and is exemplified by the National Aeronautics and Space Administration's phased programme planning (PPP) in which a new product is passed between functional specialists rather like the baton in a relay race. The authors contrast this approach with the 'Rugby' approach, in which the product development emerges from the constant interaction of a hand-picked, multidisciplinary team whose members work together from start to finish.

The rugby approach involves varying degrees of overlap between the notional stages in a project. Thus a group of engineers may start to design the product before all the results of the feasibility tests are in, or the group may be forced to reconsider a decision as a result of later information. The process is determined through the interplay between the participants rather than because of any predetermined procedure. The authors report that they have observed different degrees of overlap in different companies. For example, Fuji-Xerox inherited the PPP system from its parent company but redefined and aggregated the process to reduce the number of stages. They also introduced a measure of overlap called the 'sashimi' system, which refers to a Japanese dish where slices of raw fish are arranged on the plate with the slices overlapping.

The sashimi system rests on extensive interaction between all those involved in the development, including the company's suppliers who were invited to join the Fuji-Xerox project from its beginning. The authors observed greater degrees of overlap in Honda and Canon and a case study of this approach to development is given in the example.

Example
Interactive new technology development at Canon

This example illustrates a radically different approach to developing new technology and new products. In particular, it emphasises the productive use of chaos in creativity.

Until Canon launched its NP1100 in 1970, Fuji-Xerox were the only manufacturers of plain-paper copiers (PPC) in Japan. At that time cameras were the main business of Canon and the copier business received little attention. Despite this there was support from Canon's management for further development of PPCs. This development occurred at a time when demand for PPCs was levelling off and further decline was expected. It took the form of an attempt to develop a product to meet an apparently unmet need for personal copiers. Such a product would require a major change in technology as it would be completely unprofitable if the company continued to think in terms of cost per sheet or frequency of servicing per month. This was because, in some cases, the number of copies might only be several dozen per month.

The radical approach to this new market was undertaken by a task-force and this group was the second largest horizontal group ever established by the company. From the start the group included Quality Assessment and Cost Assessment Groups. The first group decided that the copier should aim for the level of repair frequency of home TV sets and the second worked on cost and quality allocation for achieving a predetermined sales price. The development-related groups and the team of production-engineering related groups met weekly to decide all issues. This approach did not lead to a smooth development path: 'It was more like a chaotic battle than the orderly script of a well-rehearsed play.'

The group was faced with determining what were the main concepts for the product and what were the technologies that would realise them. The product concept centred first on the elimination of servicing. This was seen as essential for a product which was to be sold throughout the country. A national service function would be too expensive. This was because many of the copiers would only be lightly used so that service costs would only be spread over a few copies. The associated requirement for high reliability would also be difficult to achieve as the product was aimed at a wide market and therefore low price was important.

The group found that 90 per cent of copier

problems concern the drum and copier companies usually strive to prolong the life of drums and cleaners. This route would not have been possible within the cost and price parameters with which the group were working. They came up with the radical solution of making the key module of the entire drum disposable, so that it would be discarded after a fixed number of 2,000 copies had been produced. Once the cartridge concept had been accepted the group then faced the problem of making the cartridge at a profitable price. This too was achieved through a process of intense interaction and was commented on by the now deputy director of the Reprographics Development Centre as follows:

In any company good products are created when production engineering and design become fused for their development . . . By becoming one with Production Engineering, one can propose uniform parts design, or assembly in one direction, how something should be assembled and in what sequence, or that one should do this or that if possible, when attempting to automate production for example. If we (in product design) are by ourselves, it is easy to prepare drawings and do what we like without thinking that far ahead. So, our discussions with Production Engineering people and working to accommodate their various requests in our own ways, I believe resulted in both tangible and intangible cost reductions.

The new technologies required for the cartridge can be divided into four main areas. First, improvements were made in chemicals. Different chemicals were required for the drum coating as this disposable product had to be non-polluting. Also, to develop new markets for the copier new colouring technologies were developed. Second, new technologies for cleaning apparatuses and chargers made possible development of a cartridge that facilitated miniaturisation, weight reduction, no maintenance, high quality and high reliability. Third, new design technologies were developed that allowed automated and adjustmentless assembly. Finally, the production technology improved. The cartridge required mass production and the actual rocess was designed in co-operation with parts and materials suppliers.

(Developed from Nonaka, I. and Yamanouchi, T. (1989) 'Managing innovation as a self-renewing process', *Journal of Business Venturing*, **4**, pp. 299–315.)

The Fuji-Xerox and Canon examples indicate clear differences in approach to the strategic management of technology in the case of new technology development. We will see similar diversity when we examine other aspects of current practice. The differences in approach are due to the inherent difficulty in understanding the process of technological change, the complexity of the technologies themselves and the diversity of the problems which companies must simultaneously address. At the root of these difficulties is the way in which managers think about technology and the ways in which they approach technology-related decision-making, to which we now turn.

HOW MANAGERS THINK ABOUT TECHNOLOGY

There has much research which has tried to analyse how companies cope with the problems of technological change or innovation in general, or which has tried to examine how new technologies are conceived and introduced, how they compete with older technologies and how they percolate through different industries and applications. Our interviews with managers show that they have a view of technology which does not always coincide with the way in which they are portrayed in this research.[4] A reason for this difference is that many researchers and writers have tried to isolate technology from its context in companies so that they can carefully dissect it. In contrast, managers spend their time in a world populated by a mess of products, processes, markets and people. Every product is based on a number of technologies, some new, some old, some acquired externally and some developed by the company itself. Each product is produced by processes which, to a greater or lesser extent, have been developed inside the firm. This production in turn depends on equipment which may be more or less well understood by the people responsible for it. Therefore, it is not surprising that managers do not have a neat approach to technology, which is capable of convenient diagnosis and prescription.

Managers' views of technology

The managers we talk to seem to have at least a twofold view of technology. First, they see that their company utilises a set or bundle of multiple technologies. This means that competitive activity for them is as much about building an appropriate bundle of technologies as it is about the intrinsic level or newness of any single technology, or indeed from where it came. Second, the way they think about the technologies they use is not in some abstract form. Instead they naturally relate the technologies to the applications for which they are used.

This twofold view leads to other factors which condition their thinking about technology. The idea of 'newness' of a technology has little absolute meaning for many managers. Whether a technology is new or not can only be considered in terms of a specific application. Examples of this thinking are illustrated in the following managers' quotations: 'Skill is being aware of (technology change) and ultimate commercial success is in packaging up what everyone else knows about, in usable form.' 'We put together heating elements and printed-circuit, laminate-board technology to make a thin, robust, waterproof heating panel . . . technologies new to this industry but not to industry in general.' 'People think this is a new technology . . . it's a concept of which the technology is not new but the application of it was new . . . certainly new for us.'

Views of high and low technology

Other commonly used terms in the literature such as 'high' and 'low' technology can have different meanings for managers in different situations. For example:

(clients) see us as a high-tech sort of business . . . the fact that we don't manufacture high-tech equipment doesn't matter . . . they see us as *users* of high-tech equipment . . . but we are not high tech in my eyes . . . the guys writing programmes in new languages don't regard themselves in a high-tech industry . . . after six months it's mundane.

most people outside see this as a high-tech company . . . (inside) most people see it as 'easy' . . . something they are familiar with . . . visitors see high requirements and standards . . . but technology is not revolutionary.

Positions on technology chains

One explanation for the above views is that these different companies are operating at various points on a 'technology chain'. In such a chain, a technology is likely to be incorporated into a base product with wide application. This product is then incorporated into other products which form subassemblies for those products down the chain. For example: 'Silicones have become a club now . . . only big boys in it . . . we have an agreement to buy raw materials and basic formulations . . . we are free to develop further formulations.'

When we get down the chain then the company may still be bringing a new technology to its customers. But this technology may in fact be something which is essentially the technology of other companies further back up the chain. Hence the company is likely to regard itself much more as a user of the technology, although it will be seen by its customers as a possessor of the technology:

we are not in a position where we are going to make technological breakthroughs . . . one of the big problems is that our industry is commonly known as high tech . . . it's really nothing of the sort . . . it's not high tech in a base sense . . . it's an agglomeration of things to make technology more usable.

Technology leaders

Customers may see a company as some kind of technology leader and as the bringer of a new technology to the world, although of course they are really referring to just their particular application. Even the idea of leadership is not at all straightforward. For example:

The reason it's difficult to identify a technology leader is that our industry is really not making technological advances . . . raw technology advances like fibre optics, micro-chips that make possible what we do that is the base technology . . . those are the sort of industries where raw technology is clearer . . . we take the output of these raw techno-logy freaks . . . making use of it, packaging it.

When we have asked managers to list their technological strengths they have often found this to be a difficult question to answer. Responses have varied considerably. For example:

'I'm not sure we've got any,' (a main board member of a large multinational company in the office equipment and communications businesses, whose strategy depended heavily on sourcing products from others); 'It is not a question of possessing a technology as such, rather we have experience in certain technologies,' (the Operations Director of a large firm in the design and project management industry, specialising in energy installations, oil and nuclear power installations); 'Classifying them would take hours . . . in a static technology position you tend not to look at it in those terms . . . you tend just to do it,' (the Chief Executive of a group of niche engineering businesses, including those in fluid transfer).

Codifying technology

Finally, when looking at how managers think about technology, we must mention the issue of the codification of technology. Codification refers to the fact that for practical purposes, a technology does not completely exist in a recorded form as drawings or specifications, it also includes knowledge and abilities that are in the heads of the individuals in a company. This has obvious implications for a company trying to introduce a technology, incorporate it into its planning process or transfer it to another company in any deal or co-operative arrangement. A technical journal article may have no difficulty in describing and discussing a new technology, pointing to how it can be introduced and noting what are its potential applications, but for a manager, trying to work with a new technology then it may not be so easy:

> Our key technology is clearly process technology and it's embodied in people more than machines. (Success) is much more about having an optimised process . . . (We are) now getting that down on paper . . . doing it methodically to optimise it . . . it's going to take away variability.
> (At the moment) we do things three times then on the fourth it's different . . . What did we do? . . . we don't know . . . We're finding that as we get more control, discipline . . . all those Theory X words keep coming up . . . that we did do something different . . . used to be no one knew where to start looking.
> (Chief Executive of a small advanced materials company)

Although this manager emphasised the value of codifying his technology, he had no illusions about the difficulty of doing this when he was acquiring new technology from other companies: 'the licensor didn't have the information codified . . . so I said we'll come and watch . . . I think that's a much better way of transferring technology . . . perhaps I'm contradicting what I said earlier!'

It is clear that any ideas we may develop on what companies *should* do with their technology must relate to the very real problems which practising managers have in conceptualising and codifying technology, in separating it from the products and processes in which it is employed and in judging the technological position of themselves and those with whom they deal.

HOW MANAGERS ORGANISE FOR TECHNOLOGY DECISION-MAKING

Companies are faced with a wide range of choices of different ways in which to acquire new technology, both internally and externally. They can also exploit their technologies in their own products and processes, license them or co-operate with others in that exploitation. They also have the task of managing all aspects of these development and exploitation activities. The range of decision-making involved in all of this may fit uneasily into conventional job titles. For example, it is unlikely that a vice-president in charge of R&D will immediately feel comfortable with a range of issues which includes decisions on inward licensing, the use of contract R&D houses or joint ventures. These different activities inevitably take the R&D manager away from his or her immediate functional orientation which is likely to centre on a corporate R&D laboratory.

Chief technology officers

Some companies have attempted to encompass a range of technological decision-making within the responsibilities of a single technology manager. A study by Adler and Ferdows investigated the extent to which Fortune 100 corporations in the USA had adopted the job title of 'Chief Technology Officer' (CTO) with broad responsibility across product, process or information technology areas.[5] Using company records they identified twenty-nine Fortune 100 companies that had corporate officers with explicit technology responsibilities and with titles other than 'VP for R&D', i.e. which extended beyond the narrower focus of internal technology development.

Twenty-five of those who subsequently responded to their questionnaire had the breadth of responsibility that their titles suggested, such as Vice-President for Technology or Chief Technology Officer. Nineteen of these Chief Technology Officers reported to their company's Chief Executive or equivalent, but they varied considerably in the extent to which they had line management responsibility. Some had full authority over technical budgets in all business units while others had no formal authority over budgets, technical appointments in the business units or even over corporate research. The main responsibilities of the CTOs were as follows:

- co-ordination between the technological efforts of business units to ensure synergy and economies of scale;
- representation of technology within the top management team;
- supervision of new technology development;
- assessment of technology aspects of major strategic initiatives, such as acquisitions or joint ventures;
- management of the external technological environment, including liaison with universities and outside research organisations.

The motivations of companies in creating the CTO position are interesting. In several cases the interviewees suggested that the trigger had been the availability of a suitable individual, but beyond this the motivations appeared to differ depending on whether the company had central R&D or not. In those with central R&D two issues appeared important. The first was the need to foster greater 'responsiveness' on the part of central R&D and greater 'receptiveness' on the part of business units. For those without central R&D the main concerns were to 'avoid duplication of businesses' R&D efforts', to ensure 'cross-fertilization' of businesses' technology efforts and to 'exercise overall leadership' in order to maintain the technology base of the company, in particular by serving as a 'window to outside technologies'.

Managing product and process technologies

The Chief Technology Officers in this study had responsibilities for both product and process technologies. It is unusual for companies to devote similar levels of attention to process as to product technology. For many companies, process technology remains a poor relation. The lack of strategic attention devoted to the manufacturing function is long established and deeply rooted, and it has been blamed for the decline in competitiveness of both US and UK industry.[6,7] Part of the reason for problems in developing new process technologies centres on the lack of effective linkages between the separate tasks in developing new product technology and turning it into something which can be manufactured, which we have already mentioned.

But the problem runs deeper in many companies. A diversity of current approach is again apparent. Steven Wheelwright contrasts those small number of companies which approach process innovation as a source of competitive advantage and which take a long-term, strategic approach. He suggests that in the majority of companies, processes are not usually developed in anticipation of new-product opportunities. Instead, process development is only viewed tactically as a way to achieve cost reductions or introduced when it is required by R&D's design for a new product[7].

Diversity of approach to technology decision-making

We should emphasise again that the establishment of a chief technology office occurred in only a minority of Fortune 100 companies and there is a wide diversity of approach in others – and frequently a lack of a coherent address to issues in the strategic management of technology. Almost two-thirds of the 800 USA managers questioned in a study by consultants Booz Allen and Hamilton thought that their companies were doing a poor job of harnessing technology to their corporate strategy. Booz Allen concluded: 'Many chief executives have surrendered control over this critical aspect of their business. While management tends publicly to espouse the importance of technology, few companies approach it as a strategic issue.'[8]

Perhaps a contributory factor in this problem is that only one Chief Executive Officer in five regards their top technologist as part of their inner circle.[9] Similarly the board itself cannot always be relied upon to exercise a coherent approach to technology: 'Both during my time and my predecessor's it was said that the Board will not comprehend this thing about product development' (The former Chairman of the Board and Corporate Managing Director of Volvo).[10]

BUYING AND SELLING TECHNOLOGY

So far in this chapter we have concentrated on what managers do about developing their own technologies. But an increasingly important aspect of technology strategy involves buying technology from others. Technology can be bought by taking a licence to use the technology from the company which has developed it, or by buying the company itself. An alternative is to buy from a research organisation that will develop technology to the company's requirements. Similarly, an important way to maximise the financial return on a company's investment in new technology is to license that technology to others. As well as its intrinsic importance, managers' attitude to the purchase and sale of technology also reveals a great deal about their overall approach to their technology.

Buying technology by buying the development company

Both General Motors and Mercedes-Benz chose the route of buying companies to get into new technologies for both their own existing applications and new ones. General Motors bought a number of companies in the early 1980s, including Hughes Electronics. Mercedes-Benz acquired aircraft makers Dornier and Messerschmitt, the electrical and electronic group AEG and diesel- and aero-engine maker Motoren und Turbinen Union (MTU). These moves had two stated goals: the first was to offset stagnating vehicle sales by expanding into high-technology growth markets, particularly aerospace; second, they both aimed to strengthen their automotive businesses by applying advanced technologies developed in the acquired companies. This latter argument was also advanced by British Aerospace for its acquisition of Rover in the UK.

There seems to be little evidence that these transfers of technology have occurred and the takeovers appear to have more logic in financial rather than technological terms. While many observers conclude that the potential for technological synergy may exist between vehicles, electronics and aerospace, many doubt that acquisitions are needed to capture them: 'If all you want is a glass of milk, why buy the cow?' (A top manager of another German automotive group).[11]

The possible financial inefficiency of the takeover route for acquiring technology must be added to two other problems. The first is the almost inevitable mistrust by those in the core business of the quality of imported technology, the so-called 'Not-invented-here' syndrome. The second problem is the feeling that hard-earned revenue in the company's core business is being diverted away from their R&D to fund unfamiliar and risky ventures.

Minority interests for technology acquisition

Some companies seek to acquire new technologies or exercise some control over important technologies by taking a minority interest in other companies, including those that are suppliers of products or components to them. There is anecdotal evidence that this type of action is relatively unpopular. One reason for this unpopularity appears to be that many companies feel uncomfortable with any arrangement which does not give them total control over technology which are important to them. According to consultants Bain and Co., many companies which try the minority approach fail to form successful links with other companies because of their desire for control.[12] They suggest that IBM is an exception to this and is perhaps one of the best examples of a flexible approach to the acquisition of technology by minority ownership. IBM have many business partnerships with smaller companies, which range from simple marketing deals to minority stakes. Their attitude can be summed up in the following remark from one of IBM's partners: 'IBM has been very sensitive . . . IBM appreciates that if they try to change the company they will lose it.'

Despite what they call the traditional aversion of UK companies to minority stakes, Bain and Co. point to some companies which have accepted their value. They mention British Aerospace which took, what was for them, the unusual step of buying a 49 per cent stake in an innovative small company. Both parties recognised that full acquisition would be suboptimal for the future of the acquired company.

A common belief exists that Japanese companies seek to exercise control over the technologies of their product suppliers by taking a stake in them. Although many do have a stake in some suppliers, it is by no means universal, nor does it often extend to majority control. For example, Toyota has shareholding in only thirty-two of the 180 suppliers with whom it deals direct and in only seven of these is its stake more than 50 per cent.[13] When we discuss technological alliances between companies we will see that Japanese companies seem willing to accept that overall control of a company as expressed by majority shareholding is not a guarantee of effective influence but that a minority stake can lead to strong influence, if it leads to the development of a productive relationship between the partners

Buying technology from contract research organisations

There has been a considerable growth in the use of contract research organisations by companies as a way of buying new technology. The OECD Basic Science and Technology statistics show that the ratio of external to internal funding of research has been increasing by approximately 2–3 per cent for the four years up to 1995. However, this growth varies between different countries and different industries. According to a survey by PA Consulting and the Massachusetts Institute of Technology, Japanese businesses would increase their percentage reliance on external technology from 40 per cent to 60 per cent between 1993 and 1996. Comparable figures for the USA were an increase from 12 per cent to 35 per cent and for European companies increases of only a few points to 24 per cent. Again according to PA Consulting, outsourcing of R&D is less common in the chemical and pharmaceutical industries, largely because of the importance of process technologies which may be more difficult to acquire externally. In contrast, the computer industry has invested very heavily in outsourced technology because of the impossibility of keeping up with technologies in a wide range of different areas.[14]

External technology suppliers range from universities, which in the UK received £122 million from industry in 1992–93 to dedicated research houses with expertise in specific areas such as Sintef in Norway and the PA Technology centre in the UK, to the research departments of industrial companies which are allowed the freedom to generate revenue in this way.

Decisions on outsourcing technology involve the same sort of strategic consideration as those for any other make-or-buy decision. Once taken, a decision to discontinue research in a particular technology cannot be easily reversed as the company may have lost the ability and the personnel to work at a subsequently more advanced state-of-the-art level. Similarly, the decision to develop a technology in-house may commit the company to a long-term project and hence inhibit its ability to develop technologies in other areas.

Licensing technology

Licensing is a relatively common method of acquiring and exploiting technology and is applicable to both large and small companies. In our studies in the USA, 53 per cent of the sample had licensed technology to others and 58 per cent had taken a license from others. Comparable figures for the UK were 24 per cent and 25 per cent respectively.

In another UK study confined to small firms, 9 per cent of the sample had engaged in licensing and a further 11 per cent had considered licensing.[15] The discrepancy between the two countries is striking. US companies in these studies were over twice as likely to be involved in licensing as those from the UK. This does not mean that the US companies have developed sound strategies and those from the UK have not. Licensing is only appropriate in some clearly defined circumstances and is not a universally applicable strategy. Indeed, in many cases, licensing in someone else's technology may be the panic reaction of a company which has failed to either plan or carry out its own internal development. Similarly, licensing out may be a sound strategy or the means employed by a risk averse management to avoid making the necessary investments to effectively exploit a technology itself. Furthermore, licensing is a strategy which under the wrong circumstances can lead to the uncontrolled loss to others of the company's main technological assets.

Organising for licensing deals

The organisation of licensing deals again indicates some clear differences between companies and may also explain some of the apparent discrepancy between the extent of licensing in the USA and UK. Perhaps surprisingly, almost 30 per cent of our US sample reported that they had a department whose primary role is expediting technology sales. In another study of large US firms, three-quarters had a central licensing department which took a monitoring and co-ordinating role.[16] In the UK it is a technical department or R&D department that is most likely to be involved in both buying *and* selling technology. Few British companies mentioned that a business development or legal department would be involved.

In our US studies, another 30 per cent of the companies said that their chief executive officer or top management were principally involved in deals and over half of the UK companies also mentioned top management. Licensing appears to be an *ad hoc*, rather than a routine, delegated activity. Further, it seems to take place without a planned strategy or purpose in many companies. The emphasis on technical involvement in the UK may also mean that many companies do not have a view of the licensing activity as an integral part of the business's plans, but rather as a purely technical, activity. This and the *ad hoc* nature of deals may go some way towards explaining the lower level of licensing in the UK.

Problems in licensing deals

The main problems which US companies report in their licensing deals are the length of time that negotiations take, the amount of professional manpower required and the price obtained or the cost of the technology. These concerns were similar to those in the UK, although British licensors also emphasised the problems of inadequate finance in their own and the licensee company. UK licensees were also concerned with disagreements over the technology which was to be included in the deal. Here again, it appears that the issues which face managers centre on planning and organisation for acquisition and exploitation of technology.

Differences between companies in licensing deals

Our studies have shown some important differences in how companies approach the idea of licensing technology. For example companies were likely to both license in and license out technology, or do neither. In the USA, 76 per cent of those companies which had sold technology had also bought it, but 70 per cent of those which hadn't bought technology from others hadn't sold any either. Perhaps predictably, large firms in both countries are more likely to have licensed in and licensed out than are small ones, and this was confirmed in the Lowe and Crawford study.[17] Also, those firms engaged in both buying and selling of technology tended to be the most internationally oriented of the companies.

We expected companies which spent more money on R&D to be more likely to have technology which they then could license to others, and this was indeed the case. More surprising was the fact that the companies, in both countries, which spent more on R&D were also more likely to license *from* other companies as well. Clear indications emerged of a separation between large majority of companies for whom licensing is simply an *ad hoc* way to deal with a problem of technological inadequacy, and a small minority for whom it is only one part of a more coherent approach to acquiring and exploiting technology.

Who takes the initiative in technology licence deals?

Our research indicated that in both the USA and the UK it is the *buyer* of the technology which was most likely to take the initiative in licence deals. This means that in the majority of cases, companies are more able to identify an inadequacy in their own technology and seek to do something about it by identifying a company to license from. Companies which may have a marketable technology appear to be less able to identify this and to seek potential customers.

The above even applies in many large international companies. In a study of twelve such US firms, only two had any formal search process to find possible licensees.[18] Comments from the companies suggested that an organised search for licencees 'never works', while one of the more active companies in the chemical industry when it wishes to license a technology simply announces its availability and 'sits back to wait and let users come'. Some companies argue against the idea of a proactive approach to licensing their technology. For example, a manager interviewed in one company which had once created a subsidiary to market its technology concluded: 'The reason it failed was the reason such companies are bound to fail – it was a missionary unit. It gave people solutions to problems they didn't have.'

In contrast, some companies emphasise the importance of careful market research as a preparation for technology sale, as the following comments made during one interview reveal:

> Following the evaluation (of the technology and of competitive technologies) we are in a position to decide how the product can best be licensed, i.e. whether it will be a patent license only, a know-how licence only or a combination of the two. Once we have determined the best method of utilization, we use all available approaches to find a licensee, such as trade publications, contacts with trade associations, Chambers of Commerce, etc. In connection with our overseas licensing program, we work very closely with the commercial attaches of the various foreign consulates and the various overseas associations, such as the British Board of Trade, to secure information on companies interested in expanding their product lines. Another fertile source of prospective licensees is our own internal-purchasing vendor lists. We work very closely with our purchasing departments, and as a matter of policy give our vendors first opportunity to qualify for a license relating to products they are now manufacturing for us.

An example of a company which takes a strategic view of the marketing of its technology is provided by the Anglo-French packaging company, Carneau-Metal Box. The company's central R&D facility is constituted as a public limited company and competes for commissioned research from operating companies within the group. Within the R&D company, the licensing company is charged with the task of marketing the group's technology to other companies. It also assesses the available market for new technologies within the areas of expertise of the R&D company and commissions research from the company for subsequent sale to others.

The importance of licence deals to companies

It is difficult to gain a clear idea of the importance to companies' sales and profits of technology which they have acquired from other firms. The results in our US and UK studies are not directly comparable, but they do indicate a wide diversity between companies in each country. In both countries, the majority of companies did not report that purchased technology was an important element in their business, although a small minority had a different experience. For example, 8 per cent of UK respondents said that at least 11 per cent of their annual turnover was generated from technology acquired from other companies. Similarly, the sale of technology to others did not seem to be important to the majority of companies, but a small minority, 5 per cent, reported that licensing generated 11 per cent or more of their revenue.[19,20]

TECHNOLOGY AND PATENTS

We now turn to the examination of managers' attitudes to more specific aspects of dealing with their technology, starting with their view of patents.

In some industries there is an increasing concern with intellectual property rights in general and with patents in particular. The concern with patents appears to centre more on the issue of general protection from loss of the companies' knowledge, rather than on the value that a patent might have in exploiting technology through licensing it to others. This concern varies in intensity between different industries. It is perhaps currently at its most extreme in the US electronics industry. After decades when the protection of intellectual property did not seem to be a major issue in the industry, it is now following the pharmaceutical and chemical industries in developing a greater concern about patents matters and an all-embracing view of property rights.

According to William Keefauver, an AT&T Vice-President and the company's top lawyer, there are three reasons for this: first is a significant gain in the competitiveness of non-US producers, coupled with an upsurge in counterfeiting; second, a higher proportion of a vendor's added value is now found in software; third is said to be the radical court ruling in 1982 which led to the creation of the US Court of Appeals, Federal Circuit, which has consistently upheld the value of patents.[21]

In a survey by the US journal *Electronic Business*[22] among the Chief Executives of small electronics companies, 58 per cent claimed to be bringing more of their engineering work in-house, rather than subcontracting it to others. Thirty-six per cent were reducing second-source agreements with suppliers for fear of technology leakage.

Patents and licensing deals

Despite this increasing concern over the retention of companies' technology, patents are generally of relatively little importance in licensing deals between both large and small firms in the UK and the USA. Only 23 per cent of US licensors and 30 per cent of licencees reported that their deals had *always* been of patented technology. In the UK, nearly three-quarters of licensors and over half of licensees emphasised the importance of unpatented technology.[23,24] In another study, Contractor found that the vast majority of international companies in his sample had obtained overseas patents. But he concluded that the crucial part of the international deals he was investigating was the unpatented know-how which was transferred to the licensee.[25] In a contrasting study of small firms in the UK, Lowe and

Crawford found that know-how and other intellectual property were at least as important in licensing deals as were patents.[26]

All of the above means that the stock of 'marketable' technology in companies extends beyond that which is patented and includes its 'softer', less codifiable know-how and abilities. But of course, these abilities are only marketable if the possessor can recognise them as such. We have already noted that buyers rather than sellers are more likely to be able to identify valuable technology and to take the initiative in licence deals to obtain this technology.

Example
Defending distinctive technology:
Renishaw plc

The need to protect distinctive technological resources is a main consideration for any firm active in product or process development. One firm has made patenting a cornerstone of a successful competitive strategy.

Renishaw was founded by Rolls-Royce engineers who, during design of the Olympus engines for Concorde, developed an innovative measurement probe as a solution to a metrology problem. Having registered the resulting patent they started up business independently, all with the co-operation of Rolls-Royce. This start, some twenty years ago, has formed the key philosophy and strategy of the firm, whose management strictly limits development to patentable ideas, which are rigorously defended. The company says, 'We only make unique products which can be sold for what they're worth to the customer, not what they cost to make'. This is explicitly what sets the sale price of any product.

In order to protect its future positions the firm has taken a similar approach to its own manufacturing methods. Unique processes have been patented to improve costs and margins, and to lead to potentially saleable products once proven in use. The philosophy is thus the creation of protected products in niche markets, which are all currently in dimensional metrology. Within this approach the company has expanded from its original probe to such things as actuation systems, linear measurement scales, laser interferometry for instrument calibration and diagnostic tools for coatings.

Strategic planning is explicitly oriented towards maintaining technological protection, and this has allowed them to be self-supporting in cash terms and all development is funded internally. The success of Renishaw's approach has produced large cash surpluses allowing high R&D expenditure, currently around 15 per cent of turnover. Renishaw plan to continue to maintain a 'patent thicket' which 'builds an impenetrable wall to the market'.

CO-OPERATIVE AND JOINT-VENTURE TECHNOLOGY DEALS

Technological development and/or exploitation has been at the core of many of the increasing number of co-operative alliances or joint ventures in recent years. Managers reported that technology development was the purpose of 20 per cent of the international coalitions in a recent European study as opposed to 42 per cent which were set up for operations and logistics purposes and 22 per cent for marketing purposes.[27]

Table 2.1 Types of technological co-operation

Type of co-operation	Total %	Customers %	Suppliers %	Horizontal units %
Mutual exchanges of technological information	22	18	24	24
Tests, trials, etc.	18	17	21	16
Special technological project	26	34	27	14
Joint development activities including project group	14	14	10	19
Long-term technological collaboration	15	14	12	18
Other (including licence agreements)	5	3	6	9
TOTAL	100	100	100	100

Source: Hakansson, H. (1989) *Corporate Technology Behaviour*, London: Routledge.

An interesting profile of the ways in which companies are involved in co-operative arrangements for joint development is provided by Hakansson's study of Swedish companies.[28] A summary of the extent of co-operation for different purposes is shown in Table 2.1. This table illustrates the percentage of these co-operative relationships which fit into the categories of joint development or the mutual exchange of technological information, etc. The table also shows the proportion of each of these relationships which were established with customers, suppliers or 'horizontal units', such as contract research houses, universities or the manufacturers of competing or complimentary products.

The most significant form of technological co-operation which managers establish seems to be for special one-off projects, followed closely by relationships which rest on the mutual exchange of technological information. These two types of collaboration appear to be particularly important in the case of relationships with customers.

Hakansson also discovered two other facts about these collaborative deals. The first of these is illustrated in Table 2.2. We can see that over two-thirds of all the technology co-operation relationships he studied were informal arrangements. Despite this, the weighted average of the length of these technology development relationships was thirteen years for customers and suppliers. Even for those relationships between different horizontal units which are not bound by a continuous flow of goods and services, the weighted average length of relationship was eight years. Second, Hakansson estimated that approximately 50 per cent of all the technology development work in the Swedish companies he investigated involved close collaboration between companies.

The findings emphasise that a key task which managers face in the development and exploitation of technology is the ability to plan, develop and manage these long-term, informal but probably complex intercompany relationships. The complexity of these

Table 2.2 Duration and formality of technology co-operation

Form of co-operation	Customers %	Suppliers %	Horizontal %
Formalised relationships			
Annual agreement	20	11	1
Long-term agreement	13	8	8
Joint company (or similar)	2	2	11
Non-formal relationships			
Part of continuing relationship	51	67	41
Other informal design	14	12	39
Duration years			
0–4 years	36	28	55
5–14 years	30	41	29
> 15 years	33	29	15
Weighted average	13 years	13 years	8 years

Source: Hakansson, H. (1989) *Corporate Technology Behaviour*, London: Routledge.

relationships is illustrated by Hakansson's finding that in 20 per cent of development relationships with customers at least ten people were involved in contact with the other company and that contact was at least weekly. The importance of intercompany relationships in technology development and exploitation should not hide the issues which must be taken into account. Obvious problems include those of selecting partners and making the relationship work and, as we have already mentioned, the control of technology leakage to the partner firm.

Joint ventures and strategy

Another broader issue in joint ventures is the place they have in long-term strategy. According to research by Hamel et al.,[29] western managers often enter technology-based alliances as a way of avoiding subsequent investment rather than as a way of acquiring new skills. They illustrate this point with two quotations from the respective US and Japanese partners to a joint venture as follows: 'We complement each other well – our distribution capability and their manufacturing skill. I see no reason to invest upstream if we can find a secure source of product. This is a comfortable relationship for us' and 'When it is necessary to collaborate, I go to my employees and say, "This is bad, I wish we had these skills ourselves. Collaboration is second best. But I will feel worse if after four years we do not know how to do what our partner knows how to do."'

A similar tentative finding was expressed by Nueno and Oosterveld[30] when they carried out a preliminary study of technology alliances in Europe. They found that alliances for the development of a technology at the pre-competitive stage and for which there was not a clearly defined end market, tended to be different to those at the competitive stage or which centred on a defined market. The pre-competitive alliances had less clearly defined objectives than those at the competitive stage and the analysis of risk was weaker. The relation between the technology itself and its incorporation into production was given less consideration in pre-competitive alliances and the alliances themselves were more unstable.

Not all companies enter into these type of arrangements, either internationally or within their own country. Significantly, our studies show that in both the UK and the USA it is those companies which have bought or sold technology via licence which are more likely to form co-operative or joint ventures with others to obtain and to exploit technology. Hakansson found a considerable range:

At one extreme were the 'isolated companies'. These were almost a quarter of those in his sample and had very limited contact with other companies for technology development or exploitation. These companies tended to be important to both their suppliers and customers in terms of volume of business between them, but not at all important from a technological point of view. They also had the lowest market share in the sample and were effectively minor players in a well-structured network of companies.

At the other extreme, were those companies with a very broad co-operation profile. These were also around a quarter of the sample and all of them had at least five important collaborative partners. Technological collaboration with their suppliers was the most important form of linkage for most of these companies and occurred in all but two of them, while just over half had co-operative arrangements with customers or 'horizontal' organisations, such as research houses. This group also contrasted with the isolated companies by having a position of market leadership and a wider range of customers. Technological development was rapid in the markets from which they bought and new products accounted for a relatively large share of their purchases.

MAKE OR BUY

To make or buy may seem at first sight an odd choice of topic to include in a chapter dealing with what companies do about technology. Nevertheless, make-or-buy decisions have a major impact on a company's technological future. A company which manufactures a product itself will be using its own product and process technologies (unless it is operating under a licence arrangement). A decision to switch to purchasing the product from a supplier will generally mean that the company will be reliant on the supplier's technology. Over time, as technology develops, the ability of the company to revert to its own manufacture will be limited by the fact that its own technology will become outdated. Similarly, and often more importantly, if a company does not consider the possibility of switching from 'make' to 'buy' then it has implicitly taken a resource allocation decision. It has decided to allocate scarce R&D funds and management time to developing the technologies for that product – at the expense of other technologies which may be more critical to its future.

Despite this, our studies in the USA, UK, Canada and Australia show that only a small minority of firms actually take a strategic technological view of these decisions.[31] We were

Table 2.3 Different approaches to make or buy

Approach	Basis of approach	Examples	Problems or drawbacks
Operational/ cost-based approach	Decisions taken individually on the basis of cost savings or operational advantage	Subcontracting transport, printing or peak load manufacture	Failure to achieve all possible savings. No relationship to any overall company strategy
Business approach	Proactive approach to make or buy based either on a system of continuing evaluation or assessment based on broader cost/ operational criteria	Use of multifunctional team (materials, finance, legal) which assesses any departmental activity for cost savings by buying in	Decisions may be made based on short-/medium- term cost savings which are cyclical Buying-in decisions may lead to strategic shortcomings
Policy approach	Based on an overview of the strategic direction of the company and its technological strengths and weaknesses	Activities based on single-minded concentration on core/essential technologies	Difficulty in integrating business policy/technology strategy/purchasing organisation

able to divide companies into three groups depending on the approach they took and this is illustrated in Table 2.3.

The large majority of firms we studied took a short-term, cost-based approach to make or buy. Decisions were taken on an individual basis and mainly involved moves to contract out such activities as cleaning, printing or subcontracting activities where an obvious cost saving could be achieved or where union difficulties could be avoided. A second group took a business approach. This involved a more systematic examination of possible areas for contracting out, often carried out by a committee also charged with the task of monitoring the cost savings achieved. In contrast, a small number of companies adopted what we called a policy approach which involved taking an overview of the nature of the company's activities and those technologies which were critical to its future, and investing strongly in those. This approach was summed up by a manager as follows:

> The general trend towards buying-in services and products has been well-established for several years and we have found that results have been in line with our basic objective, which is to concentrate on doing those things which (a) we can do well and (b) are absolutely essential to the core of our business.

The policy approach may or may not lead to an increase in subcontracting. What it does seem to lead to is an increase in understanding those technologies which are the keys to the companies future and which should be held in-house, and for which the company should develop its links with others.

TECHNOLOGY ACTIVITY AND TECHNOLOGY STRATEGY

These studies all point to a clear division between the approaches of companies to technology activities and strategy. On the one side are a relatively small number of companies, the 'technologically active' which have an integrated approach to the management, acquisition and exploitation of their technology. These companies use a number of different methods to acquire technology, such as their own in-house or contracted-out R&D, licensing and joint ventures. They are likely to take a strategic view of their make-or-buy decisions on long-term technological grounds. Similarly, they are likely to use a combination of exploitation methods, such as incorporating technology into their own products or processes, subcontracting manufacture to others or licensing where appropriate.

They may, for example, seek to capitalise on their technological strengths by licensing to others when they are in the position of market leader. As we might expect, the largest group of those which sold technology to others were market leaders at the time of the deal. They may also seek to defend their long-term market leadership by licensing from other companies as appropriate. Perhaps less predictably, the largest number of those which acquired technology from others were also market leaders.

The technologically active tend to be larger companies and are more likely to be concentrated in particular industries. For example, in the USA over 70 per cent of companies in the chemicals, petroleum and coal industries had both sold technology to others and bought it. Technologically active companies tend to have a higher level of R&D spend. They are more open to joint ventures with other companies for manufacturing, marketing or product development and are also more involved in international markets.

Technologically active companies also exist among small firms. In the UK, a subgroup of small firms was also identified which was involved in both licensing in and licensing out. This subgroup saw the development and exploitation of technology as a less *ad hoc* activity than in the majority of small firms. They thought of licensing as a useful tool to be considered in tandem with the alternative options of in-house development of contracted R&D.[32] The predominant technology sale for these technologically active companies has been of manufacturing technology or design/formulation for a specific product. Over a quarter of these companies have sold technology while it was still at the R&D stage and so is not yet incorporated into their own products.

The above gives a strong impression that this small number of technologically active companies take an overall view of their technological position and their technological assets, and make a considered attempt to utilise all appropriate means of acquiring and exploiting technology.

We can contrast these companies with the large majority of 'technologically passive' companies. These companies seem to exist in all industries, but appear to be more concentrated in some than others. For example, less than half of those in the US rubber and plastics, stone, clay and glass and in fabricated metal industries had bought or sold technology. Less technologically active companies, from whatever industry, are less internationally orientated and are unlikely to be involved in many different ways of exploiting or acquiring technology. It appears that for these companies, licensing is more likely to be reactive than proactive, let alone have any strategic thrust. According to a report by consultants Bain and Co. the lack of a strategic view of technology by these companies can be summarised by their view of licensing: 'There is still a regrettable attitude in some British companies that "real men don't license".'[33] We could probably go further and say that for the majority of firms technology decisions are simply not taken. Instead, the companies' technological position is the result of individual product, process or marketing decisions or decisions, on R&D programmes or projects, rather than by any coherent view which takes technology as the unit of analysis.

CONCLUSIONS

This chapter has attempted to sketch a picture of some of the things which managers seem to do and to think about technology. Of course, companies do not fit neatly into one category or another and many are more thoughtful and accomplished in some areas than others. Nevertheless, we can conclude that the concept of technology strategy is not well established in many companies, but that for some it is the basis of their existence, even though it may not be articulated in those terms. Companies have widely different approaches to technology and we can distil some of these differences into the following slightly less than serious types of approach. You are invited to speculate which well-known firms exhibit these characteristics:

1 *Technology machismo.* Technological strength is the basis of these companies' potency. This means that if a new technology emerges anywhere near their area of operations they feel they have to develop *their* version of it. These companies believe it is beneath their dignity to buy anyone else's technology and that they can 'out-R&D' anyone else. These companies are likely to suffer major problems when they have acquired a history of failed versions of technologies which are different to the industry standards, or because they can no longer fund their enormous R&D activity.
2 *Virile technologies.* This group is rather similar to the first group in approach but is found in those companies that have a particular technology which they regard as so central to their operations that no amount of money is too great to be spent on it. These companies are likely to be so secretive about this technology that they will not consider any co-operation with others in its development and may even lose the chance for wider co-operation in more general areas. They will squander opportunities to license or sell the technology to others, even in quite separate areas of application. This approach is often associated with particular individuals in a company who believe that only they can know and direct its future.
3 *All-or-nothing.* This approach could frequently be subheaded 'and frequently nothing'. It is particularly common in small firms and is based on the idea that a company must do everything for itself. We saw it clearly in a group of small electronic companies all located close together in a particular Scandinavian country. Each was built around a single but different product technology and each had difficulty in process development and marketing. Not only did they not talk to each other, but they did not think of subcontracting some or all of their manufacturing or marketing to others. The result was that management and budgets were impossibly stretched in technology development for all areas of their business.

4 *The seedcorn approach.* This approach occurs in companies that have an inflated view of the value of their technology which they regard as the seedcorn for their future. They dismiss the chance to license their technology to others because of what they see as the danger of licencees competing with them. This view is held until the technology no longer has any value, by which time potential licencees have all disappeared. Hence the companies lose valuable revenue and fail to optimise the return on their technological investment.

5 *The trained-monkey syndrome.* Managers with this approach act as if they believe that the world is divided into two classes, a class which understands and can use technology – the trained monkeys – and a superior class which takes pride in its lack of ability in this area. This approach may be found among some MBA-trained managers. It leads to an emphasis on financial engineering, short-term style changes, product modification and company growth by acquisition. It de-emphasises the importance of long-term technological development and organic growth.

6 *The hollow-corporation approach.* This is a further extension of the approach and is exemplified in the idea that production is inherently difficult and dirty, and leads to bad labour relations and low rates of return on capital employed. The only sensible strategy, they argue, is not to produce anything but to concentrate on badge engineering and buying in product from elsewhere, preferably the Far East. Such an approach is viable but only as long as the company has an absolute edge in marketing and distribution skill, which may be easier for competitors to match than product or process technology.

7 *The joint-venture approach.* Companies with this approach are in some ways similar to the previous ones. They have frequently fallen behind competitors in process or product technology and have formed joint ventures with other, often Japanese, companies to manufacture or, more usually, to distribute their products. Instead of using the time gained by these joint ventures to recover their own product or process technology, they continue to rely on their partner until development means that it no longer needs their production or distribution.

8 *The marketeers approach.* This approach is based firmly in the marketing concept. Its followers are passionate that their companies must be marketing led. Implicit in their approach is the idea that no product is so out of date that good packaging can't save it and no product is so badly made that good advertising can't sell it. They emphasise minor product change within unchanging technologies and seek to limit R&D spend and to transfer the money into the marketing budget. These people probably were raised in the days of 'tranquil technology' in the 1960s and still long for the time when all the ingredients for business success could be found in the pages of undergraduate marketing textbooks.

9 *The sleepy approach.* This final approach is the simplest and probably the most common. People who have this approach believe that their technology is OK – isn't it?

REFERENCES

1 Pavitt, K. (1984) 'Sectoral patterns of technical change: towards a taxonomy and a theory', *Research Policy*, **13**: 343–73.
2 Koerner, E. (1989) 'Technology planning at General Motors', *Long Range Planning*, **22**(2): 9–19.

3   Takeuchi, H. and Nonaka, I. (1986) 'The new new product development game', *Harvard Business Review*, January–February: 137–46.

4   Clarke, K., Ford, D. and Saren, M. (1988) 'Technology and strategic management of the firm', paper presented to the Strategic Management Society Conference, Amsterdam, October.

5   Adler, P. and Ferdows, K. (1990) 'The chief technology officer', *California Management Review*, Spring: 55–62.

6   Hill, T. (1985) *Manufacturing Strategy*, London: Macmillan.

7   Wheelwright, S. C. (1985) 'Restoring the competitive edge in US manufacturing', *California Management Review*, **XXVII**(3), Spring.

8   Booz Allen and Hamilton (1984) *Management and Technology: a Survey of European Executives*, USA: Booz Allen and Hamilton.

9   Willder, S. (1985) 'Directing technological development – the role of the board', *Long Range Planning*, **18**(4): 44–49.

10 Grandstrand, O. (1982) *Technology Management and Markets*, London: Pinter.

11 De Jonquieres, G. and Fisher, A., 'Chart the obstacles Daimler-Benz must overcome if its diversification strategy is to succeed', *Financial Times*, 15 March 1991.

12 Bain and Co. (1990) *Innovation in Britain Today*, London: Bain and Co.

13 Macmillan, J. (1990) 'Managing suppliers: incentive system in Japanese and US industry', *California Management Review*, Summer: 38–55.

14 *Financial Times*, 6 January 1995.

15 Lowe, J. and Crawford, N. (1984) *Innovation and Technology Transfer for the Growing Firm*, Oxford: Pergamon.

16 Contractor, F. J. (1981) *International Technology Licensing*, Lexington, MA: Lexington Books.

17 Lowe, J. and Crawford, N. (1984) *Innovation and Technology Transfer for the Growing Firm*, op. cit.

18 Contractor, F. J. (1981) *International Technology Licensing*, op. cit.

19 Ford, D. and Jongerius, C. (1986) *Technology Strategy in British Industry*, Milton Keynes: Base International.

20 Ford, D. (1985) 'The management and marketing of technology', in R. Lamb and P. Shrivastava (eds), *Advances in Strategic Management*, vol. 3, Greenwich, CT: JAI Press, pp. 103–34.

21 Kerr, J. (1988) 'Fight for your technology rights', *Electronic Business*, 15 August: 44–48.

22 Ibid.

23 Ford, D. and Jongerius, C. (1986) *Technology Strategy in British Industry*, op. cit.

24 Ford, D. (1985) 'The management and marketing of technology', op. cit.

25 Contractor, F. J. (1981) *International Technology Licensing*, op. cit.

26 Lowe, J. and Crawford, N. (1984) *Innovation and Technology Transfer for the Growing Firm*, op. cit.

27 Nueno, P. and Oosterveld, J. (1988) 'Managing technology alliances', *Long Range Planning*, **21**(3): 11–17.

28 Hakansson, H. (1989) *Corporate Technology Behaviour*, London: Routledge.

29 Hamel, G. and Prahalad, C. K. (1989) 'Collaborate with your competitors and win', *Harvard Business Review*, January–February: 133–39.

30 Nueno and Oosterveld, 'Managing technology alliances'.

31 Ford, D. and Farmer, D. (1986) 'Make or buy – a key strategic issue, *Long Range Planning*, **19**(5): 54–62.

32 Ford, D. and Jongerius, C. (1986) *Technology Strategy in British Industry*, op. cit.

33 Bain and Co. (1990) *Innovation in Britain Today*, op. cit.

Chapter 3

First steps in technology strategy

INTRODUCTION

It is now appropriate to move on to the central issue of how a manager can develop a strategy for technology. In this chapter we first examine three different views of the relationship between technology and strategy. This leads to a definition of technology strategy which will form the basis of the remainder of the book. We examine the technological interdependence that exists between companies and provides a categorisation of three generic types of technology which will be used in subsequent chapters.

So far, we have explained the complexity of technology issues for companies and described some of what managers do and think about technology. We believe that a strategic approach to technology is as much about attitude as about plans, and as much about ideas as about structure. A strategic view of technology is more likely to emerge slowly through careful thought and self-analysis, rather than be produced by a conscious, deliberate strategy development programme. This means that we should not start our discussion with a view that 'strategy' means the same as 'plan'. Instead, we see company strategy more as the formation of perspective[1] and this book is about the development of that perspective.

THREE VIEWS OF TECHNOLOGY AND STRATEGY

It is important to make clear the exact relationship between technology strategy and the more general concept of corporate strategy and hence the precise area of our attention in this book. We can think of three aspects of this relationship. First, there is a technological dimension to overall corporate strategy in the same way that there is a financial, production or marketing dimension to it. Each dimension is an area to which attention must be devoted, each provides ingredients for the strategy development process and each is a way in which strategy is implemented and through which the effects of strategy become apparent. Thus, a corporate strategy to achieve a low-cost position can be implemented through process technology improvements to achieve lower production costs. This strategy also has a product technology element as design improvements can lead both to product cost reductions and a smoother production flow. Further, a low-cost strategy will affect the brief given to the purchasing department on the types of components which should be bought and the product technology on which they are to be based.

Second, technology can be used as a unit of analysis in evaluating a company's behaviour and performance as a basis for strategy development. This is similar to the way in which we could evaluate a company in terms of its financial or market performance. Thus, if we have the tools of analysis we could consider such factors as technological leadership, exploitation performance, technology share, etc. In this book we are involved with questions of evaluation of a company's overall technological position and performance. We argue strongly for the value of an analysis in technological terms as a basis for strategy building and suggest that this is particularly important in today's conditions of rapid technological change and uncertainty.

Third, we can consider the development of strategy for the acquisition, management and exploitation of the company's technology. This is the view of technology strategy with which we are mainly concerned in this book. The elements of technology strategy are illustrated in Figure 3.1.

The acquisition of technology includes far more than conventional R&D. Technology can be acquired internally, through the company's own R&D, or externally, by licensing from other companies, or from contract research houses, or via joint ventures with others or from suppliers of products, etc.

Similarly, technology can be exploited internally, by incorporating it in the company's own products, processes or market offerings or externally, by licensing it to others, by turnkey deals, by contract manufacturing for others, by designing or marketing products for them, or by joining in joint ventures with them.

Finally, technology management includes a variety of activities:

- the development of long-term strategy for technology;
- the co-ordination of different means of acquisition and exploitation of technology;
- effectively transferring of technologies between different operating units within the company;
- efficiently inserting new technologies where they are needed;
- integrating the different technologies which are held by the company and those around it to meet the requirements of any chosen customer.

Our approach to technology strategy is not confined to the issue of technological innovation, because introducing innovative technology may be irrelevant to a company at any one time. Instead, it may be vital for that company to concentrate on strategy for the fullest exploitation of its existing technology. This exploitation may involve difficult choices between a variety of different means such as new product introduction, licensing

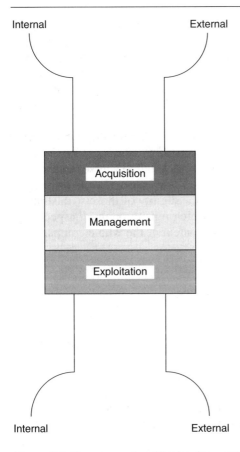

Internal   External

Internal   External

Figure 3.1 The elements of technology strategy

or joint ventures, all of which can have both short- and long-term consequences for the company. Perhaps even more importantly, we would argue that a strategic approach to technology is vital even for companies that may see themselves as being low-tech or would never think of being involved in innovation. These companies also need a clear understanding of the technologies on which their companies are based, their respective positions in these technologies and their performance in exploiting their technological assets.

TECHNOLOGY STRATEGY

We use the following working definition of technology strategy: Technology strategy is the tasks of building, maintaining and exploiting a company's technological assets, no matter what their level or newness when compared to other companies in the same or other industries.

This definition emphasises that technology strategy is central to a company, whether it is a 'high' or 'low' technology company, a product or service provider, a technological 'innovator' or a 'follower'. This means that in order to make sense of technology strategy we cannot simply concentrate on what is to be the content of that strategy. Instead, we must look at technology strategy in its wider organisational and corporate strategical contexts, both of which have such an impact on the outcome and success of strategy. For example, collaboration between different functions in the company is vital for success in the technological innovation process.[2,3]

A company's technology is the sum total of its abilities – including that which exists inside the heads of all its staff. Technology strategy is not something which can be separated out as the responsibility of a single department. It cannot be relegated to a terse request from marketing or elsewhere for R&D to produce 'something new and quick'. Nor is technology a question of detailed implementation and hence beneath the dignity of those with strategic responsibilities. On the contrary, technology is a thread which runs through *all* aspects of a company and hence it can only be understood within the context of the whole company and its culture.

BASIS OF ANALYSIS: TECHNOLOGY AS ASSETS

A prerequisite for the development of strategy is a process of self-analysis to establish current position. This analysis must be expressed in a language which is appropriate to the subject of the strategy. Thus our language must be about technology and not about products or markets. Technology is embodied in products or services and these are the final outputs from technology strategy, not its ingredients. Technology strategy is not just about managing R&D, or the process of introducing new technology into the company. Nor is it just about new ventures or new products. An approach to technology strategy must start with the following questions:

1 What are the technological assets on which the past, present and future success of the company depend?
2 Can these assets be divided into those which are core and those which are more peripheral?
3 How can we assess the strength of our assets, relative to those of our competitors, how can we maintain them and how can we grow them?
4 How can we ensure that we achieve the best possible return on the investment we have made in these assets?

Our view of technology strategy looks at least one level behind a conventional listing of strengths in terms of products and markets. Instead of taking these products and markets as the units of analysis, we believe that we must examine and evaluate the underlying technologies which form the basis of its products and processes: 'The core of a company is not its products or its markets, but what it knows and what it can do.'[4]

Internal and external technologies

The distinction between internal and external technologies is important in the development of technology strategy. Internal technologies are those which the company owns or controls, possibly because they were developed by the company itself. External technologies are those from which the company benefits but does not own, such as those that have been developed by companies which supply it with products or services. The management task in developing technology strategy includes decisions on which areas of technology the company wishes to develop internally. It also includes decisions on which technologies it should not develop for itself, but on which it will continue to depend. These external technologies are increasingly vital as the cost and range of technologies needed to operate in any market escalate. Therefore, relationships with product or service suppliers must increasingly be seen in technological terms, rather than as routine, cost-reducing, fail-safe activities which are labelled as 'purchasing'.

Ideas such as those concerning partnership purchasing, if properly conceived, can tie together the existing and potential technologies of both buyer and seller companies. But a failure by a company to effectively use and develop the technologies of its suppliers means that the sum total of the technology which the buying company has available is restricted to its own internal 'stock', or that which it is able to develop internally. The value of external technologies was illustrated by Kenichi Ohmae when he spoke of 'the heart of IBM's accomplishment with the PC is its decision – and its ability – to approach the development effort as a process of managing multiple external vendors'.[5] (We discuss how technological assets are related to what have become known as the 'core competencies' of the firm in the final chapter of this book.)

Example
Externalising technology:
The interrelationship between distinctive and external technologies over time

This example shows how the technologies controlled by the firm can change in value and lose their distinctiveness as technical change elsewhere impacts upon them. In this case the development of microprocessor technologies for applications in other industries made redundant some of the central skills of the company.

This datacommunications firm manufactured and sold a range of products, services and systems to business users. One of its core product groups, modems, was traditionally supported by substantial R&D expenditure, particularly on system software. The ability to use standard circuitry, adapted to differing product and customer needs by varying software configurations, was considered a key distinctive skill.

Within the microprocessor industry however, major investments were being made in the development of integrated circuits aimed at specific applications. In this way, manufacturers sought to counter the growing 'commoditisation' of chips. In due course the communications industry was targeted with the development of the 'modem on a chip'. Much of the functionality of earlier combined hardware and software could now be integrated on to a single microprocessor.

The result for the company was that many of its product technologies based on its own design skills in this area became obsolete. In response it elected to rely on external sources of product and process technology rather than invest heavily in updating its own. The company concentrated on maintaining its market skills and developing new skills in managing critical supplier relationships (marketing technology). It accepts that a key technology is now external to the firm and gains access to this technology through a purchasing relationship.

Example
Externalising technology: Massey Ferguson

Snowballing development costs have led to rationalisation in the tractor market. Survivors have had to reduce development resources and activities, and learn to rely more on specialist suppliers.

Massey Ferguson, a long-established tractor maker has, along with its competitors, faced hard commercial times over the last ten years. It used to make a full range of tractor models and related equipment such as combine harvesters.

Now, under the same sustained competitive pressures which led Ford and Fiat to merge their tractor operations in 1992, it makes two middle-market tractor ranges in the UK and France respectively, and fills in its product range by selling badged models sourced mainly from Japan. More fundamentally, it is re-examining its engineering and development activities and deciding which areas of tractor design should remain in-house and which should be left to suppliers. In future Massey Ferguson aim to compete by 'maintaining a core tractor knowledge and utilising outside resources as and when appropriate for specific design tasks'.

To this end a major reorganisation has taken place at the two manufacturing locations. At the UK factory in Coventry, tractor assembly and marketing is now separate from the manufacture of components and subassemblies. Internally manufactured parts consist of gears and driveshafts, major chassis castings and the linkages to towed implements such as ploughs. Towed imple-

ments are to be outsourced, in line with a strategy to produce only transmission and associated castings internally. While the logic underlying this simplification of business philosophy is clear, it creates new management tasks and changes priorities both within and between functional areas.

For engineering, a major task now is the overseeing and co-ordination of design activity within suppliers and contracted design houses. In general, a more modular overall product design philosophy has had to be adopted to allow components and sub-systems to be effectively integrated.

More specifically, intense design collaboration is needed. For example, in developing a new range of tractors to replace its current basic models (which derive from a 1950's design), Massey Ferguson decided that even in the core area of transmissions, specialist design input was desirable for four-wheel drive models. A four-wheel drive firm was contracted to provide leading edge knowledge in this area. Because the bulk of this firm's experience was in road and rally cars, considerable joint activity was needed to link these skills to Massey Ferguson's knowledge of tractor performance, reliability, operating conditions, etc. As a result a team of Massey Ferguson engineers has been sited with the supplier for the duration of the project. In a similar example for engines, the need to trim external designs to specific requirements has led Massey Ferguson to 'do more engine design in the last 12 months than in the last 20 years'.

For the purchasing function, a routine

order management role has been transformed by the need to manage these critical supplier relationships. For bought components such as fuel injection systems, tractor firms represent a small niche market in comparison to mass-production car makers.

A major challenge for Massey Ferguson will therefore be persuading suppliers to meet its particular technical requirements. Skill in choosing co-operative suppliers, and in carefully managing relationships with them will be a key to its future competitive success.

TECHNOLOGIES AND INTERCOMPANY NETWORKS

We have already emphasised that an understanding of technology and its management needs to take place within the context of the network of competing and co-operating companies within which all firms are enmeshed. A technology in itself has no value. It is simply a passive resource which is only activated when its owner interacts with another company which places some value on it – either because the other company wishes to acquire the technology for its own use, or because it wishes to buy products or services based on the technology, or plans to combine this technology with its own skills to provide something of value to others in the network. The value of a technology is specific to the other company and will be related to that company's own technologies and to its view of the technologies of other companies in the surrounding network.

A company which seeks to meet the requirements of its customers will use its own technologies and those which are embodied in the products and services of other companies which supply it. In order to meet customer requirements it may also seek to acquire other technologies directly, from licensors, contract research houses or those with which it has a joint venture. In this way it builds a 'bundle' of technologies suitable for its own customer (Figure 3.2). It may also use the services of other companies that provide the means by which the bundle of technologies can reach the customer, such as distribution companies or subcontract manufacturers, etc. Of course the company will not control this bundling process entirely. Other companies will have their own ideas of the importance of the company and its customer, and their own role in the network. Thus for example, a component maker may seek to influence how its components are used and who the final products are sold to.

The interaction between a company and those that surround it is not simply to acquire the use of their technologies. This interaction is not a zero-sum gain; both sides benefit by the exchange which takes place and by the learning which occurs from each other through the interaction, perhaps over many years. In this way the technological resources of both parties can grow through that interaction.

Interaction and product development

This brings us to a second reason for emphasising the interdependence between companies. A large proportion of new products are not developed by suppliers alone or by buyers, but interactively between them. Because of this, our ideas of the nature of the product development task in industrial firms may need to be revised and the question of intellectual

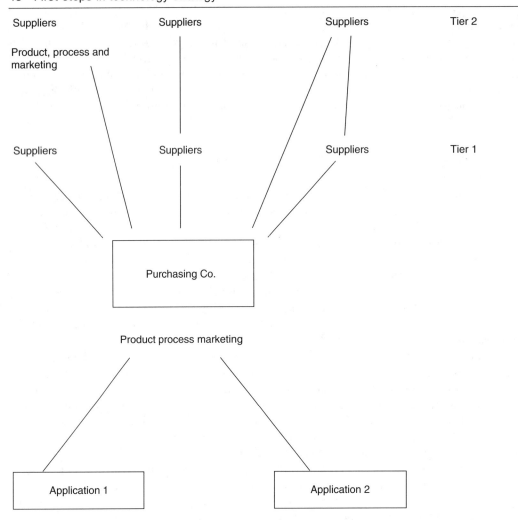

Figure 3.2 Technologies and networks

property rights becomes much more complicated. Additionally, companies will need to think very carefully about how the product development task carried out with any one partner will affect its dealings with others. Even more importantly, interdependence between companies means that a notionally independent company is not surrounded by a solid boundary, but by one which is permeable. In fact, when we look at many companies which buy and sell from each other or develop products together, it is rather difficult to identify the boundary between them or where the areas of each companys' responsibility, ownership or even culture start and finish. The extent to which a company will allow others to influence its nominally internal activities and will seek to involve itself within others is an important issue of managerial decision-making and control. For example, when a company

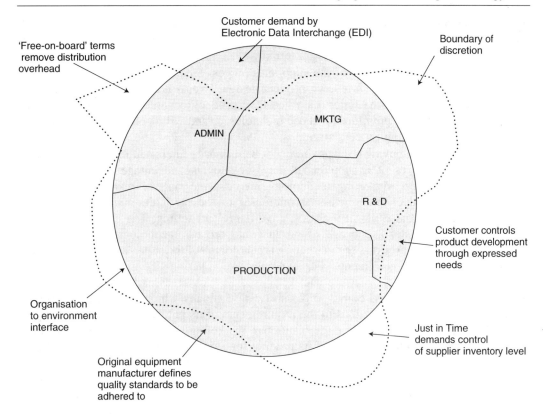

Customer demand by
Electronic Data Interchange (EDI)

Boundary of
discretion

'Free-on-board' terms
remove distribution
overhead

MKTG

ADMIN

R & D

Customer controls
product development
through expressed
needs

PRODUCTION

Organisation
to environment
interface

Just in Time
demands control
of supplier inventory level

Original equipment
manufacturer defines
quality standards to be
adhered to

Figure 3.3 Discretionary boundaries

is developing a new product it will often be influenced in that activity by the product development departments of a customer or its own suppliers. Similarly, the production plans for a new product will often be largely determined by the quality specifications of a main customer. Lake and Trayes[6] describe this interaction as occurring across 'discretionary boundaries' and this is illustrated in Figure 3.3.

TECHNOLOGY STRATEGY, PRODUCTS AND PROCESSES

A technological perspective on analysing a company may give a different view of the activity of buying products or services. For example, a customer may appear to choose a supplier because it wishes to buy its particular products. However, that supplier's products may be absolutely standard and unremarkable. Instead the buyer may have chosen the supplier because of the distinctive way in which it produces these standard products, which provides greater consistency of quality. In this way the purchase is actually determined by the process technology of the product supplier. The customer values these skills of the supplier, either because of its own lack of production capacity or because it does not have the necessary process technology itself. This may mean that if it produced the product itself its costs of production would be higher or its quality lower. In this way the company is treating these process technologies as 'external'.

In some cases the importance of the supplier's process technology is reinforced because the customer may be buying to its own product design. Even when this is not the case and the product is designed by the seller (based on their product technology), the customer may not be prepared to pay a premium for those technologies and will decide between suppliers on the basis of competing process strengths.

On the other hand, a buying company may not be primarily interested in either the product or process technologies of a supplier. It may seek to take advantage of the supplier's Marketing technology. Marketing technology includes the skill of market analysis, the ability to tailor product and process technologies to the particular requirements which have been analysed and skills in logistics, advertising and selling. These skills are necessary in order to transfer a package of product and process technologies to a particular application. In many cases it is the marketing technologies of the seller which are critical in meeting the buyers' requirements. For example, the functionality may be very similar between many proprietary software packages used in such areas as business logistics. In these circumstances, success comes to the software company which is best at tailoring its offering and its sales presentations to the requirements of its potential clients. Similarly, in many consumer markets it is often the distinctive marketing technology of a manufacturer which enables it to build the appeal of its product for a particular group of customers, even though its product is functionally identical to others in the market.

Marketing technology requires similar investments to develop as product and process technologies. It is also exploitable in a number of different ways, such as when a company uses its skills to market the complementary products of another company on an agency basis. More importantly, a bundle of product, process and marketing technologies is needed to meet any set of customer requirements. For example, many companies have the product technology suitable for a particular group of customers, they may also be able to develop the process skills to manufacture for that application. But, they also need the appropriate marketing technology to determine those customers' requirements precisely, tailor, package and communicate their offering, and transfer it to the customer at an appropriate price. Without this marketing technology they will fail, or have to use the services of someone else who has these skills or form a joint venture with another company to assemble a package of the requisite technologies. For example, when Arm and Hammer decided to introduce their baking-powder toothpaste internationally they obviously had the necessary product and process technologies. However, they did not have the skills or marketing resources to support the launch of the product in unfamiliar markets. For this reason, in the UK, they used the resources of the marketing agency Food Brokers to provide the necessary marketing technologies.

Definitions of the three types of technologies are given below:

1 Product technology is *knowledge* of the physical properties and characteristics of materials and the *ability* to incorporate these into the design of products or services which could be of value to another company or individual.

2 Process technology is *knowledge* of ways of producing products or services and the *ability* to produce these so that they have value to others.

3 Marketing technology is *knowledge* of ways of bringing these product and process technologies to a particular application and the *ability* to carry this out. This involves the skills of market analysis, branding, packaging, pricing, communications and logistics.

THE INTERDEPENDENCE OF COMPANIES

The second major issue of technology and interaction centres on the interdependence of companies. It is a false picture to see a company as the master of its own destiny, building its independent strategy and trying to get a favourable reaction from the market – such a view is more appropriate to the rather colourful newspaper accounts of the lives of famous industrial 'barons' than it is to an understanding of industrial reality.

There are a number of reasons for this. It is difficult to imagine a company which is able to meet any application in a modern market solely on the basis of its own technologies. A hundred years ago, railway companies brought-in raw timber and billets of iron and created locomotives, carriages and wagons using their own skills and abilities. Nowadays, the products of most companies depend to a great extent on the technologies of others, whether they are supplying technology in its 'pure' form via licence etc., or whether the technology is incorporated in the products or services which the company buys. Increasingly, both the pace of technology change and the escalating up-front cost of R&D mean that it becomes more and more difficult for a company to maintain a position in even a relatively narrow technological area, much less in a wide range of technologies. A company is faced with the difficult question of which technologies it should continue to devote its resources to maintaining and developing internally and which it should regard as external technologies it has the benefit of, such as when the company buys products based on external technologies but does not own them.

CONCLUSIONS

This chapter has introduced the idea of technology strategy as three interrelated tasks of acquiring, managing and exploiting technology. The tasks are interrelated because the process of technology acquisition takes place with the specific purpose of, and frequently in parallel with, the exploitation of that technology. The task of managing technology has both short-term and longer-term strategic aspects. It involves managing a set of resources, only some of which are tangible, and many of which exist in the form of the knowledge and abilities of the company's employees and, indeed, in the culture and collective experience of the company. A good analogy for this management task is that of the farmer who seeks to exploit the assets of his land, but at the same time seeks to replenish those assets and leave the land 'in good heart' for his successors.

Although some technologies are individually important, a bundle of product, process and marketing technologies are needed to meet the requirements of a company's markets. In some cases it is prowess in only one or a subset of these technologies which makes for competitive advantage. In other cases none of the company's technologies will be distinctive when compared to other companies. But it is the company's skill in assembling the appropriate bundle of technologies to deliver the requirements of its customers which is distinctive. No company has all of the technologies which are needed to satisfy the requirements of a market. A company must work with others around it and use their skills as external technologies so as to assemble the required bundle of technologies. This bundling will involve many companies; the process of bundling may be more or less controlled by all the companies in a wide network ranging from component manufacturers to retailers. The management of a company's position and interactions in that network is a major issure of strategy. Through those network interactions its technological resources acquire their value to other members of the network and to final customers.

REFERENCES

1   Quinn, J. B. and Mintzberg, H. (1991) *The Strategy Process: Concepts, Contexts and Cases*, Englewood Cliffs, NJ: Prentice-Hall.
2   Ford, D. (ed.) (1990) *Understanding Business Markets*, London: Academic Press.
3   Nonaka, I. (1990) 'Redundant, overlapping organization: a Japanese approach to managing the innovation process', *California Management Review*, Spring: 27–38.
4   Ford, D. (1988) 'Develop your technology strategy', *Long Range Planning*, **21**(5): 85.
5   Ohmae, K. (1982) '*The Mind of the Strategist – the Art of Japanese Business*', New York: McGraw-Hill.
6   Lake, K. and Trayes, A. (1990) 'Technology and networks', unpublished MBA project report, University of Bath.

Chapter 4

The technology audit as a basis for technology strategy

INTRODUCTION

This chapter examines the processes by which a company can audit its technological resources and compare them to the companies with which it competes or which may affect its future. It is difficult for the manager to decide at what level of detail such an analysis should be carried out, and could lead to an attempt to list and evaluate every technical activity which the company performs. Because of this it is worth emphasising that the aim of the exercise is to obtain an understanding of the overall technological position and of the important technological issues the company faces. This chapter presents an outline of the type of questions that can be used to provide that understanding. The chapter starts with a discussion of some of the complexities in the task of auditing technology.

COMPLICATIONS OF A TECHNOLOGY AUDIT

There are a number of complications in attempting a technology audit and which distinguish it from the more commonly experienced marketing[1] and financial audits. These complexities are outlined below.

Basis of comparison

Technology audits are made complicated because a company's technology cannot be assessed solely by examining the company itself. Nor will it be sufficient to compare a company's position relative to where it was at some previous time. Simply comparing over time would make it difficult to answer such questions as: How reasonable was the time it took us to develop and commercialize a technology? What was the quality of the technology we developed and how successful was the company in exploiting it?

A better perspective for understanding a company's position can be achieved by comparing a company's technology with that of its immediate competitors. But even this comparison may not reveal important technological issues which the industry as a whole may not have faced. Just as a single company can 'miss the tide' of technological change occurring in other industries, so too can a whole industry operate without knowing about a particular technology which could transform it.

For example, the oxygen systems supplied to high-performance military aircraft traditionally stored oxygen on the aircraft in tanks under very high pressure in order to save space. The oxygen was then delivered to the flight crew at the correct pressure via a complex set of valves. Companies competed in the design of these systems and in their attempts to save weight and space. However, there already existed an entirely different technology which was widely used in other applications, but which was unknown to this industry. This technology was molecular filtration. Within a very short time of the first company finding out about the technology, this specialised industry was transformed. Now on-board oxygen systems have dispensed with bulky tanks and substituted a small scoop and filter which captures oxygen molecules in the rarefied upper atmosphere in which these planes fly.

Such a transformation would have been possible earlier if the companies involved had taken a wider technological view. Any company doing this would have been at an obvious advantage in an industry with a small number of orders, each of very high value and where a technical advantage can exclude competitors for many years.

Even those companies which are technologically ahead of their immediate competitors are vulnerable to the danger of invasion of their industry by those from elsewhere using newer technologies. There have been many examples of such invasions, such as the impact of Japanese companies on the mechanical watch industry, or the move of electronic component companies into the calculator industry. This type of move was at the expense of well-established companies such as Facit in Sweden. Facit was a leader in its industry, but operated with a mechanical technology which was out of date when looked at from a wider perspective. A wider perspective for analysing technologies can also form the basis of a phased exploitation of a single technology across different industries and applications. This was once a stated policy of Texas Instruments. Their operating guidelines included an aim to 'exploit microprocessor strengths . . . and expand into contiguous segments'.[2]

Single technologies

A second complication in a technology audit is that it is difficult to analyse the acquisition or exploitation of a single technology alone. For example, the successful exploitation of a particular new product technology is likely to take place as part of a bundle which includes a number of other support technologies. These support technologies include other product, process and marketing technologies. The successful exploitation of a new technology in a particular application can be prevented by the absence of a necessary support technology that may be specific to that application.

Example
The importance of support technologies in a new tea product

Four out of five British people drink tea, but volume is declining as more people switch to coffee. The constant need to increase margins to cope with this decline has led to producers promoting a move from loose tea to tea bags and to other innovations of varying appeal such as instant tea, one-cup bags and round bags.

Recently, one manufacturer launched what they described as, 'the first real advance in the quality of tea since it was introduced into the UK in the seventeenth century'. This innovation rested on a new process technology. Research found that certain volatiles in tea change drastically when exposed to air in the first ten weeks after picking. To avoid this, tea needs to be isolated from oxygen and so the new product was picked, dried and vacuum-packed within twenty-four hours. Once in the UK it was sealed in nitrogen flushed bins until blended and put into tea bags.

Exploitation of the new process technology depended on the availability of suitable packaging. The Typhoo company is using foil pouches. This support technology had been developed independently of the process technology at the core of the innovation. Without it, the project could not have proceeded.

Conceptualising technology

Another complication in a technology audit is that managers often have difficulty in conceptualising their technologies or clearly articulating their position. We have already noted that it is natural for managers to concentrate more on the applications of their technologies in products or processes and to think in terms of useful bundles, rather than individual technologies. For example, even a simple electric hand-drill is based on the product technologies of motor design, plastics and metal alloys. It also rests on the process technologies of armature winding, plastic extrusion, automated assembly, etc. Any and all of these may provide opportunities for competitive advantage or innovation. However, for this to take place the company must separate these technologies and assess its position in each of them relative to its immediate competitors and to technological movement in a wider arena.

Technology and customers: the technology gap

Another complication in technology assessment is the importance of relating a company's technological position to that of its customers. We have already emphasised the idea that a technology itself is of no value and that value only exists through interaction with others.

Suppose an auto manufacturer is keen to buy fuel-injection equipment from a particular component supplier for use in a range of diesel cars and light trucks. The buyer may favour this supplier because it has the latest product technology, based on electronic control, and gives the greatest performance. He may be prepared to pay a premium price for this performance and even accept poor consistency of quality from the supplier, perhaps because the product is based on a process technology which is either less advanced or, as yet unproven. At this early stage the gap between the knowledge of the new product technology held by the seller and that of the buyer will probably be large. The customer is an unskilled buyer of the new technology product and will need, and usually pay a premium for, the supplier's advice as to how the new technology will be appropriate for the customer to use.

This situation is unlikely to last. Over time, the buyer's knowledge of the technology on which the product is based may increase. This increase could be because the buyer has become familiar with using the technology through its interplay with work on developing the company's vehicle engines. Alternatively, it may simply be because the technology has diffused widely and become part of every other suppliers' offerings. For whatever reason, the customer is now a skilled buyer of that product technology. He or she will now be less likely to pay the same price as before for what is now regarded as a commodity or for the seller's advice and problem-solving skills. In this situation the seller will only be able to retain a premium in the business with that customer if one of three things can be achieved:

- create new distinctiveness in the product technology;
- create distinctiveness in the process technology and therefore the consistency of quality;
- create distinctiveness in the marketing technology through relationship management skills or superior ability to deliver a standardised product to the buyer based on logistics ability.

Many companies hit hard times when they build an organisation on the assumption of a wide technology gap with their customers, with high levels of customer service, high margins and high overheads, only to find that such an organisation is unsustainable when the technologies in their products becomes commoditised. The most obvious recent example is the personal computer industry, where the margins achieved by manufacturers when dealing with uncertain new buyers could not be sustained as the knowledge and skills of these buyers increased after a number of purchases. A diagramatic representation of the buyer–seller technology gap is given in Fig. 4.1.

It is worth noting in Figure 4.1 that the lines indicating the technological knowledge of the seller and the buyer cross. There are many examples were the buyer understands more about a product technology than does the seller. In this case the buyer and not the seller is contributing the product technology to the relationship and the seller is making to the design of the buyer. There are instances where the buyer is also contributing the process technology to the relationship. In this case the seller is simply contributing production capacity or labour, plus perhaps any marketing or logistical technology that may be required. This situation is common in buying from some third world countries in the early stages of their development,[3] and is increasingly common in the relationships between retailers and their suppliers where the retailer often develops innovative products and provides the manufacturer with both the product design and the specification for its production. A recent example where this has involved considerable technological change has been in the development and mass-marketing of chilled, prepared or 'value-added' food products by Marks and Spencer in the UK. Marks and Spencer provides product, process and marketing technology. Their suppliers trade-off the low margins they receive as the company which brings little or no technology to the deal against the advantages of a long-term relationship with the retailer.

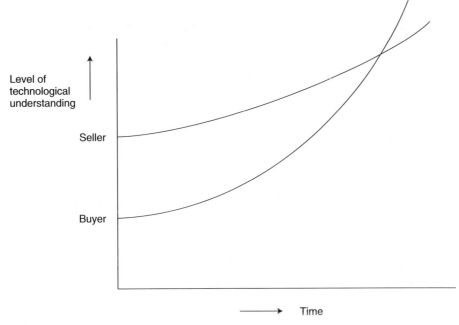

Figure 4.1 The buyer–seller technology gap

Example
The technology gap at an alloy manufacturer

A UK company was a pioneer in the development of nickel alloys. These initially found application in jet aircraft engines and later in petrochemical plants and the nuclear industry. Typically, a customer would approach the company with a problem involving high-temperature, acidity or vibration. The company would then develop a suitable alloy and present this to the customer. No charge was made for this development work and the company recouped its costs from the revenues received when the production alloy was delivered to the customer.

Over time nickel alloys started to be used in other applications; the cylinder heads of car-engines and the elements of electric cookers. Standard types of alloys became known in the market and the company found that it was being approached by customers requesting a price quotation for a standard alloy.

The company's first reaction was to ask customers if they were sure that this product was the right alloy for their requirements. This often produced an impatient response, 'What's the price and what's the delivery?' Clearly, the company's product technology was no longer valued by the market. What now was of importance was the ability of a company to supply a standardised product technology cheaply and efficiently.

The emphasis had changed to process and marketing technologies and the company went through considerable traumas as it tried to cope with a market which no longer valued what it regarded as its primary skills. The company had to change almost its entire culture as it sought to cope with work which it had previously thought was beneath its dignity.

Example
Other technology gaps

When US banks expanded into international markets, they were initially successful because they could move funds between countries more quickly and efficiently than the existing national banks. On the back of this ability they found that they could gain good loan, letter of credit and other work all at acceptable margins. Eventually, these clients and the national banks became familiar with the technology on which the funds transfer work was based. The US banks found that their clients felt able to 'cherry-pick' between banks for different elements of a commodity-type service at consequently lower margins.

The technology gap also provides an explanation of the old adage that, 'no one ever got fired for specifying IBM'. In the early days of computers, potential buyers knew little of the technology on which products were based; the technology gap was wide. Consequently they felt the need to rely on the strength of IBM's brand name. This became known within IBM as the FUD factor – fear, uncertainty and doubt! Somewhat later these same customers gained a greater knowledge of the technologies involved in computers. Although they could not design one for themselves, they knew the technological parameters which were involved. Now they were not prepared to pay such a high price for the no-longer-needed reassurance of IBM and were more inclined to buy from a plug-compatible peripheral manufacturer.

Technology bundles and time

A further complication in assessing a company's technological position is that the technological bundle it must assemble to satisfy customer requirements is likely to change over time. Mathur has suggested that this change can be seen as three separate stages.[4] In the first stage, a customer buying for the first time a product based on a particular technology is likely to buy a complete 'system' which consists of a bundle of the technology and other support technologies as well. This is partially caused by the customer's lack of knowledge of individual elements of the bundle of technologies which are needed, but also because the customer lacks skill in integrating different technologies from different sources. Using our fuel injection example again, we can imagine a customer in the early stage of applying this new technology being likely to buy a complete system of fuel pump, piping, controls and injectors, etc. from one supplier. In the second stage, when the customer's knowledge has increased through experience it is likely to 'de-systemise' its purchases and construct its own system. Therefore, the customer now is able to evaluate the different technologies involved and choose individual items separately, perhaps from separate manufacturers. Later still, in the third stage, this particular bundle of technologies may become commonplace in the customer's application so that it ceases to be a source of competitive advantage to the customer. Because of this the customer will seek to minimise the managerial and design resources it devotes to these technologies and will revert to buying a system again.

The issue of bundling also becomes important as more and more companies adopt a structure of 'tiered' suppliers. In this structure a company seeks to reduce its supply base and to rely on a small number of main suppliers. These in turn deal with and manage a larger number of suppliers, thus acting as system integrators for the main customer. The ultimate customer in this arrangement is effectively buying from its first-tier suppliers their ability to bundle together the respective technologies of suppliers further back in the chain. We shall return to this idea shortly when we will discuss the issue of external technologies in more depth.

DIMENSIONS OF A TECHNOLOGY AUDIT

The complexity of the concept of technology, the difficulty in describing it and the interrelationship between product and process technologies all cause difficulties in auditing. Some authors have attempted to apply sophisticated methods of analysis to 'measure' technology, such as the Q-sort approach used by Shrivastava[5] and Souder and Souder and Shrivastava.[6] However, we propose to use a more qualitative basis of assessment to concentrate on overall strategic issues in technology, though a series of questions which apply to the three areas of the company's product, process and marketing technologies. Ten questions applicable to a technology audit are listed below:

1 What technologies does the company possess?
2 Where did the technologies come from?
3 What is the range of our technologies?
4 What categories do our technologies fit into?
5 What is our standing in our technologies?
6 How new are our technologies?
7 What is the life-cycle position of our technologies?
8 What is our performance in acquiring technologies?
9 What is our performance in exploiting technologies?
10 What is our performance in managing technology?

We now look at each of these questions in turn.

WHAT TECHNOLOGIES DOES THE COMPANY POSSESS?

This analysis initially is at the level of technological resources. We have said that a technology itself is of no value, but that value is a function of the importance of the technology to others. Nevertheless it is a good starting-point to simply list the technologies which the company employs. Such a list may be long and may appear intimidating. It need not be detailed and many technologies can be omitted if they are common across a wide range of industries. The value of the list is to form a basis for a number of further questions.

WHERE DID THE TECHNOLOGIES COME FROM?

Were they developed internally, did they come from customers or suppliers or were they licensed in from others? These questions start to give an indication of the pattern of the company's technology acquisition activity. They may show that the company has been wholly dependent to date on internally acquired technology. In contrast to this one US chemical company in our early research reported that, 'Half our current technology either started with or is still under licence'. Another company's current position may be very largely dependent on the technology it has acquired from its customers, either formally or informally. Perhaps such a company will have developed the habit of carrying out work for one customer under this customer's guidance and then applying this newly acquired knowledge with others.

Further questions are raised. In the chemical company mentioned above, that was heavily dependent on licensed technology, it would be natural to ask questions about its R&D activity, particularly if it had been making major (and unsuccessful) R&D investments over many years with the aim of achieving more technological self-sufficiency. This may lead to the conclusion that it had either failed to generate valuable technology internally, failed to develop an appropriate bundle of technologies for a particular application or failed to commercialise successfully its technology.

More generally, these questions lead us to analyse the appropriateness and quality of the company's technology acquisition activity. We would ask about the balance between different methods of acquisition, the long-term implications of the company's acquisition methods for the quality of its technology base, as well as its overall performance in acquiring technology. We will refer further to these questions in Chapters 5 and 6.

WHAT IS THE RANGE OF OUR TECHNOLOGIES?

Grandstrand and Sjolander defined the 'multi-technology corporation' as being a company which operates in at least three different technologies.[7] We suggest that virtually all companies are multitechnology firms, especially when we consider process as well as product technologies and marketing technologies. It is obvious that not all of the technologies which a company uses are of equal importance to it in terms of achieving competitive advantage. Nevertheless, it is important that companies have an appropriate competence in all the technologies which they use.

However, many companies attempt to maintain leadership in a range of technologies which is far too wide for their resources, perhaps because the company drifts into investing in a wide range of internal R&D projects through a lack of strategic direction or the costs of a full range of R&D may escalate beyond that which can be funded from a restricted sales volume.

For example, the UK helicopter manufacturer Westland needs to maintain technological resources in a wide range of technologies: advanced structures, composite materials, avionics, gearboxes, rotor-blades, aerodynamics, ordinance, etc. However in its core operations, these resources can only be exploited in the sale of a small number of helicopters – perhaps five or ten in a good year! Such a company must either seek to reduce its total spend on acquiring new technologies in some of these areas by joint venture, licensing-in or buying product components from competitors, or it must seek wider applications for its technologies. Decisions on which technologies to maintain a position in, which to manage through joint venture and which to exploit in wider applications are of great strategic significance. Westland is in fact employing a variety of methods of acquisition and areas of exploitation. However, both it and its competitors jealously guard their technological independence in some areas which they regard as being critical for their long-term position, such as the design of helicopter rotor-heads. They are also conscious that unplanned licensing in of technology from other companies would be fraught with the risk that the company would lose its ability to ever again enter these fields of technology. Westland also understand that to seek a wider application for their technologies is extremely seductive for many companies but is often unsuccessful. This because the company may lack the necessary support technologies, often in the process and marketing areas, which are necessary to reach particular applications. We consider this issue further when we examine technology exploitation in Chapters 7 and 8.

Finally, there is one more reason why a company may attempt to maintain a position in a range of technologies which is too wide for its resources: because of the technological machismo we mentioned in Chapter 2. One manifestation of this is when the R&D manager or, often, the chief executive of a small (or large) firm sees his or her position exemplified in the pre-eminence in a particular, or indeed in ALL the technologies on which the business depends, often with disastrous results!

WHAT CATEGORIES DO OUR TECHNOLOGIES FIT INTO?

The company's range of technologies must now be separated into three categories in order to ease our analysis. This categorisation is illustrated in Figure 4.2, and has become known as the 'magic triangle', after being so described by a French manager with a strange idea of geometry.

Basic technologies

Basic technologies are those on which the company depends and without which it would not be able to operate in its markets. For example, in a car manufacturing company the process technology surrounding the operation of an assembly line is an essential prerequisite for a place in the industry. However, it may well be that a higher rate of technological investment in its assembly line may not at this time produce a worthwhile increase in competitive advantage when compared to investment in, for example, computerised design technology.

When managers in an industrial manufacturing company carried out a technology audit it found that approximately 70 per cent of its current R&D spend was into process technologies that would not be seen as a source of competitive advantage by its market. Their recommendation was to adjust investment levels in these basic areas in order to maintain the company's standing at a level approximating to the industry average and to switch more investment to those areas where it could achieve distinctiveness.

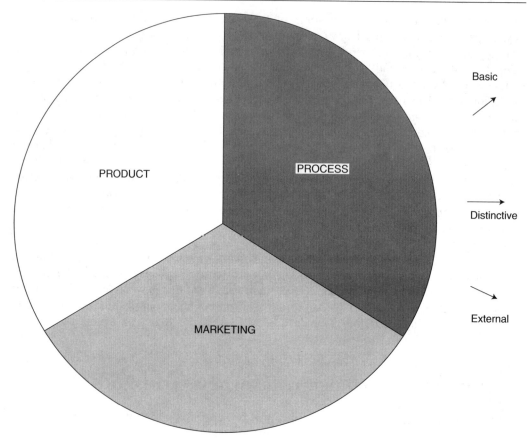

Figure 4.2 The 'magic triangle': three types of technologies

Distinctive technologies

Distinctive technologies for a company are those which are seen by its customers to provide a differential benefit when compared to the offerings of other suppliers. This distinctiveness can occur even if customers do not fully understand the technological basis of the benefit. For example, many customers believe in the safety skills of Volvo, even if they do not have much idea of the detailed technological basis of that skill. Customers *know* that it is a safe car. Distinctive technologies are those which confer competitive advantage. This competitive advantage can be either because the technology provides a cost advantage to the holder or because it enables the company to provide an enhanced product or service (of course, a cost advantage will only be recognised by customers indirectly or in the form of lower prices). For some car manufacturing companies the product and process technologies which provide corrosion protection may be distinctive, as long as they are recognised as such by the market. This may be the case with the German company Audi. For BMW a distinctive product technology could be the design of 'the world's smoothest straight-six auto-engine'.

Companies which compete in the same market can operate on the basis of distinctiveness in different technologies. *Distinctiveness is always defined by the market's view, not the view of the company.* The notion of distinctive technologies helps us to understand competitive position. Describing a company as the leading technological company in a particular market is rarely of much value. Not only do such positions change over time but they are specific to particular technologies or groups of technologies. For example, a senior manager in the UK automotive components industry said recently that he regarded Volkswagen as the leading product technology company in the European car industry, Nissan was the best in the production area and Ford was the leader in running a dealer network and in getting products to market, which we refer to as marketing technology. Of course for completeness of analysis we would need to examine the overall groups and look at individual technologies within the product, process and marketing areas.

The separation between basic and distinctive technologies is an important one. We refer to the absolute level of a company's competence in a technology as its 'standing' in that technology, and this is discussed in more detail below. A high standing in a technology will not guarantee competitive success. Only if that standing is perceived as distinctive by the market can it form the basis of competitive advantage. It may be a single technology which has distinctiveness in the eyes of the market and which may be directly observable by its effects, such as the new stain-removing characteristics of a particular detergent. Alternatively, a company's success may be built on several technologies which are distinctive, but less readily observable. These could also have effects which are well known to the market, for example the reliability of Toyota's vehicles is largely a function of various process technologies. Finally, we see later in this book that there are many examples of competitive advantage being achieved without distinctiveness in any one technology, but because of the company's ability to assemble a bundle of technologies which together meets the requirements of an application better than those of competition.

There is great danger for any company which assumes that just because it has a competence in a particular technology it automatically has a source of competitive advantage. We have met managers who use terms such as 'core' or 'key' technologies to describe the technologies of which they are proud. Further analysis may show that, although the technologies are important, they are basic and therefore a prerequisite to operation in the market; they only form a *basis* for competitive action based on other technologies.

Competitive advantage is a function of the ability to assemble an appropriate bundle of basic, distinctive and external technologies for each application. It is also a function of the company's ability to mobilise its technologies into features of value to the customer, or into operations having a cost advantage. Mobilisation can be a complicated task and may be immediately apparent to the customer in a product or service, or much less apparent in the way in which that product is provided. Technological standing can also be mobilised in terms of cost reduction which enables the company to offer an enhancement of product or service in other areas well removed from the original technology.[8]

An example of less apparent mobilisation of technology is provided by a company in the aerospace components industry. The company carried out a technology audit and this highlighted a high standing in its business systems technology. Its marketing staff asked the question, 'How can we sell this to a customer?' Clearly, this was a technology well removed from the more obvious skills of the company in component design and production.

The company's task was to mobilise this technological standing into features that the customer felt would give value. These features included improving flexibility in schedules and increasing stock-turn during projects, in turn reducing the customer's liability and lead time when required product changes were required. Of course these improvements were only seen to be of value when they were communicated by the company's marketing staff, who were now more aware of the company's technologies after the audit. Finally, there is a danger that technologies may be consigned to the 'basic' category and starved of investment. Although basic technologies may only be a necessary condition for success in a market, they are essential and some may still require major investment.

External technologies

We have already referred to external technologies as those which are not possessed by the company but are used by it. These technologies are embodied in the products and services that it buys. We have also noted that decisions on which technologies the company will acquire for itself and which it will acquire from its suppliers are of major long-term strategic significance. The separation of a company's technologies into the categories of basic or distinctive is also an important basis for strategy building. To seek to build distinctiveness in an area in which the company is not strong is likely to be both expensive and slow, and must be based on the soundest of strategic analyses. To unconsciously allow a distinctive position in a technology to wither away is a huge act of managerial neglect. Levels of investment in basic technologies must be appropriate to the position that the company wishes to maintain and must not be based on a grandiose idea to achieve 'overall distinctiveness', which is also likely to be expensive, probably unnecessary and ultimately fruitless.

Example
Using the magic triangle in an industrial distributor

This company is a highly successful international distributor of industrial components. It sells through a catalogue which contains many thousands of lines, backed up by a specialist sales force and trade-counters. The company's 'product' is the service to its customers, which includes the quality of the contents of its catalogue, its design and the service which provides technical advice and next-day delivery throughout its international territory.

Thus, its product technology is its ability to design and continuously develop this offering. The company's process techno-logy is the ability to actually provide this service, which includes skills in locating and buying products, managing relationships with suppliers, inventory management and order processing Marketing technology in this case consists of the ability to research and understand the needs of a market and to create tailored offerings to meet the needs of particular segments.

The company prided itself on the fact that its catalogue and its delivery performance was second to none – that its product and process technologies were distinctive.

Unfortunately, other companies began to offer very similar catalogues and to match its delivery performance, which had in effect become an accepted standard. Both technologies had become basic. Also, analysis showed that it had never had any distinctiveness in marketing technology and had simply offered a standardised offering to the whole market. Despite having a large sales force it had not developed strong skills in segmenting and tailoring its offering, and had little real idea of who within the companies it delivered to actually used its products. It faced increasing competition from companies which had the marketing technology to serve the requirements of particular segments of its markets.

This analysis led to a major change in strategy. The company continues to develop its product and process technologies so that they are at least at the state-of-the-art level. However, it acknowledges that these alone are unlikely to be a major source of competitive advantage.

The company's main strategic thrust is to build a defensible position of distinctiveness in marketing technology. By developing its skills in this area the company seeks to be able to spot and rapidly serve emerging requirements in new technologies as well as tailoring its existing offerings to different subsets of its current markets.

Range and distinctiveness

The matrix in Table 4.1 illustrates a number of the points we have made so far. It shows the range of technologies across the different companies in a single group. Grandstrand and Sjolander refer to these technologies as 'key'.[7] This approximates to our idea of distinctive technologies and is defined by them as the technologies which directly influence customer-relevant product performance and quality parameters or which allow for major cost reductions. The table shows how wide the range of technologies can be in a single company and the number which can contribute distinctiveness, and also illustrates the scale of the management task in husbanding these resources, particularly when they are spread widely

Table 4.1 Technology–company matrix for Saab-Scania Combitech group.
Source: Grandstrand, O. and Sjolander, S. (1990) 'Managing innovation in multi-technology corporations', Research Policy, 19.

Technology	Company									
	C1	C2	C3	C4	C5	C6	C7	C8	C9	C10
Electronic hardware	X	X	X	X	X	X	X	X	X	X
Man/machine communication		X	X	X	X	X	X			
Electronic packaging	X	X				X				
Micro-mechanical design		X	X	X	X	X	X			
Software		X	X	X			X			X
Computer communication	X			X		X				
Electro-optics		X	X			X	X	X		
Infra-red technology	X	X				X		X		
Microwave technology				X	X		X			
Laser technology		X						X		
Hydro-acoustics		X		X						
Image processing				X	X		X			
Artificial intelligence		X	X	X	X	X	X			
Systems technology		X	X	X	X	X	X	X		X

across different divisions within the company. This task is particularly important if the company is to effectively co-ordinate its resources so that all divisions can have the benefit of the appropriate technologies which the company holds. Table 4.1 also highlights the potential problem of overlap and duplication of effort which can occur if intra-organisational communication and learning are imperfect. All of these issues are included in the management of technology and we return to them at various points in the book, but particularly in Chapter 9.

WHAT IS OUR STANDING IN THESE TECHNOLOGIES?

The standing of a company in its technologies is different from the idea of being basic or distinctive. Standing is an objective measure of the technological resource the company has. We have often explained this concept to managers by saying that standing is a measure of the score the company would receive if it were to take an examination in its technology! Distinctiveness depends on how that standing is seen by the company's customers and, therefore, whether it is a source of competitive advantage. The latter depends on the requirements and perceptions of other companies in the network and the actions of the company itself in communicating its standing. Standing, most narrowly, refers to the relative quality of the company's technologies when compared to those of its immediate competitors. More broadly, quality is compared with companies which may operate in other applications or which may have initially developed that technology. A technology can form the basis of a number of products, so the assessment process is more complex than would be the case with individual products themselves.

We have found wide variation in the assessment of a company's standing in a particular technology, between those whose role has been to develop the technology and those who have been responsible for bringing it to the market. Neither of these groups is likely to have a similar view to those in customer companies where again views may vary between, for example, engineers and buyers.

Outside consultancy

This difficulty of achieving an objective assessment of technological standing is one reason why many companies use the services of outside consultants for the initial audit of their technologies. Even if outsiders are used, we will see later that the company's management will still have the task of continuously monitoring technology standing as the basis for acquisition and exploitation decisions. More importantly, an assessment of technology standing gives a clear idea of the technological resources that a company has to work with.

Standing in different applications

We should emphasise that the assessment of technology standing is not something which can be considered either in general across all a company's technologies or in abstract. The standing of a technology is application specific. A company can have a high standing with a particular technology in one application area, but a much lower one in another application area where competitors are more advanced. This can be a major problem when a company seeks to widen the application of its technologies. However, a company may choose to operate with a low standing in a specific technology if it does not wish to build that particular distinctiveness. Obviously, a high technology standing in those areas where the company claims distinctiveness is of greater importance than where it chooses to operate with a basic technology. Because of this a company needs to relate its standing in each technology and each application to those companies which are following a similar approach to its own strategy. For example, if it seeks to achieve distinctiveness in a particular technology then its acquisition programme must have regard to that of any competitor taking a similar approach. If it wishes to operate at the basic level in a technology then it must watch those of its competitors that are following a similar 'entry-ticket' approach.

Wide analysis

Different technologies are to a greater or lesser extent tailored to specific applications. The standing of all technologies in any company must be judged initially according to the requirements of the application for which they are intended. However, it is also important that these technologies are evaluated against those of other companies in other application areas. It is unlikely that in many cases a complete analysis either could or should be made. Nevertheless, some idea of more general relative standing is important so that the company may become aware of the possibility of exploiting its standing in applications where the incumbent competitors have lower technologies. A wide analysis may also serve to forewarn the company of the possibility of competitive entry by another company from another application area or the prospect of a more immediate competitor acquiring this technology from the same area.

HOW NEW ARE OUR TECHNOLOGIES?

We are all familiar with the sort of statements which proud managers make, 'Sixty per cent of our sales come from products which we have introduced in the last three years'. These statements in themselves say little about the newness of the products or of the technologies on which they are based. The products can be new to that firm but similar to those previously launched by other companies into the same market. The products may be based on product or process technologies which are entirely new or which have been used by this or other companies in many different applications.

Therefore, a clear understanding of the newness of a technology will depend on separating out different aspects of newness. The ability to assess the newness of a technology is an essential prerequisite to understanding competitive position and a basis for developing strategy for its exploitation in particular application areas.

Figure 4.3 shows the interrelationships between different aspects of newness of products and technologies. Cells 1, 4 and 7 refer to the situation where a new product is based on a

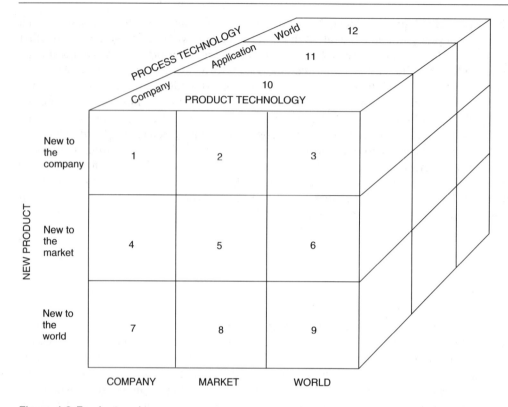

Figure 4.3 Product and process newness

product technology that is new to the company, but which has previously been used by others. Cell 1 refers to a product which is new to the company but not to the market or application and is based on a product technology already used by others in that particular market. This is an extreme form of 'me-too-ism' and if it were to be successful the company would have to have the advantage of lower input costs in the form of labour or raw materials, more advanced process technologies (cells 10–12), marketing technology or a willingness to accept a lower price. This me-too-ism may be quite common. For example, a components manufacturer recounted that he had just been sent the drawings for a main customer's next-generation new product. The manufacturer's analysis showed that the customer appeared to have arrived at this product by buying and reverse-engineering the current product of a successful competitor!

Cell 4 involves the launch of a product which is new to the market but which is based on a product technology which has previously been used by others in that market. An example would be the introduction of a new IBM-compatible personal computer, which used existing technologies in a more user-friendly way. A product launch such as this could depend on the company's marketing technologies for its success or it may rely on innovative process skills to obtain competitive advantage (cell 11).

Cell 7 is the launch of an entirely new type of product based on a product technology which is new to the company, but which has previously been used by others in that market, is a higher level of innovation than cell 4. Cell 7 represents an important, but often undervalued aspect of business. It has at least two manifestations. The first when a late-comer to a market may use its greater knowledge of the requirements of that market to rearrange the technologies used in a product which has already been launched by someone else. In this way the follower produces a product more acceptable to the market. The company could also use its greater knowledge of support technologies to transform the product offering, perhaps in terms of product reliability or customer perception, etc. For example, Bic transformed the shaving market when it applied its process technology previously used in making ball-point pens to produce disposable razors (cell 11), using a product technology that was new to the company. The second manifestation of cell 7 concerns the introduction of later generations of product based on a single generic technology through what might be termed a process of 'technological refinement'. A company often has to make a critical decision as to whether it should further refine an existing technology to provide minor product modifications, or make a major change to a new technology with all the costs and risks that may involve. We examine this issue in greater depth in Chapter 5.

Cells 2, 5 and 8 refer to the first use of a product technology in a particular market. In cell 8 the company is using the technology to produce a product which is not only new to the specific market (cell 5) but is new to the world. An example would be the Sony Minidisc, which took existing compact disc product technology (with some modification), used it in the mobile entertainment market and produced a product that was new to the world. In cell 2 the technology is new to the market and the product into which it is incorporated is new to the company. Unless the company has used the technology in other applications then it is making both a technological and a product innovation. The distinction between the two innovations is important for strategic analysis. A simultaneous product and technology change is likely to produce more strain on a company than a conventional new-product introduction within an existing technological, or the insertion of a new technology into an existing product.

Cells 3, 6 and 9 refer to what is conventionally thought of as technological innovation where a new technology is launched for the first time into the world. But there are differences between the three categories. Cell 9 represents the most extreme form of innovation where the company is launching an entirely new product based on a product technology which has had no previous application in this or any other company. Apart from the obvious technological and market risks in this type of project, such an introduction will probably require the company to develop support technologies for itself or to use the services of others to provide them. For example, the originating company may wish to have a new product manufactured or marketed by another company. But in this extreme case it may have difficulty in finding other companies that have the necessary product, process or marketing technologies and with which it can establish the links to bring the product to market.

Cell 3 represents the introduction of a new technology into a product area which is new to the company but which already contains other competing products. An example of this is when a technology has arisen incidentally to the main thrust of a company's research. The company may decide to exploit the technology even though it has no experience of the product area. It is thus inserting this new technology. In these circumstances the company would also be likely to lack the appropriate support technologies. However, here it is more likely to find other companies with the necessary marketing, and possibly process technologies, with which it could interact. More difficulty may be expected in forming links with those who possess the necessary marketing technologies where the company planned to launch a product into a new application area (cell 6). We will look in more detail at the issue of the integration and matching of technologies from different companies when we examine technology exploitation decisions in Chapter 8.

For simplicity this discussion has referred to products and product technology. We could draw a similar diagram for processes and process technologies, or indeed for the interrelationship between process technologies and products or vice versa. The important issues are that our analysis must separate technologies from their applications. In this way we can make sense of the underlying basis of products and processes, and develop a clear view of the nature of technology and application changes and how their interrelationships affect the firm.

High and low technology

In the same way that the newness of a technology is a relative term, so the often used terms of high and low technology are equally relative. Throughout this book we have tried to avoid using them, simply because they seldom add to the debate. A technology may be considered 'high' and therefore 'new' in one particular application while simultaneously being viewed as 'low' by a competitor which is familiar with its use elsewhere. This reinforces the importance of analysing technology newness from a wide perspective and so avoid the problems caused when high technology is rendered obsolescent by the entry of a product based on technology which is new to that market, but well established in another application.

WHAT IS THE LIFE-CYCLE POSITION OF OUR TECHNOLOGIES?

The analysis of the newness of a technology only provides a snapshot of its position and gives no idea what has happened to it and what might happen in the future. In order to obtain a more complete picture we need to use the concept of the technology life cycle (TLC) to enable us determine how well the company has managed the 'careers' of these technologies. Marketing tasks change through the life of a product from introduction to deletion. Similarly, the tasks facing a manager also change when he or she seeks to achieve the optimum benefit from exploiting a technology over its life. Life-cycle management includes the tasks of selling products based on the technology, perhaps licensing the technology, to others and managing the interrelationships between a product technology and the process and marketing technologies on which it depends. These technology interrelationships will probably change through the different stages in the life of the technology.

The idea of the TLC has been used by a number of authors with more or less precision. The early Ford and Ryan article emphasised the importance of looking at the life of technologies rather than products.[9] It identified a series of stages in a technology life cycle

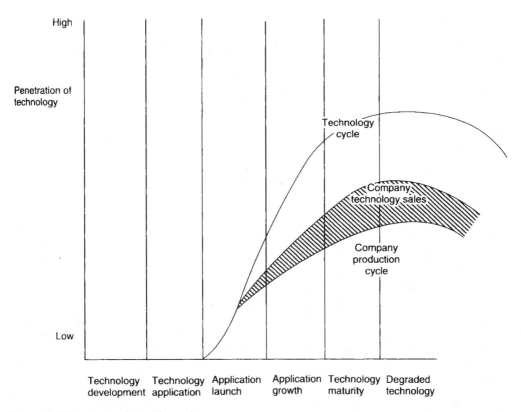

Figure 4.4 The technology life cycle
Source: Ford, D. and Ryan, C. (1981) 'Taking technology to market', *Harvard Business Review*, March–April.

and examined the different managerial decisions involved in each of them. An idealised TLC is shown in Figure 4.4.

The diagram refers to a single technology and is drawn from the perspective of the originator of the technology. For simplicity we will discuss the cycle of a product technology, although a similar cycle could also be drawn for both process and marketing technologies. The top line in the diagram, the overall Technology Cycle, plots the penetration of the technology. This is the extent of the use of the technology by all companies in all applications when compared to the use of other technologies in the same applications. The lower line, the Company Production Cycle plots the sales of the originating company's own products based on the technology. This is the company's in-house exploitation of the technology. The area between this and the middle line, Company Technology Sales, is a measure of the potential revenue which could be generated by direct sale of the technology by the originating company to others by licensing, or as part of a joint venture. We describe the TLC from the perspective of a company introducing a technology which is new to the world, but the diagram could be used for other companies subsequently introducing their own versions of a technology.

Stage 1: Technology development

Stage 1 is the pre-launch phase for a technology that is new to the world. It occurs before an application for the technology has been determined and is a stage of research rather than development. At this time the critical strategic question is whether or not the technology should be developed further. Normally, development continues if:

- the technology has an obvious application in a readily identifiable market that fits within the company's overall strategy;
- the company has the financial resources to develop the technology and the technology is compatible with that company's production and marketing skills.

However, the situation is often less clear-cut. The technology may have several potential applications which may require quite different supporting process or marketing technologies. For example, one application may need a product to be produced by mass-production methods at a low cost while another may require higher quality levels at lower outputs. A further application perhaps might be reached by subcontracted distribution but yet another may require the establishment of an entirely new, dedicated sales force.

   Whatever the case, it is important that those involved in the decision on whether or not to proceed have a sufficiently broad perspective. All too frequently these decisions are taken by R&D staff alone, who are unlikely to have a broad enough perspective of the potential applications of a technology. This does not mean necessarily that conventional product marketing staff should take the decision on further development. Marketing staff are frequently accused of taking a short-term approach and of emphasising the immediate exploitation of existing product and market assets at the expense of long-term development. This is often said to be a function of their generally short job tenures. Even those who are able to take a more strategic perspective may have an inappropriate idea of what constitutes the long term. Their view will be based on their experience of product life cycles which are likely to be much shorter than the cycles which characterise technologies. We examine the general issues of staffing, organisation and decision-making for technology exploitation in detail in Chapter 8. For the moment we emphasise the importance of a wide analysis and a strategic perspective among the group of people involved in the development decision. The issues involved in this analysis include the following:

1 Should the company find a partner which has the resources to help fund the development of the technology or which has the process or marketing technologies necessary to achieve success in wider or different applications, and so enhance the potential returns?
2 Should the company try to sell the technology 'whole' if it does not have an immediate application within the company's present markets or strategy?

   Selling a technology to another company at this stage is likely to be difficult because it does not have a recognisable application and so it will not be easy to value, by the developer or any potential buyer.

Stage 2: Technology application

This is the stage which occurs after a company has decided to incorporate a new technology into a product. As we have already discussed, this may mean that the product itself is wholly new or that the company is inserting the new technology into an existing product type. Whichever the case, it is now that the company starts to incur major costs. These costs consist not only of the costs of developing the technology itself, but also of acquiring the necessary support technologies of process and marketing. Now that the application of the technology is clearer, a realistic assessment of at least the immediate potential of the technology becomes possible. Also, it will become easier to identify the required support technologies, and determine which should be developed internally and which must come from partners. These partners could include companies that supply goods or services based on the developer's technologies. The suppliers often would need to invest capital or to develop their own technology in order to provide the products required by the developer. Partners could also include another company which would join a joint venture to exploit the technology. Joint ventures are more likely to be set up at this stage, as a potential for the technology can be more fully demonstrated at the prototype or pre-production stage.

The company could decide that although the technology has exploitable potential it does not fit the company's strategy. This could be because the company lacks the necessary financial or technological resources or because it would take the company away from its strategic direction. In this case the company could seek to sell the technology to another company for a fee, which would probably involve abandonment of the company's own development work in the area.

Licensing a technology to others may also occur at this stage. The value of a technology for licensing is likely to increase when it can be demonstrated to have marketable applications. But, licensing-out decisions are almost always difficult, at least if they are properly thought through. We have already stated in Chapter 2 that licensing seems most often to occur at the initiative of the licensee. Therefore, in many cases the decision to license-out is reactive and so is not based on a full evaluation of all the alternatives by the licensor. At this early stage it may be even more difficult for the owner of a technology to assess whether it is appropriate or not to license or to be able to find and effectively communicate with potential licencees.

Unfortunately, there are no neat rules-of-thumb for taking licensing decisions at this stage. Too many variables enter the equation: the initial development costs of the technology; the company's cash-flow position; its other development load; the technology's potential; the availability of suitable licencees; the possibility of segmenting the applications into discrete areas; and, perhaps most important, the extent to which the technology is essential to the company's present or future activities. We will examine these variables in some depth in Chapters 7 and 8.

Stage 3: Application launch

Paradoxically, the time immediately after a technology has been developed and incorporated into a product is likely to be a period of considerable product change. The initiator of a

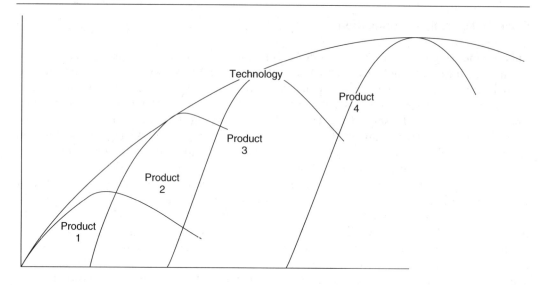

Figure 4.5 Technology and product life cycles
Source: Ansoff, H. I. (1984) *Implementing Strategic Management*, Englewood Cliffs, NJ: Prentice-Hall.

new technology and any imitators will all be involved in what may appear as a frantic rush to refine the technology and introduce a succession of new product variants based on the refined version. These may be more and more tailored to the requirements of a particular application but at this stage the emphasis is likely to be on general performance enhancement rather than on segment targeting. This stage corresponds to the 'performance maximising' phase described by Abernathy and Utterback.[10]

The technology may have been developed to this point with the involvement of a potential user. If so, the company faces decisions about the possible wider application of the technology, away from its initial use, and the introduction of successive generations of product. Such decisions may be taken jointly if the technology has been developed with a user, and they will start from a firmer base and perhaps be less urgent than when a user is not involved.

Without user involvement the considerations facing the company are more complex. The company which originated the technology, having faced the high costs of its development must now fund the introduction of the first application of the technology. The company must commit or acquire the necessary marketing technologies to enable it to analyse the market, build a tailored offering to specific segments, communicate the new product concept and deliver it to customers. Additionally, it will have to consider the timing of successive product introductions and the interrelationships between product and technology changes. Even at this early stage of a technology's life the company must base its actions on a view of the probable life of the technology. At this point the company is most likely to be concerned with the costs, characteristics and timing of the introduction of successive new products based on the technology. But each product introduction is a contribution to the total return on that technological investment and each product is itself a further investment in that technology. Each product must be judged on the basis of the overall financial return on investment and not in isolation.

The timing of successive product introductions within a technology is an important factor in competitive action. If the company has a clear view of the application *and* the life of a technology then it can plan the introduction of new products timed to meet or forestall competitive launches. This is rather like the way in which a product originator can preplan price reductions to meet competitive actions. Economists often refer to this as 'sliding down the demand curve' and perhaps we can write about 'sliding round the TLC curve' with a programme of preplanned product launches. Figure 4.5 illustrates the interrelationships between product cycles and technology cycle.[11]

Stage 4: Application growth

The fourth stage corresponds approximately to the 'sales maximising' phase described by Abernathy and Utterback in their discussion of product and process cycles.[12] Sales maximising is when sales of product based on the technology are growing rapidly. During this stage the issues facing the company change. The introduction of successive generations of product within the original application is still important, but the wider exploitation of the technology becomes of greater significance. If the originator of the technology wishes to exploit it in different applications then different support technologies may be required. For example, the originating company may require the co-operation of another company with channels of distribution which are able to reach the new application (marketing technology). The decision on which new applications to pursue is not simply one of deciding which areas offer the most sales or profit potential. Other considerations include:

1 The costs of developing product for the new application and of acquiring the necessary support technologies. These costs may involve the recruitment of a specialised new sales force or of process development to achieve the low product costs necessary for the new application. The costs may also be expressed in terms of lower margin achieved by the use of other companies' technologies on a joint-venture or subcontract basis, when compared to an alternative application.

2 The potential of the new application. A company may find that it has the resources to exploit a technology which it has developed in only a relatively narrow area. It may lack the financial or technological resources to effectively enter different and larger applications with the necessary speed, i.e. before the technology is overtaken by a later rival. This may lead the company to consider licensing as an alternative means of exploitation at this time.

3 The prospects for technological leadership. A decision to go it alone in exploiting a technology which is seen by competitors to be successful is likely to lead to these competitors intensifying their efforts to develop their own version of the current technology or of a later generation. In contrast, a willingness to share the technology on a licence or joint-venture basis may be used as a way of ensuring that others do not develop their own versions and therefore remain as technology followers. This decision should be based not just on the immediate cost and revenue issues, but on a strategic awareness of

whether the company's strengths do lie in the area of technological innovation. If not then it is unlikely to be able to continue to maintain the technological leadership it is seeking.

4 The issue of standardisation. The issue of formal government standards and both formal and informal industry standards is often vital in the growth phase of a technology. Standardisation can mean increased revenue for the standard through increased product sales and through licence revenue from other producers. The originator of a technology has the advantage that as the first product on the market, its product *is* the standard, at least initially. But, by the growth stage competitors, perhaps with more resources, may bid to achieve standardisation. Informal standards are those which are widely accepted, although not legally enforced. Examples include the VHS system for video recorders and the MS DOS operating system for personal computers. Standardisation is not always achieved by the technical excellence of a particular product technology, but because that technology has achieved the greatest share of the market in a particular application. This was the case in the well-known battle between the VHS, Beta and Philips 2000 video systems; the marketing technology strengths of Matsushita led it to victory over its rivals.

Example
Standardisation and licensing:
Dolby Corporation

Standardisation is also sometimes achieved through an early decision to license a technology to others. This licensing can be within a single application or with many applications. A good example of licensing within a specific application was Ray Dolby's noise-reduction technology for tape recorders.

Dolby developed the product technology to take the high-frequency hiss out of tape recorders. He did not have the necessary support product, process or marketing technologies to launch a new product on to the consumer market, nor was the technology of proven value in the minds of potential users. Dolby proved his technology by producing tailor-made products which incorporated the technology for use in the professional recording studio application. He did not license the technology to rivals in this application.

Even after the technology had been proven, he still did not have the resources to launch a product in the consumer area where he would also have faced retaliation from much larger competitors. So he offered licences to all the manufacturers of consumer tape recorders at an initial fee of 50 cents per unit. Part of the licence deal was that he guaranteed them access to any future developments in the technology.

Thus he not only achieved standardisation for his technology, indicated by the famous double 'D' symbol on tape recorders, but he also effectively removed them as future rivals in developing noise-reduction technology. He used the revenues he generated to fund the development of this technology and sound technology for other applications, most notably the famous 'Dolby Sound' used in cinemas.

Stage 5: Technology maturity

A mature technology will have been modified and improved by the originator and by other companies which have developed their own versions. It may also have been used by many companies in a number of applications other than the initial one. At this stage some technologies will still be owned by the originator, because of either its continuing patent protection or unique knowledge. In some cases the originator will receive licence fees from other companies for using the technology. In other cases the technology will be more freely known and available to many companies, irrespective of whether or not the originator is still responsible for the majority of sales of products which use the technology. As well as patent protection, the use of mature technologies depends on the width of its possible applications, the likely length of its life before being supplanted by others and the speed of its penetration of different application areas.

Technologies make a clearly observable progression through different applications. A technology will arrive and be used in different applications at different times and therefore will be seen as being both new and mature at the same time by those involved in different applications. A major task for those using a technology is to plan and take advantage of its exploitation in areas where it is not yet mature. Such a task often involves diversification for the company. This diversification imposes problems for a company with, for example, a product technology which has possible application in areas where it does not have the necessary process or marketing technologies. It is often difficult for such a company to conceive of these diverse applications because its marketing function will probably have no ready knowledge of them. The company may find it difficult to recognise the relatively few applications where it would be worthwhile to invest management and financial resources either alone or with others, rather than to concentrate on the applications it is more familiar with. This problem re-emphasises the importance of scanning with a wide perspective when evaluating the company's technological position. Technology scanning is also important from the perspective of a company working in a particular application, perhaps relying on mature technology. These companies need to look outside the areas of their current applications and the technologies which they employ, to search for technologies which have not yet reached their application. For these companies, scanning can avoid the problems caused by the sudden introduction by a competitor of a technology into a new application.

But perhaps the biggest issue facing the company with a mature technology is when it should introduce a product based on a *new* technology rather than another version of product based on the existing technology. Such a technology change is likely to produce the same problems caused by inertia and emotional attachment as occur when companies are involved in the deletion of existing products. These problems are likely to be more acute in the case of a technology for a number of reasons:

1 A technology will probably have been an important part of the life of the company for longer than a product and may have spawned several generations of products.
2 A technology will represent a greater level of development investment than a product (although not necessarily a greater total investment when marketing costs are taken into

account). Any change will involve the company in writing off this investment of money, experience and ego and embarking on a similar major investment.

3 The requirement for a product change is clear-cut and ultimately is signalled by the market. What is less clear-cut is whether that product change should be accomplished by minor modification or a radical technology shift. The technology on which a product, or even more strongly a process, depends often will be 'hidden' from the market, which will have little knowledge of it. Technologies can also be 'hidden' from the company's management, so that they are taken for granted until such time as its obsolescence is made obvious by the market offerings of its competitors.

Of course, a technology is not always developed because of an identified market requirement and, indeed, if technology decisions must wait until a requirement becomes apparent then almost certainly the technology will be too late on the market. The process is much more accurately seen as one in which the development of new technology parallels the exploitation of the old. Success depends on the quality of the bridges which the company is able to build between the two activities and the appropriateness of the distance between them.

Stage 6: Degraded technology

Stage 6 is reached when a technology has reached the point of virtually universal exploitation. By this time patents and most licence agreements will have expired and the technology will be so well known as to be of no commercial value for direct sale. All companies operate with a mix of technologies of different maturity, but those in the degraded category are unlikely to be of major significance to successful companies. However, there two points of significance for us here:

1 If an analysis of a company's portfolio of technologies reveals a substantial number in the degraded category then this indicates either a comprehensive lack of competitiveness or a dependence on a very few technologies. Further, such a diagnosis would throw up urgent questions about which areas of technology should be addressed in order to rectify the problem and how the necessary technology should be acquired.

2 The fact that a technology has become degraded within one country or one area of application does not mean that it is universally degraded. There is a market for many seemingly degraded technologies in third world countries where they are more likely to fit with other available technologies than are newer ones. Very often the sale of such technologies is not a direct financial transaction, but part of a buy-back deal involving products produced using the technology and the local low-cost labour.

The TLC we have described refers to a single product technology. It would be possible to describe a similar cycle for a process or indeed a marketing technology. For example, database marketing is a marketing technology which involves the building manipulation and use of databases built on psycho-demographic data. This technology is probably best described as being in the application growth stage of the cycle at the moment. Also, we have described the technology life cycle from the perspective of the originating company. This means that the starting-point of the cycle is at the point of inception of the technology in that originating company. Any other company with its version of the technology, or using the originator's technology, will be joining the cycle at a later stage even though to that company the technology is new. This corresponds to cells 1, 2, 4, 5, 7 and 8 in Figure 4.3. This reinforces the point that life-cycle position and therefore relative newness is a more valid description of a technology than the idea of 'high' or 'low'. The description of a technology as being 'high' will be subjective and will relate to a particular company or application. The development of a strategic view of technology depends on a perspective which sees technology in a wider context than simply within one firm.

WHAT IS OUR PERFORMANCE IN ACQUIRING TECHNOLOGIES?

We have already noted that a company can acquire technologies in a number of different ways in addition to via conventional in-house R&D. Auditing acquisition performance includes investigating the company's decision-making on which technologies it should enter. This involves questioning whether it has made the right choices between alternative technologies for a particular application and whether those choices have been made at the appropriate time. More fundamentally we are concerned about whether the company has been taking the right decisions about if it should acquire the technologies it needs or whether they should have remained as external technologies. We should question whether the company has been devoting R&D resources to developing product technologies, or financial resources to taking licences, when it should have chosen to buy product from a supplier.

Similarly, we should examine if the company has been acquiring process technologies to manufacture product for itself when it should have had product made for it, perhaps to its own design, but using another company's process technologies. All of these questions concern the direction of the company's technology, whether resources have been devoted to those areas which build on the company's development skills and technological strengths or whether R&D has taken directions which are inappropriate.

We must also consider whether the company has chosen the appropriate source for those technologies it has chosen to acquire. This involves decisions on whether technology should be developed internally or sourced externally. There are then questions to be faced over which external source should have been chosen between contracted R&D, licence, joint venture or company acquisition. Finally we are concerned with the quality of decision-making within those choices, covering questions of which R&D contractor should be used – internal or external.

The quality of decisions on acquiring technology depend on the quality of the criteria which are developed, which functional areas are involved in the decision-making and the procedures which are adopted for the decision-making. All of these factors are addressed in Chapters 5 and 6 when we consider the process of technology acquisition in full.

WHAT IS OUR PERFORMANCE IN EXPLOITING TECHNOLOGIES?

Technology exploitation is the task of achieving the optimal return on the company's technological investment by all available means. Exploitation performance touches on a number of areas, some of which are rarely considered. We can outline these as follows.

Commercializing

The first area to examine in technology exploitation is the company's performance in commercializing its technology. By this we mean the process of taking the technology which the company has obtained, from whatever source, to the stage at which it is ready for launch in its first application. Commercialization is likely to involve the use or acquisition of the necessary product and process support technologies, financial analysis, market assessment and liaison, and prototyping, perhaps with a lead user. Many companies do not fail in their efforts to acquire new technology because of inadequacies in the technology itself. Instead, failure comes from an inability to bring that technology to market quickly enough, at the right development cost, with the right support technologies to enable it to be translated into a marketable product which can be produced at the right price.

Questioning must focus on past performance in commercialization and lead from this to the appropriateness of the managerial approach to commercialization. Questioning must determine whether past failures in new technology introduction have been due to the intrinsic inadequacy of the core technology itself or to problems with the quality of support technologies, whether the organisation for commercialisation has been at fault and if these faults have been to do with timing, cost overrun, interfunctional liaison or market analysis.

Return on investment

Many companies have an attitude to the return on their technology investments which contrasts with the way they view all other investments. For example, before a company invests in a piece of capital equipment it usually will examine the likely rate of return on that investment as well as the pay-back period. In contrast, R&D expenditure is frequently treated as an overhead expense with little accounting for the return achieved on the investment. In other companies the assessment of likely pay-back on an R&D investment is expressed in purely qualitative terms such as, 'This R&D is necessary to maintain our place in this product area and it will cost £x'. Even when attempts are made to assess the likely return on an R&D investment, often no comparison is made between the opportunity costs of investing scarce R&D funds in different projects, and the costs and benefits of different means of acquiring technology.

Once a technology has been acquired the evaluation of performance in exploitation is likely to be even less thorough. Generally, a company will be concerned at the market performance of the products it produces using the technology it has acquired. It may be able to relate the sales and profit achieved by these products to the technology investment made.

However, this will be made difficult because no product will be based on a single technology and any one 'piece' of technology may have a number of applications.

A technology audit needs to assess the return on particular investments in technology and to compare the company's history of return on both its investments in general and specifically in internal and external acquisition. Such analysis can show up the extent to which the company's return on its technology investment matches its investment criteria and whether any one means of acquisition is more profitable than others. Of course, such an analysis is intimately tied in to questions of R&D organisation. If R&D is organised on an operating company basis then R&D costs and the costs of other acquisition means can be more readily assigned to the recipients. Such an arrangement has clear accounting advantages, but exacerbates the problem of interdivisional transfer of technology when compared to having a centralised R&D.

For the purposes of a technology audit we are also concerned with a broader issue which is seldom addressed in many companies: the assessment of the return on a company's technological investment when compared both to its competitors and to what could have been achieved. We can illustrate the importance of this by using the following example.

Three companies separately develop their own versions of a new product technology. Company A uses the technology to launch a product into a particular application and achieves considerable success measured by market share in that application and by profit. Company B launches a similar product on to the same application market. It achieves a lower market share and less profit than A. However, it also develops a second product for a different application, using the same product technology and different process technologies, and achieves considerable profit in that market.

Company C uses the technology to form the basis of a product for one of these applications, but achieves a lower market share than A or B for its product. But it also licenses the technology to several other companies. Some of these other companies use the technology to achieve sales in the two application areas of A and B, others employ the technology in other national markets for the same application, and yet others combine it with their own product, marketing and process technologies to exploit it in different applications. Further, company C also enters into a joint venture with another company which has certain process strengths and this enables the two companies to dominate an entirely different application.

These wider aspects of technology exploitation are shown in the hatched area of the diagram in Figure 4.4. This may seem like an unrealistic example, but it illustrates that the return on a technology investment needs to be examined in a wide context. Company A will have viewed its investment as a success; after all it achieved both profit and market share. But it was only successful in terms of the profit on a single product and when set against a very narrow view of the potential for the technology. Company B probably achieved a much greater return on its technology investment, when compared to its competitor, by taking a wider view of the potential for the technology, while company C could favourably compare its return against its competition *and* against the optimum exploitation of the technology in all its potential applications.

Assessing the productivity of technology investment

Auditing the rate of return which a company has achieved on specific technology invest-ments will probably only be worthwhile for those relatively few major technologies in which it has been the originator or has taken a leading role. In many cases it is probably more important to assess the company's overall performance in exploiting technology. The dimensions of this assessment are illustrated in Figure 4.6. This time we discuss the diagram by referring to process technologies.

Figure 4.6 plots the relative expenditure of the company on acquiring technology in any particular area when compared to its competitors and sets this against the market and technology share achieved. This expenditure includes R&D funding and expenditure on licensing in and contracted-out R&D. Market share is defined in the usual way and in the case of process technologies refers to the share achieved by the company's products based on the technology. Technology share is somewhat similar. It is the share of the overall use of a particular technology which is accounted for by the company's version of that technology. This share includes sales of the company's products based on that techno-logy, either independently or as part of a joint venture and its sales of the technology to others by licence, etc.

In cell 1 of the matrix a company has managed a high market share in its own product sales and a high share of the technology as a whole by its broader application. The company has been productive in acquiring technology and successful at commercialising that technology and developing products based upon it. Its success in market share may also have been due to its competence in applying marketing technology to its process skills. However, a company in cell 1 has reached its high shares at the cost of relatively high expenditure on acquiring technology, when compared to its competitors.

A company in cell 2 has achieved high market and technology shares but with lower levels of expenditure. Its high market share could have resulted from more productive acquisition, such as better planned or directed R&D, or sound decisions on what and from whom to license. On the other hand perhaps its success has been because it has linked together its process, product and marketing technologies more effectively. Companies in cell 2 also include those that have been successful at lower relative cost in gaining technology share. This success could be because of greater productivity in technology acquisition, more 'bang for its bucks' in R&D or because it has been more effective in exploiting its technology. Cell 2 seems to indicate success, but being in this cell could be a warning to a company. Perhaps its current technological achievement is a result of past spending or fortuitousness – luck or 'living on the past'. The company may have cut back on technology expenditure after the first generation of a technology and, therefore, it may be vulnerable to losing both market and technology share in the future.

Although the matrix does not show it, it is of course quite possible for a company to have a high market share based on a technology but a low technology share, as company A in the previous example. Similarly it is possible to gain a high technology share with only a low market share as in the case of company C in the same example.

Cells 3 and 4 show low market and technology shares. Cell 3 illustrates a company which has failed to win high market or technology share despite relatively high expenditure. This

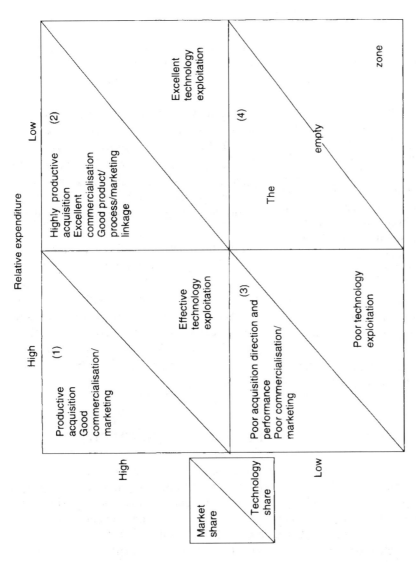

Market share is the proportion of total sales of products accounted for by the company's sales of product.

Technology share is the proportion of the productive use of a technology accounted for by the company through in-house application or sales of the technology to others.

Figure 4.6 The productivity of technological investment

failure would need further diagnosis and could be the result of poor performance in any area of acquisition, management or exploitation.

Cell 4 refers to low share achievement and low spend – the 'empty zone'. This can mean either that the company has sensibly refrained from major investment in an area of little opportunity or that it is missing a major opportunity!

Example
Excellent technology exploitation:
Black and Decker and Pilkington Glass

Black and Decker is an example of a company which has been successful at applying its marketing skills to the task of developing and selling new products. This success has been based on what it regards as its distinctive technologies, particularly its process capabilities in the manufacture of small electric motors and in automated assembly.

Instead of just using its process technology to make electric drills the company has found many new products to 'wrap around its motors'. In this way the company has achieved its high technology share by wider exploitation of the technology than could have been achieved just by using it in its initial product area.

The Pilkington Glass company in the UK developed the process technology to make float glass. In this process flat glass is produced by continuously pouring molten glass over a bath of molten metal. This process offered a dramatic improvement in product quality and a reduction in production costs when compared to previous methods which involved grinding the glass to make it flat. The company used the technology in its own production. However, it was aware of its universal potential and lacked the resources to produce float glass for the entire world market.

For this reason it offered to licence the technology to other glass makers. Virtually all of the world's flat-glass makers took a licence for the technology and for a number of years Pilkington's profits from licensing were greater than its total profits from all its manufacturing. This revenue also funded its costs of further development in other areas of glass technology.

WHAT IS OUR PERFORMANCE IN MANAGING TECHNOLOGY?

This book is based on the idea that technology is the core of a company and that the tasks of acquiring and exploiting technology in interaction with others defines the company's activities. The management of technology is the enabling activity for this acquisition and exploitation. It has a number of ingredients which we will examine in some detail in Chapter 9. All of these ingredients must be assessed as part of a technology audit.

The first aspect of technology management which needs to be audited is whether or not the company has a satisfactory approach to technology strategy-making. We have already noted that strategy in this area is likely to 'emerge', rather than be the outcome from some formalised process alone. Therefore, a company seeking to develop strategy in the area must have the elements of both formal structure and informal culture which can facilitate this process. An audit must examine not only the quality of any written strategy which has emerged, but also the way in which the company goes about the development process.

A key element of this process is the links between different functions within the company. An audit needs to examine these links in general and specifically between such critical areas as marketing and R&D.

Another aspect of technology management which requires analysis is the company's performance in interdivisional management and transfer of technology within the company. This refers to the common problem of a company where one division may have acquired a particular technology which could be of value to another *if* that other only new about it! For example, a discussion of technological assets in a seminar with managers from a multidivision company revealed that one of these divisions had developed an effective filter for use with hydraulic systems. This division had been forced to do this because it produced a narrow range of hydraulic units for a single application which had a very harsh operating environment. It had no other application for the technology and so was not developing it further. Another division in the company produced hydraulic components for a wide range of, but typically less severe, applications. It did not have the pressure of the requirements of the first-mentioned application, but had been trying for years to add a filter to its range without success. It knew nothing of the technology developed in the other division.

A full technology audit will seek to determine if the company is effectively maximising the use of its stock of technology located throughout its operations. It will also examine the more detailed aspects of the management and organisation of technology acquisition and exploitation such as R&D, licensing and subcontracting, etc.

CONCLUSIONS

The ideas on a technology audit that we have advanced in this chapter could involve a company in a major task of investigation, possibly using outside consultants. On the other hand the process of questioning the company's approach to technology can be productive even if formal analysis is restricted. Our research shows that even the initial attempt to see the company's activities in technological terms can be extremely productive. Other companies may wish to analyse their technology by taking examples of significant activities from different divisions and carrying out an audit on them. This will serve to highlight issues, problems and performances which require immediate managerial attention, and establish a methodology for future analysis and throw up issues which subsequent analysis may find to be general across the company. A technology audit, however carried out, is an essential prerequisite for improvement in a company's acquisition and exploitation performance. More important, a process of questioning about the company's technology serves to raise the level of the debate about technology in the company, and that in itself is of tremendous value.

Example
Technology audit in a food ingredients company

This technology audit is not just interesting for its outcome, but also for the fact that it was carried out in a company which would conventionally be described as 'low-technology'. The company manufactures a wide range of additives which add flavour, colour or texture to food. An audit of the company's product and process technologies was carried out and this led to the matrix in Figure 4.7.

The matrix shows the company's main product and process technologies according to whether they are basic or distinctive. Thus, both the product technology in designing sausage seasonings is well known to all those in the industry, as is the process needed to produce them. In contrast the product technology to design snack food seasoning is recognised by the market as a distinctive technology for the company and a source of competitive advantage. Although emulsifiers, which bind water and fat together in food products are a well-known product technology, this company is seen to have a distinctiveness in their production. Only in the technologies surrounding textured wheat protein for use as gluten in vegetarian and pet foods is the company seen to have distinctiveness in both the product and process areas.

Further analysis led to the figures in the matrix. These show that two-thirds of the company's gross contribution came from areas where it had no distinctiveness from its competitors. The company only earned 1 per cent of its gross contribution from distinctive process technologies alone and 13 per cent from those areas where it was distinctive in both product and process technologies.

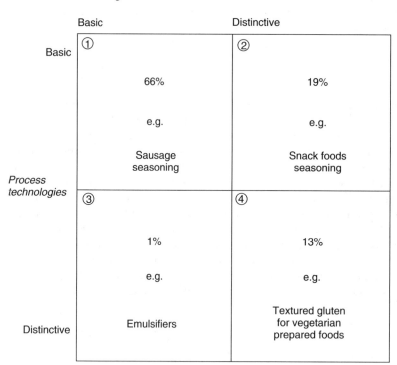

The percentage figures refer to the proportion of the company's total gross profit contribution generated from each technology

Figure 4.7 The contribution of different product and process technologies

The company believed that all its activities tended to drift into cell 1 of the matrix as its technologies lost their distinctiveness. Cell 1 activities produce a lower percentage gross margin per unit of sales because they are essentially commodities, widely available from other producers.

This analysis led to further thinking by the company. First, it was puzzling that the company was so financially successful on the basis of such indistinctive technologies. This caused the company to examine its marketing technology. The company's offerings were in most cases similar in nature to each of the food manufacturers which formed its market (although product formulations varied in many cases). The company diagnosed that it did have distinctiveness in its marketing technology. This distinctiveness was in its ability to spot emerging trends in the food industry, but more important for marketing people to liaise effectively and speedily within the company to assemble the appropriate bundle of product and process technologies to meet customer requirements (often in less than forty-eight hours). Brewer refers to this as the marketer playing the role of quarter-back and orchestrating the 'play' in each customer interaction.

Having diagnosed the seeds of its current success, the company looked more nervously at the future. First, it decided that this would have to be based more on the development of distinctiveness in its product and process areas. Table 4.2 illustrates the issues here.

The table shows the company's assessment of the proportion of its managerial resources which were currently devoted to short-, medium- or long-term activities in the three areas which were respectively: customer specific, i.e. conventionally marketing; to do with exploiting its existing technologies; to do with acquiring new technologies. The largest proportion of the company's efforts were devoted to responding to the immediate demands of customers, an area where it had acquired a distinctiveness. However, the company devoted virtually no efforts to longer-term relationship-building. The other activities received very much less resource allocation. In particular the longer-term acquisition of technology was grossly under-represented.

This analysis has led the company to seek a more balanced approach to the different areas. Its chief executive has mandated that all the company's management must spend a greater proportion of their time on 'technology issues'. The need for this was demonstrated at a meeting

Table 4.2 Resource allocation in different technology areas

Technology area	Time-scale		
	Short term 0–1 month (%)	Medium term 2–12 months (%)	Long term 12 months + (%)
Customer-specific activities (demand pull)	33	13	–
Technology exploitation activities (technology push)	–	30	7
Technology acquisitions	3	10	4

called for the company's 'senior technology people'. Of the thirty-eight attendees, only two were from marketing and no one was there who had responsibilities for the company's process technologies! More

generally, the company's strategic planning process is now built on a realisation of its technology position, and aims to achieve a more balanced approach to the activities in the table.

(From the work of R. Brewer, research student)

Example
Technology strategy in a Japanese company

Japanese industry suffers because of the mobility of process technologies. For example, Thailand and Malaysia now make more televisions than does Japan.

Keyence is an Osaka company which designs and markets magnetic and optical sensors for use in production lines. It has sales of $274 million. Eighty per cent of its manufacturing is subcontracted and the company president, Takemitsu Takizaki, aims to raise this to 85 per cent. Only those manufacturing steps which involve trade secrets are kept in-house and only sixty out of its 900 employees are engaged in manufacturing or in overseeing manufacturing suppliers. Over a five-year period the company's operating profits grew threefold.

The company's success depends on its concentration on distinctive technologies in

marketing and product design. It has broken away from the Japanese norms of jobs for life and promotion on seniority. Keyence poaches staff from others to increase its creativity and pays according to success, not age. The company also does not use the conventional Japanese system of marketing through separate wholesale companies. It has an in-house sales team which accounts for half its workforce. This is partly because of the complex product technology of its product, but also because its sales force feeds back information on product requirements to the research department.

Because Keyence operates on the basis of its distinctive product and marketing technologies, its assembly costs account for only 5 per cent of its sales value. Its sales overseas, where Japanese companies are most vulnerable to the rising yen, were up 30 per cent in the year to March 1993.

(Developed from *The Economist*, 15 May 1993)

REFERENCES

1   Kotler, P., Gregor, W. and Rodgers, W. (1977) 'The marketing audit comes of age', *Sloan Management Review*, Winter: 25–43.
2   Kerin, R. A. and Peterson, R. A. (1987) *Strategy Marketing Problems*, 4th edn, Boston: Allyn & Bacon, p. 548.
3   Wortzel, L. W. and Wortzel, H. V. (1981) 'Export strategies for NIC and LDC based firms', *Columbia Journal of World Business*, Spring: 51–59.
4   Mathur, S. S. (1988) 'How firms compete: a new classification of generic strategies', *Journal of General Management*, **14**(1), Autumn: 30–57.
5   Shrivastava, P. and Souder, W. E. (1987) 'The strategic management of technological innovations: a review and a model', *Journal of Management Studies*, **24**(1), January.

6 Souder, W. E. and Shrivastava, P. (1985) 'Towards a scale for measuring technology in new product innovation', *Research Policy*, **14**: 151–60.
7 Grandstrand, O. and Sjolander, S. (1990) 'Managing innovation in multi-technology corporations', *Research Policy*, **19**: 35–60.
8 Prahalad, C. K. (1993) 'The role of core competencies in the corporation', *Research. Technology Management*, November–December: 40–47.
9 Ford, D. and Ryan, C. (1981) 'Talking technology to market', *Harvard Business Review*, March–April: 117–26.
10 Abernathy, W. J. and Utterback, J. M. (1975) 'A dynamic model of process and product innovation', *Omega*, **III**(6): 634–56.
11 Ansoff, H. I. (1984) *Implementing Strategic Management*, Englewood Cliffs, NJ: Prentice-Hall.
12 Abernathy and Utterback, 'A dynamic model of process and product innovation'.

Chapter 5

Technology acquisition: Opportunities and threats

INTRODUCTION

So far in this book we have been concerned with a general approach to the technology 'problem'. We have described some aspects of how companies think about technology issues and how they deal with them. We have presented a series of questions which can be used to analyse a company's position and approach to technology, and we have suggested that technology strategy comprises the three areas of the acquisition, exploitation and management of technology. The remainder of this book is devoted to the tasks which are involved in each of these areas; this chapter and the next deal with the acquisition of technology.

Here we provide a context for understanding the ways in which companies acquire new technology. In particular we examine the issue of the supposed advantage of moving first to market with a new technology. This is followed by an examination of the implications for technology acquisition, of the process of technology change across industries and the trajectories of individual technologies. We then look at the implications of this general view of technology change for the assessment of technological opportunities in a company.

HOW FIRMS ACQUIRE TECHNOLOGY

The value of each of the possible means of acquiring technology will be discussed in greater detail in the following chapter. Here we examine the incidence of use of the various means which are available based on a survey of 703 UK companies in seven industrial sectors.[1] Table 5.1 lists the methods of technology acquisition which were reported by the companies in this sample. The most common method of acquiring new technology after that of internal

R&D is licensing-in technology (33 per cent of the total firms) followed by acquiring the company to obtain its technology (22 per cent). The use of external R&D houses was reported by 18 per cent of the sample, while 15 per cent of the firms used joint ventures as a method of acquiring technology and 10 per cent sought to acquire technology by entering into a franchise agreement.

The number of acquisition methods used by different firms is related to their size, their R&D intensity, their level of exporting activity and varies between different industrial sectors. These relationships are shown in Tables 5.2, 5.3, 5.4 and 5.5.

Table 5.1 Methods used by firms in acquiring technology

Acquisition method (%)	Method	Exploitation method (%)
	LICENSING	
25	Between companies	26
8	With research organisation	–
10	FRANCHISING	11
	CONTRACTING OUT FUNCTIONS	
–	Marketing/distribution	16
18	Research and development	–
	COMPANY OWNERSHIP SHIFTS	
17	Acquisition (100% ownership)	–
5	Acquisition (minority interest)	–
–	Spin-off (100% ownership)	14
	JOINT VENTURES	
6	Separate company formation	13
9	As a project	17
6	RECIPROCAL TECHNOLOGY EXCHANGE AGREEMENTS	17
8	OTHER	–

Table 5.2 Technology deals and company size

Average no. of exploitation methods	Business size	Average no. of acquisition methods
0.9	< £5 million	0.8
1.4	£6–20 million	1.4
0.9	£21–£50 million	1.1
2.3	> £50 million	2.1

Table 5.3 Technology deals and R&D expenditure

Average no. of exploitation methods	R&D expenditure as % of turnover	Average no. of acquisition methods
0.8	0–1	0.8
1.4	2–5	1.4
1.5	6–10	1.1
2.1	> 10	1.4

Table 5.4 Technology deals and exports

Average no. of exploitation methods	Exports as % of sales turnover	Average no. of acquisition methods
0.8	0–10	0.9
1.2	11–40	1.2
1.7	> 40	1.5

Table 5.5 Technology deals and industry

Average no. of exploitation methods	Industry	Average no. of acquisition methods
2.0	Processing industries	1.7
1.1	Construction industries	1.4
0.7	Metal manufacturing	0.6
1.1	Mechanical engineering	1.1
0.9	Electrical/electronics	0.9
1.2	Transportation equipment	2.2
1.0	Instrument engineering	1.0
1.4	Service industries	1.4

Table 5.6 Types of technology acquired

Types of technology	% of companies that have acquired this technology
Design of formulation of a specific product	61
Product technology with a wide application	25
Manufacturing technology for a particular product	34
General manufacturing technology with a wide application	9
Turnkey operation	8
Technology at the R&D stage	17
Management know-how	5
Marketing know-how	3
Financial know-how	3

Certain types of technologies appear to be more commonly acquired than others. Those which have a specific application and which are clearly linked to tangible hardware are more often involved than generic and separated technologies. Table 5.6 shows that many more firms have acquired design technology (61 per cent) or manufacturing technology (34 per cent) for a specific product than product technology (25 per cent) or manufacturing technology (9 per cent) with a wide application. Also, technology at the R&D stage is less often acquired than at the product development and manufacturing stages.

It appears that technologies are more likely to be acquired if they can be clearly associated and applied to a specific product, material or manufacturing process. This is hardly surprising, but it does illustrate the extent to which technology is viewed and used by firms, not as a separate resource in its own right, but as inextricably linked to tangible items of hardware.

A strategic approach to technology acquisition requires that firms take fully into consideration all of the possible means of acquisition. Those 'technologically active' companies we identified in Chapter 2 are involved in a variety of methods of technology acquisition. Additionally, our discussion of technology auditing has shown that companies need to look widely at the trends and competitive positions in technology of companies not only in their immediate competitive arena but also among companies which could invade their markets.

THE TIMING OF TECHNOLOGY ACQUISITION

Technological change reorders the shape of industries and alters firms' competitive positions by their success or failure to take advantage of the new conditions it creates. Therefore, a strategic approach to technology acquisition by a company must not only involve the company's own immediate technology requirements, but must also take fully into account its industrial and technological context. A major issue which faces companies in technology acquisition is that of timing; specifically whether it is more sensible to be first to market with a new technology or to follow others in its industry or elsewhere.

First-mover advantage and disadvantage

The first firm to acquire a new technology need not be the one which benefits most from it. A first-mover advantage is not always translated into a sustained competitive advantage. Others can and have profited more from a new technology than the firm that first used it. An example which illustrates the failure of a first-mover is provided by the EMI body-scanner, which was based on computerised axial tomography research. This technology enabled EMI to produce a machine for generating cross-sectional pictures of the human body.[2] The company introduced its first product in the USA in 1973, but within six years competitors had brought out their own versions based on the same technology and EMI had lost its initial market leadership position. Two years later it dropped out of the body-scanner business altogether.

This example shows how a company with an excellent new technology (the inventor won the Nobel Prize in 1979) and meeting a clear market need can still fail to profit from it, but imitators succeed. The problem for EMI was that the scanner was of much higher technological sophistication than most hospitals were accustomed to. It therefore needed much more support, servicing and training than products using established technologies. This is where EMI failed. They did not have the marketing technology to support the product technology. The company could not buy in dedicated support services easily and was in any case slow to realise their importance. Furthermore, the technology itself had very little intellectual property protection through patents. The equipment could be reverse-engineered and its essential features imitated. Two competitors already had the necessary technical capabilities and experience in marketing medical equipment (GE and Technicare) and were able to develop and launch competing scanners within three years of EMI. In this case, the second-movers won because of the superiority of their marketing technology, not their product technology. The example also illustrates that speed in technology acquisition is not in itself a guarantee of success.

A contrasting example to EMI is provided by Searle's NutraSweet brand sugar substitute. In 1982, NutraSweet achieved sales of $74 million, which had reached $1 billion by 1988. By then they had secured the leading share of the sugar substitute market in the USA and five other countries. The absence of a successful challenge to the first-mover in this case can be explained by the strategy which Searle adopted. Searle cleverly established and protected their technological advantage partly by pushing for extended patents and early approval from the Food and Drug Administration, which made it difficult and time-consuming for a potential imitator to follow them. They also took pre-emptive action to maintain their competitive position once the patents expired by maximising the exposure of the brand identity by requiring the NutraSweet name and trademark to be carried on all goods licensed to use the ingredient. In addition, they invested heavily in R&D for their own exclusive in-house production technology in order to establish a manufacturing cost advantage over competitors.

In this case the first-mover was able to maintain its product technology advantage initially through patents and then, when these expired, it defended its competitive position by means of a superior process technology.

These two examples illustrate the importance for the firm of thinking strategically to maximise the benefits from their technologies at the time when those technologies are acquired. This issue will be examined further in a later section when we discuss how firms should manage the exploitation of their technologies. However, for the moment we should emphasise that having available a technology before competitors does not guarantee a long-run advantage for a company. Equally, if a competitor is first to acquire a technology and exploits it effectively, it is still possible for the company to lose market position irretrievably. So, decisions about whether, when, where and how to acquire a technology are extremely important.

TECHNOLOGY CHANGE AND APPLICATION ACROSS INDUSTRIES

We have argued that a company must carefully evaluate the opportunities and threats which technologies pose for it as a basis for decisions about the acquisition of new technologies. Managers need to take a view, whether expressed explicitly or implicitly, of the future path of development of important technologies in order to make a strategic assessment of their potential. To do this effectively they need an understanding of the process and dynamics of technological change and its spread through firms and industries. This understanding depends on the key concepts of technology chains and technology trajectories.

Technology chains

Technology is likely to be very unevenly distributed throughout the network of customers, suppliers, competitors and others that surround the company. Even those companies which compete directly with each other may use different technologies. In the adhesives business, for instance, firms can use mechanical, metallurgical, or chemical technologies – or a mixture of these. These firms will have different linkages to other companies which assist in the development or use of these technologies. Also, a particular technology can find application across very different industries. For example, measurement and testing technologies are by their nature more generally used than, say, medical technologies.

Therefore, a complex pattern of technological interdependencies exist between industrial sectors. New technologies are usually initially applied in one industry but they often find subsequent application in others. All the users of those technologies have a common interest in research and development in that area and any new applications and developments which may arise from it. This common interest creates clusters of firms based on their technological proximity, as distinct from groups based on their common industry, products or customers. It is important for a firm to recognise that its technological 'neighbours' need not necessarily be its market competitors and this emphasises the collaborative as well as the competitive opportunities afforded by technology. For example:

> The CEO recognised the existence of Crown's strong skills in metal formation and built on these to specialise in 'hard to hold' applications for steel cans. He developed strong relations with the steel companies and convinced them to adapt a major external technological innovation – the two-piece can – initiated by an aluminium company for use with steel. He did not want Crown to have an R&D department, but developed strong links between a highly competent technical sales force and an applications-oriented engineering group to be able to provide complete technical solutions for customers 'filling needs'.[3]

Over time, technologies can be seen to cascade down and across industries. This cascading can take a number of different forms:

1 The use of a technology can spread as it is embodied in new products and processes, which then flow from suppliers to customers through a succession of primary, capital and consumer goods sectors.
2 A new device may be copied by firms in different sectors. For example a new food processing and storing technique may find initial application in food manufacturing, then subsequently it may be adapted and applied to the agribusiness sector and later to food retailing.
3 A product or process technology may be licensed to other more or less related technologies across a network of companies.
4 A firm may diversify its operations or acquire other companies. It can then apply the technologies it used in its original areas to new product areas such as those of its original suppliers, customers or into completely different industries.
5 Distributors and agents may apply the technologies of their principals to the problems faced by a wide range of industries with which they deal.
6 Independent R&D companies are likely to serve several industries and search for new applications for the technologies or skills which they may have developed while working for one industrial customer. For example, they may search for new markets for their computer software skills or biotechnology development abilities.

We call these flows of technology between firms and sectors 'technology chains'.[4] A technology chain links a network of interacting firms, in and across industrial sectors. It is not confined to a movement from technological leaders to followers within the same industry. A technology chain may occur in the progression from the initial specialised development of the technology to its wider application or in its progression from a generic form to its use in a specific application in a particular industry. Either way, the technology is likely to develop incrementally at various stages with a consequent impact on companies located both before and after this.

A firm's position along such technology chains significantly influences the strategic issues it must face about how to use and exploit its technologies. Thus, the further towards the end of a particular chain it is located, the more important it is for the company to select the right, well-developed technologies from the supplier chains and combine them with its own skills. For a company in this situation, the technologies will remain external as the company will use them in the form of components or services without actually acquiring them. The further down a chain that a company is located will increase the importance for it of modifying or tailoring these technologies to the increasingly specific requirements of the applications with which it deals. The company's acquisition skills will probably centre on appropriate support technologies, perhaps in the process or marketing areas which are needed to meet the particular requirements of its applications. For example, an instrument manufacturer must select the most appropriate electronics supplier based on that supplier's technology and choose which possibilities to offer its customers through its own product design and development.

The manager of such an instrument company, when interviewed, expressed his position as follows:

> Raw technology advances like fibre optics and microchips that make possible what we do are the base technologies . . . Those are the sort of industries where raw technology is clearer . . . We take the output of these raw technologies . . . making use of it, repackaging it.

Companies can usually draw on a number of chains to assess and select which technologies to acquire, and how to acquire them. In the short run, the firm's options for using technology will be determined by its existing position along the chains. However a strategic approach to technology requires the firm to look more deeply. For example, the company must assess which technology chains it should relate to and how it should best enter and position itself in such chains to obtain access to their technologies. The company must also question whether it should seek to acquire the technology for itself, perhaps by licensing it, or rely on buying products from a supplier manufactured using that technology.

Technology trajectories

Technology trajectories describe the directions of technical development. These directions are both cumulative and self-generating. They follow particular paths with their own momentum. Thus, once a solution to a technological problem emerges the possible routes of future developments are likely to be limited by the nature of the new technology. For example, the development of the internal combustion engine excluded other notionally possible alternatives. Furthermore, once a particular design becomes dominant it then defines how progress within the design is to be measured in technical terms.

We can illustrate the nature of technology trajectories using the examples at the end of this chapter. The form and characteristics of a new technology define the subsequent direction of progress within it. The trajectory consists of a series of technical developments and improvements along a path which have common features in their application of the same principle or their application to the same technology.

Technology thresholds

The trajectory of a technology will eventually reach its technical limits with respect to these defined measures of progress. This is called the technology 'threshold', beyond which the technology ceases to advance. The threshold can be defined as the highest level that can be reached on a trajectory in terms of the relevant technical dimensions by which progress is measured. For example, the technology threshold for conventional propeller-driven aircraft was reached at a speed of around 500 m.p.h. When the technological threshold is being approached and progress within it has ceased to advance there is a strong incentive for new technologies to be developed and applied to provide new and better solutions. This is unless there is no need for it to advance further along this dimension, which was clearly not the case with aircraft. The approach to a technology threshold is one way in which mature technologies are superseded by new ones.

An example of the impact of a technology threshold is provided by metrology where the limits of existing mechanical measurement technology is now being reached. The speed and efficiency of mechanical measurement has ceased to advance and now other technological possibilities are being explored and applied to this field, such as electronics, ultrasonics, optics and laser technologies.

The manager must be aware of the nature and direction of the technologies on which he depends. Further, the impact of technology thresholds means that acquisition decisions must relate to both long-term changes in technologies as well as short-term market requirements.

TECHNOLOGIES AS SOLUTIONS

The manager who is responsible for decisions on technology acquisition must also be aware of the ways in which technological change can be stimulated. One important way is to provide the solution for a new problem which existing technologies cannot solve – even if they have not reached their thresholds. But it is important to recognise that the problems to which technological solutions are addressed are not supplied only by market demand. Technological change is not simply a passive and mechanical reaction to market needs. The range of potential market needs is in reality so large that it is effectively infinite. Market signals alone cannot explain why and when specific developments occur rather than others. An explanation based on needs also neglects changes in technological capabilities which do not have any direct relationship with changes in the market. This means that it is not enough for the firm to identify customers' latent needs (even if they could) and then search for technologies to meet them. The problems to be solved (and thus the performance requirements of the technologies) may be generated by forces other than market needs; such as political, environmental and macro-economic pressures.

For example, the development of American space technology in the 1960s through the agency of NASA was primarily motivated by political pressure from the Kennedy administration with the national objective for the USA of getting a man on the moon first. Ecological considerations have exerted powerful pressure for developments in anti-pollution, recycling, nuclear and agribusiness technologies. For example, ecological pressures had a dramatic effect on the strategy of Associated Octel which was a world leader in the production of lead-based additives for automotive fuels. The company had to embark on a major programme of acquisition and development to eliminate its dependence on the threatened technology. Macro-economic conditions and consequent price/cost changes largely account for the drive to develop new sources of energy since the multiple escalation in the real price of oil in 1973 and 1979. Technological advances in wave power and wind power were stimulated by changes in the relative economic costs of other fuels. Sometimes, the problem can be caused by the existing technology itself, for example the air pollution effects of the internal combustion engine are stimulating the development of alternative propulsion systems.

The possible paths of development of a technology are largely set by the trajectory which that particular technology solution defines. Market signals or other needs can only affect the area of application of the technology and the process of development within the limits set by the technology itself. The key issue which arises from this for the technology acquisition strategy of a company is how its managers can use an understanding of the process of technological change to identify and assess the opportunities for the acquisition of technology which exist.

Example
Acquiring and exploiting enzyme technologies

The acquisition of a new technology can come about for a range of different reasons and in a number of different ways. The extent and types of knowledge required to 'put the technology to work' in product applications cannot always be predicted in advance. This problem of predicting both the direction of application of a technology and the resources required for its exploitation is illustrated by an animal feed manu-facturer attempting to acquire and use enzyme technologies.

The active proteins known as enzymes have long been employed in industrial applications as varied as detergent formulation, brewing and food manufacturing. Laboratory work at universities during the 1960s showed that enzymes could be used to free the nutrients held in barley, which was a common ingredient in animal feeds but was coarser though cheaper than wheat. The company's nutritionists, like those of their competitors, were sceptical of the commercial value because the feed-mixing process tended to break up the delicate enzymes.

In 1989, the company's local sales staff saw evidence that enzymes were increasingly being applied in the poultry feed market. Some large customers, many of whom produced their own feed formulations, were responding positively to marketing moves made by a large chemicals firm and a specialist Scandinavian feed manufacturer. Both of these companies were promoting enzyme additives as a method of processing barley.

Anxious to avoid being left without a competitive product, the company's sales management pressed for a development programme. Support was forthcoming from the raw materials function which saw the opportunity to use cheaper ingredients more widely. A low intensity investigation of the possibilities was agreed and commenced.

By early 1991 it was clear that enzyme technology was here to stay and that the company needed to develop its capabilities in this area if its products were to remain competitive. With strategic funding committed, the Agriculture division turned to the parent group's UK food laboratories which had experience of food applications. A development project was established (in some secrecy) with the following aims:

- To achieve better use of current raw materials.

- To investigate the use of cheaper raw materials presently considered unsuitable.
- To obtain feed performance benefits (i.e. faster weight gain, and easier management).

A promising and apparently cost-effective combination of enzymes was identified quickly. With heavy customer and sales force pressure to launch, it was decided to move directly to market trials. Immediately, major mistakes in the analysis of costs were revealed. The additives as developed were not financially viable and it became clear that the company could not complete this project alone. Its food laboratories did not possess the knowledge required of either the fundamental technologies involved in designing and manipulating enzyme combinations, or the particular features of the feeds manufacturing environment. In short, development partners were needed.

Since then development relationships have been established with an industrial enzymes specialist and with a small, 'high-tech' feeds firm, to fill these technology gaps. The company believes that this relationship is likely to be formalised in the near future and will continue indefinitely as the partners move up their respective learning curves. More such relationships, for other technologies and other livestock species, are planned.

Example
Dealing with the pace of technological change: Hewlett Packard

The sheer pace of changing technical standards, potentialities and expectations can be daunting in certain sectors. For an information technology company seeking to acquire technology in an area where several dynamic

technologies meet there is no room for error or delay. Hewlett Packard's UK factory in Bristol produces mass-storage devices, most recently based on digital audio-tape (DAT) technology. As with other parts of the computer industry, customers expect increasing performance at decreasing prices. The following outline demonstrates the pressures that the company faces.

Performance change for the tape travel mechanism itself is relatively slow. In this industry that means matching a historical rate of change across similar storage methods over the last twenty-five years of 25 per cent per year. The company believes that there is no reason to expect these expectations to change in the future, although they may be difficult to achieve due to external limitations imposed by standards, etc.

The picture is more startling for the data channel. Customer expectations here are driven by the performance of their hard discs systems, which are in turn driven by the increasing demands of new programmes. The historical rate of change in this area is a doubling of capacity every twelve to eighteen months. Because of this, Hewlett Packard use a technological 'road map' aiming for a doubling of capacity every two years, with an implicit expectation that performance will have to move at the same pace.

At the same time, customers expect prices to fall by 4–5 per cent per quarter. So while product technologies are developed, process technologies must also keep pace.

ASSESSING TECHNOLOGICAL OPPORTUNITIES

Industries differ in the opportunities they have to exploit new technologies because of significant differences in each sector's principal activities, sources of technology, requirements of users and potential benefits.[5] Firms in some industries, such as telecommunications, are involved in activities which are based on new technologies to a higher degree than other industries, such as textiles, and therefore firms in such industries have access to and can benefit more from new technological developments.

Firms within each industry, however, face a common set of technological opportunities defined by existing technology thresholds and trajectories. Differences in their success at technology acquisition can be explained by the differences in individual firms' technological competencies, capabilities and strategies.

The development of the firm's acquisition strategy requires the identification and selection of feasible technological opportunities. These must be selected from, and are constrained by, a common possible set of relevant technology trajectories and thresholds. In order to look at these, managers need to diagnose the current technological circumstances facing the firm. This diagnosis should seek to identify the following factors:

1 New, emerging and existing technologies which may be important for the firm's future operations in the widest sense.
2 The state of development of these relevant technologies in terms of their established techniques and trajectories.
3 The appropriate technical and economic measures of progress along the trajectories.
4 The current state of development of these technologies in terms of the potential thresholds of their trajectories.
5 What technologies should be acquired by the firm and which provide the best opportunities for it.

We can illustrate how these questions can be addressed by using an example of a company which attempted to diagnose and integrate the technological opportunities in a particular area.

Example
Assessing technology opportunities: Oliver Guage Company

This firm is a traditional UK metrology company which had achieved market leadership in quality inspection equipment. It began to decline and was acquired by a larger engineering group in 1984. At this time the firm's product range was becoming technologically outdated and the market segments in which it was concentrated were declining in value terms at 18 per cent per year. The new managing director, after consultation with Group HQ decided to undertake a modernisation programme for the entire product range.

Their existing inspection and measurement products were based on mechanical devices and techniques. The technology issue here was initially defined as one of identifying potential future developments in the application of metrology. An external search was undertaken of research bodies, university departments and independent experts in order to locate current research which was under way and to identify potential new developments in these areas.

It became clear that a number of different technological solutions to the problem of improving measurement devices were being developed. For example: information technology was being applied to improve the read-out and analysis of results of measuring systems; electronics and robotics technologies were being used to develop *in situ* measurement techniques which save time and labour in the production process; ultrasonics, optics and laser technologies were being applied to develop non-contact measurement devices which can conduct non-destructive measurement of 'soft' materials and which can operate in a relatively hostile environment.

Thus, a variety of separate technological routes were being explored to solve different problems with measurement which occurred using existing mechanical technologies. The company's next step was to conduct a technological diagnosis of the current situation. This diagnosis can be summarised as follows.

Existing mechanical measurement technology was approaching its absolute limit of progress. It was in the mature phase of its life cycle and this was demonstrated by the fact that its trajectory had ceased to advance as measured by improvements in its performance capabilities. Furthermore many firms had reached that threshold and so the relative technological advantage of different firms had given way to other forms of competition. Scope for new applications and improvements in the existing technology had become extremely limited.

A new technology had not yet emerged to replace the old one. This was shown by the fact that several different technological possibilities were being explored. The problems which were being addressed, the principles which were being applied to them and the material technologies employed had been selected but which technological solution would emerge as the dominant one in future was as yet unclear. Thus the future trajectory was undefined and the techno-economic dimensions by which it would progress were unknown. In this situation of technological flux the technological opportunities for the firm were not constrained by any single dominant technology or trajectory. The number of potentially feasible opportunities was very large and the company faced a critical selection process from among those it is exploring.

This diagnosis enabled a clear statement of the technology acquisition issues and objectives for Oliver Gauge to be constructed. The key factor which management had to ascertain is which of the possible techniques will emerge as the dominant solution to the problems with current measurement technology?

CONCLUSIONS

This chapter has emphasised that decisions on technology acquisition must be taken within a wider context. This context comprises the company's position in the chain of technology and the trajectory of any technology under consideration. The example of the Oliver Gauge Company also shows that this context provides the basis for what must be a detailed analysis of the technological opportunities open to the company. An important criterion in selecting which technologies to acquire must be potential for exploitation and the sustainable competitive advantage which they can create for the firm. Thus, any technology acquisition decision must be integrated with a strategy for its exploitation. Factors which affect acquisition decisions, in addition to those discussed in this chapter, should include the prospect of patent protection, ease of imitation, competitors' expected technological strategies and range of potential applications. We will examine these when we look at issues in the exploitation of technology. Also, the extent to which each of these factors are important will depend in part on the choice of acquisition method which is chosen, and it is to this that we now turn in Chapter 6.

REFERENCES

1   Ford, D. and Jongerius, C. (1986) *Technology Strategy in British Industry*, Milton Keynes: Base International.
2   Teece, D. J. (1986) 'Profiting from technological innovation: implications for integration, collaboration, licensing and public policy', *Research Policy*, **15**: 285–305.
3   Burgelman, R. A. and Rosenbloom, R. S. (1989) 'Technology strategy: an evolutionary process', *Research in Technological Innovation, Management and Policy*, **4**: 1–23.
4   Clarke, K., Ford, D. and Saren, M. A. J. (1988) 'Strategic management and technology strategy', proceedings of 8th Strategic Management Society conference, Amsterdam.
5   Pavitt, K. (1986) 'Sectoral patterns of technical change: towards a taxonomy and a theory', *Research Policy*, **13**: 343–73.

Chapter 6

The technology acquisition task

INTRODUCTION

In this chapter we will examine the tasks involved in technology acquisition. Because of its overall importance, much of the chapter deals with a single method of acquisition – internal acquisition or R&D. However, we also emphasise the importance of integrating different methods of acquisition, each of which may be more or less appropriate depending on the circumstances facing the company. For this reason we start the chapter by examining the critical issue of how a company can choose between the different methods of acquiring technology.

CHOICE OF ACQUISITION METHODS

The acquisition of new technologies or the use of other companies' technologies are essential prerequisites for the long-term survival of a company. There are a number of methods of acquiring technology which may be more or less appropriate in different circumstances. Technology acquisition and R&D are not synonymous, nor does a company have to acquire a technology in order to make use of it.

Table 6.1 examines four different methods of acquiring technology and compares these with the choice of not acquiring the technology. It suggests the circumstances when each choice may be more or less appropriate. The first method is that of internal acquisition through the company's own R&D. The following three methods are all of external acquisition. A joint venture for our purposes here refers to the situation where two or more companies combine their resources with the intention of developing a new technology. We will look at the role of joint ventures in technology exploitation in Chapter 8.

Table 6.1 Choices in technology acquisition

Acquisition method	Company's relative standing	Category of technology	Urgency of acquisition	Commitment/ investment involved in acquisition	Technology life-cycle position
Internal acquisition Internal R&D	High Low	Distinctive or basic	Lowest	Highest	Earliest
External acquisition Joint Venture	High Low	Distinctive or basic	Higher	High	Early
Contracted-out R&D	Low	Basic or not present	Higher	Lower	Early
Licensing in	Low	Basic or not present	High	Lowest	Later
Non-acquisition, i.e. buying in product or service	Low	External	Highest	No commitment/ investment	All stages

Contracted-out R&D is where a company uses the services of a contract research organisation or some other body, such as a university, to develop a product or process. Licensing in
refers to the conventional situation where a company takes a licence for the use of a product
design, a process or a marketing package on a franchise basis, or for some combination of
the three. Finally, non-acquisition is when a company does not develop or externally acquire
a technology but buys product or service from another company based on that technology.
For example, a datacommunications company could choose to buy in modems from a
supplier, rather than develop and manufacture its own. Similarly, it could use the services
of a value-added reseller to market its final products, rather than develop its own sales
organisation.

The first two columns in the table can be considered together. We have already noted that
a company's standing in a technology refers to an objective measure of its technology when
compared to others. The category into which a technology falls depends on whether that
standing is a source of competitive advantage to the company, that is, whether or not it is
distinctive. The urgency of acquisition refers to extent of the company's need to have the
technology in use quickly. Urgency will be great when a competitor has already developed
its version of the technology, or when a technology previously only applied in another
application is transferred into the company's competitive arena or when a lack of planning
has left the company with a suddenly obsolete technology on which it depends. Technology
acquisition will be much less urgent when it forms part of a planned succession, or if it is
intended to support technology changes in other areas which are not due for introduction
until some considerable time in the future. The commitment/investment column refers to
two issues. The first is the extent to which the company sees the technology as a major area
in its future operations, such as would be the case with a process technology which was
likely to form the basis of a number of products, or a product technology which was
essential for a major market. The second issue is closely related to the last mentioned
and refers to the level of investment which is necessary in order to operate in this area.

Internal R&D

A company is likely to choose the internal acquisition route of its own R&D in those areas
of technology in which it has high standing and which are a major source of competitive
advantage for it, that is, in which it is distinctive. For example, Volvo would be expected to
have a major investment in internal R&D in the area of safety technology. Companies may
also invest in internal R&D in those areas in which it has lower standing. The company
could make this choice in order to upgrade its long-term position, or because the strategic
significance of the area is increasing. Alternatively, internal R&D may be important for
basic technologies simply because they represent the core of a company's operation. Even
though these basic technologies are not a source of positive competitive advantage, the
company could lose its market position if it was seen to be lagging behind its competitors.
The car industry again provides an example of this. Some years ago, a major source of
competitive advantage for Japanese companies was the build-quality and hence reliability of
their cars. This was based on their distinctive process technologies. Over the years most
manufacturers have invested heavily in their own processes and vehicle build-qualities have
improved dramatically. So much so that reliability, although still improving, is almost taken

for granted by today's car buyers. The process technologies involved have become basic. However, if any one manufacturer allowed its process technologies to fall behind those of its competitors, it could be an important source of competitive *dis*advantage.

Internal R&D will probably be a slower method of acquisition than some external means, except in those situations where the company has a much higher standing than others in its network, including research contractors. Therefore, internal R&D is likely to be most appropriate when the urgency of acquisition is low, such as when the company currently has an offering which is successful in its markets and the acquisition is part of a planned succession process. Internal acquisition requires the highest organisational and resource commitment of any of the methods. This, combined with its relative slowness means that it is most appropriate for technologies at the earliest stage of their life cycle, before competing companies have established their own versions of the technology. The company then stands a realistic chance of achieving a worthwhile return on its investment over a relatively long life. Alternatively, if a technology is already well into its life cycle in a version developed by other companies, then it is likely to make more sense to consider the relatively cheaper and quicker means of acquisition via licence.

Joint ventures

A joint venture shares the risks and costs of acquisition between two or more partners and is valuable when these are high. It is an appropriate acquisition method when these costs outweigh the company's commitment to the area, so that internal development would not be considered. A joint venture may be valuable for technologies in which the company's standing is either high or low and where the company has either a distinctive or basic position. The reasons for this are similar to those for internal R&D. The combining of resources in a joint venture may mean that a quicker result could be expected than with internal R&D. However, this speed of result may be thwarted by the problems the companies have in working with each other. If more rapid acquisition can be achieved then a joint venture may be appropriate in more urgent situations, such as when competitors have a head start. For similar reasons, a joint venture may be feasible for technologies later in their life cycle.

Contracted-out R&D

Contracting with a third party to develop a new process or product technology is suitable for those situations where the company has a low standing in the technological area. Because a research house can be chosen which already has a competence in the area, this method is suitable for situations which are more urgent than those which favour internal development. External acquisition means that the company is unlikely to learn as much through the process of acquisition as would be the case with internal development and so is only suitable for technology areas to which the company is less committed.

Licensing in

Licensing in is suitable for those situations where the company has a low objective standing in the technology compared to potential licensors. Licensing is also favoured where the company either does not choose or is unable to fund what might be the considerable investments needed to redress this situation. For example, a company is unlikely to want to make these investments in areas which the company does not regard as vital to its interests and to which it is not strongly committed. Licensing has the benefit of speed when compared to internal acquisition, at least when a suitable licensor can be found. This speed and its low relative cost is likely to be of considerable benefit for technologies which are further on in their life cycles, where the cost of internal acquisition cannot be justified and when entry into the technology will only be worthwhile if it can be achieved speedily.

Non-acquisition

The decision not to acquire a technology, but to purchase products or services based on it means of course that the company retains its technological investment capital for those areas where it already has a high standing or where it seeks to gain one. Analysis may indicate a number of technology areas which are basic to the company's operations, but which do not merit further investment and could more productively be transferred to the external category.

INTERNAL TECHNOLOGY ACQUISITION: RESEARCH AND DEVELOPMENT

Research and development (R&D) is regarded by some firms as a form of corporate life insurance: 'Our research laboratory was a development of the idea that large industrial organisations have both an opportunity and a responsibility for their own life insurance. New discovery can provide it.'[1]

If this analogy is correct then R&D charges companies an extremely expensive annual premium for its insurance cover. Total US expenditure on R&D was $140 billion in 1989, $145 billion in 1990 and $151 billion in 1991. Excluding federal support, the amount spent on R&D by US companies in these years was $70 billion, $73 billion and $76 billion respectively.[2] In 1983 total R&D spending in Japan was $52 billion, increasing to $75 billion in 1988, of which industry funding accounted for 80 per cent – a much higher proportion than in other industrialised countries.[3]

It is apparent that it is the firms in the fastest moving, riskiest sectors that spend proportionately most on R&D 'insurance'. Table 6.2 compares US industrial sectors' forecasted R&D expenditure for 1992. It shows that this expenditure will be greatest in the computer and office equipment industry at over $21 million, with the highest proportion of sales (13.2 per cent) in the software business sector and highest spending, as a percentage of companies' margins, in the aircraft industry at 26.8 per cent.

Although R&D is greatest in the high-risk industries, this does not mean that it should be regarded simply as a premium which firms pay to insure against failure. This defensive view

Table 6.2 Twenty largest R&D spenders (by SIC group)

Industry	SIC no.	R&D spending (millions $) 1991	1992	R&D $ as % sales	R&D $ as % margin	Annual R&D % growth
Aircraft	3721	2180	2361	3.1	26.8	8.8
Aircraft engine, engine parts	3724	1579	1628	3.8	14.5	3.1
Chemicals & allied products	2800	5505	5940	5.2	13.6	8.9
Computer & office equipment	3570	19987	21127	8.9	18.2	6.5
Electr., other elec. equip. except computers	3600	6948	7327	5.1	13.4	5.4
Electronic computers	3571	2674	3028	9.0	18.0	14.4
Farm machinery & equipment	3523	1219	1321	2.7	11.3	9.3
Food & kindred products	2000	2215	2413	1.3	3.0	9.3
Household audio & video equipment	3651	1688	1814	4.7	11.1	7.7
Motor vehicles & car bodies	3711	15061	16038	4.4	23.8	7.9
Petroleum refining	2911	5080	5454	0.6	2.7	7.6
Pharmaceutical preparations	2834	11563	13063	9.6	14.0	14.0
Phone comm. except radiotelephone	4813	15710	16400	4.5	9.3	4.0
Photographic equip. & supplies	3861	4200	4467	6.2	16.3	8.0
Plastic matl., synthetic resin	2820	1834	1923	3.4	10.8	5.4
Prepackaged software	7372	1746	2019	13.2	21.2	17.0
Radio, TV broadcast, comm. equipment	3663	1555	1747	7.3	20.6	12.8
Semiconductor, related device	3674	2378	2545	10.9	26.5	7.3
Srch, det., nav., guid., aero systems	3812	1884	1952	4.7	18.6	3.9
Tele. & telegraph apparatus	3661	2066	2244	11.2	23.5	11.3

Source: Grady, D. and Fincham, T. (1990) 'Making R&D pay', The McKinsey Quarterly, no. 3, McKinsey & Co. Inc.

of R&D ignores its key role as part of the firm's technology strategy. For example, in our research we found that the investment in a new, purpose-built research laboratory in Britain by the Japanese company Kobe Steel, has a far more central role in the strategy of the company than simply that of insurance:

> Traditionally a steelmaker and machinery manufacturer, Kobe decided four years ago to enter the world of advanced materials . . . in particular, to break into polymers and composites. At the time the company was not active in polymer technology . . . Most polymers were invented in Europe or the US . . . The company's research will be directed at producing materials for automobiles and the mass market in general.
>
> The move into Britain is also part of the company's strategy to change direction and to move away from its dependence on steel and other metals. Saito [the general manager] says the company's R&D strategy is an important part of a broader plan to move into the polymer business.

In order to take account of the long-term technological and competitive implications of big investments in research such as this we need a broader strategic view of R&D than simply as an expensive long-term insurance cover. Our approach explicitly views R&D as one of several technology acquisition mechanisms within the firm's overall acquisition portfolio. The key function of in-house R&D should be to facilitate technology acquisition in accordance with overall strategy, by generating its own new technology and by complementing and enabling other means of acquisition, such as licensing and joint ventures.

The philosophy of R&D

The purpose and practice of industrial R&D is rooted in the large, centralised laboratories which were established before and during the Second World War. It was companies' involvement in government-directed military R&D, particularly in the USA at that time, which transformed the way in which industrial R&D was organised and viewed. With the aerospace and electronics sectors in the forefront, supported by high government spending, manufacturing companies began to invest heavily in large, centralised R&D laboratories aimed at longer-term commercial applications: 'The revolutionary change was the institutionalization of R&D activity within the boundaries of the firm.'[5]

The basic idea of these laboratories was to discover some new invention which could be used to create a new product or process that had the potential to transform both the market and the industry to the advantage of the firm which made the discovery. Lowell Steele calls this its 'Holy Grail':

> R&D organisations saw their primary mission as one of discovering and inventing – in other words, demonstrating in-house creativity . . .
>
> The Holy Grail of industrial R&D has been the major invention or discovery that creates an entirely new kind of capability or that establishes a new level of capability, preferably in the form of a new product or, secondarily, a significant new process. This is not to say

that all resources have been centered on such an objective, but it has been the gleam in the eye which both motivated and guided people in trying to come up with creative ideas.[6]

We argue that for today's modern company this approach to industrial R&D is too narrow. This may be surprising because it is based on a science- and technology-driven rationale with a distinct and central company R&D function with a mission to discover new technologies. Surely it would be expected that this would help the firm to better develop and implement a coherent technology strategy? One problem with the 'Holy Grail' approach is that the major discovery is just one of R&D's functions in the acquisition of new technologies. We saw in the example of Kobe's new R&D laboratory in the UK, described earlier, that the primary objective was to 'break into' polymers and composites technologies. However, their new R&D facility will not achieve this purely through new inventions:

> Many people are trying to make new blends of polymers but have no basic understanding of what happens . . . Setting up an R&D operation is a relatively inexpensive way of putting a toe in the water . . . The aim of the research programme is to *become familiar* with the science of polymers and then apply Kobe's metals processing techniques to the plastics industry [our emphasis].[7]

This is typical of the way in which many Japanese companies have creatively used and modified existing technologies. Although this technology strategy is highly dependent on R&D, its power as a competitive weapon does not usually involve 'Holy Grail' research. Rather, it is based on the improvement of existing technologies. Thus, to achieve a more complete view of the role of R&D in technology strategy we should consider it to have four main functions – support, access, improvement and discovery:

1 *Support*. This provides technical research support for the existing business units and product lines of the company through the maintenance of sound internal relations and an understanding of the demands of their customers.
2 *Access*. This contributes to the company by keeping it up to date with external developments in a range of potentially relevant technologies. It develops the company's access to external technology networks and this is a key input to technology decision-making at the strategic level.
3 *Improvement*. This is the search for incremental improvements or combinations of existing technologies, as opposed to focusing solely on the discovery of radical new technologies.
4 *Discovery*. This is the initiation and conduct of research projects, both in-house and in collaboration with others, to acquire new technologies and information about their potential for the company.

INTERNAL AND EXTERNAL RESEARCH AND DEVELOPMENT

Of these four functions of R&D, only that of access *must* be performed within the firm. This function is to perform the role of gatekeeper. It must be carried out internally, otherwise there has to be internal specification, management and monitoring of external R&D contracts. Someone inside the company has to maintain knowledge of and access to the

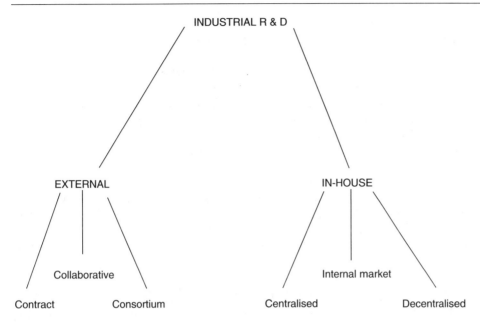

Figure 6.1 Organising research and development

providers of relevant external technologies. There must be an R&D manager even if there is no internal R&D department.

The other R&D functions – support, improvement and discovery – can potentially be contracted out. But, as with other company functions, just because some activities *can* be performed outside does not mean that it is best to do so. Some theorists would examine the transaction costs involved to decide which of these functions should be made internally or bought externally and thereby prescribe the most efficient boundary of the firm.[8] However, there are other factors which managers should consider in determining the right balance between internal and external R&D for their company.

The main methods of organising both in-house and external R&D are shown in Figure 6.1. We now move on to discuss the issues involved in managing each of these.

INTERNAL RESEARCH AND DEVELOPMENT

What managers want

Here are some recent comments from business managers about what they want from R&D:

> Anticipate tomorrow's needs today. Listen to the customer; be in touch with the market you're trying to serve. Keep ahead of new and emerging technologies; don't let them pass you by. Don't concentrate solely on 'basic inventions'; innovate on these basic inventions.

> Technological innovation is not the premier weapon in our strategic plan. Therefore, R&D leaders must work in concert with other groups (marketing, manufacturing and sales) to integrate the innovation process into successes in the marketplace.[9]

The importance of getting the firm's R&D organisation right is illustrated by the following descriptions of what seems more likely to happen in practice:

> The works would have a problem they couldn't solve themselves. A bunch of boffins would arrive; sit in the plant so it was overmanned with PhDs and BScs rather than hourly-paid blokes who left school at fourteen; run it for about three days; disappear back to [central R&D]; and about two months later a report would arrive saying there wasn't much of a problem and the works should have been able to solve it themselves. The works manager would read the report and decide it was the last time he would use that lot.[10]

> The operating divisions were strikingly uninvolved with R&D – even in projects that were ostensibly done on their behalf. Managers complained that the researchers' role was 'to invent things' and that their hit rate was far too low . . . Open cynicism flourished about research's ability to deliver. Budgets for R&D were based on history: division managers allocated money as though research was a charity rather than a vital part of their business.

> Both research and the [operating] divisions shared a sausage machine mentality about research: You put the problem in at one end, the researchers would get to work, and a solution would pop out at the other end. Only when researchers had 'the answer' would commercial considerations be taken into account . . .[11]

We now look at how the three main ways of organising in-house R&D – centralised, decentralised and using an internal R&D market to see how they relate to the problems we have outlined above.

CENTRALISED RESEARCH AND DEVELOPMENT

There are three main reasons for making corporate R&D a centralised function:

1 *To facilitate 'blue-sky' research.* One advantage of centralised R&D is that it enables more basic, theoretical and speculative or 'blue sky' research to be conducted, some of which is expected to produce far-reaching technological advances in the future. The problem is that it is not possible to predict *which* project will pay off. Novo Nordisk, Denmark's leading pharmaceuticals company, has 600 of its 1,800 R&D staff devoted to corporate research 'which comprises mainly the longer-term aspects of drug studies, such as theoretical work in genetic engineering'.[12]

   The company's operating divisions would not carry out such long-term theoretical work in their own divisional research groups because it is not directly related to their main business areas of industrial enzymes and health-care products, directed towards diabetes.

2 *To achieve technological leadership.* Simon Holberton of *The Financial Times* argues that if a company wants to be a technological leader in its industry then R&D should be a separate, central function, regardless of whether the company is a single business or a diversified collection of businesses. He cites the example of Volkswagen:

Volkswagen, the German car maker, aims to be a leader in automotive technology: it wants to control all significant automotive technologies necessary to maintain a three–four year lead in power train design and vehicle handling. The company's R&D unit is separate in funding and structure from engineering so that it may concentrate on longer-term R&D projects and not be dragged into assisting engineering with current problems.[13]

3 *To gain technological synergy*. A recent report for management consultants, McKinsey, on corporate technology found that one of the biggest benefits of having central R&D resulted from the synergy of ideas and business opportunities between the operating units and the corporate R&D. A US executive in the Lighting Group of General Electric explains how this works:

> Our lighting business benefits tremendously from the strength of our corporate R&D. We could never afford the level of expertise in say tungsten metallurgy that they have there. They have it because their metallurgical research supports not only us but other businesses as well.[14]

The extra benefits to the operating units come from the ability of central research to maintain and advance state-of-the-art technology in areas in which several of them have a common interest.

Problems with centralised R&D

In Richard Whittington's recent study[15] of six large companies in which R&D had previously been centralised, a number of problems were identified which highlight the potential drawbacks of central R&D. The three main problems were:

1 *Poor liaison with operations*. The R&D staff had been perceived to have suffered from 'excessive professionalism, proneness to overdesigning, and ivory tower mentalities'. The majority of them had little experience outside the laboratory. This was partly held to account for the complaint that R&D staff were poor at liaising with operating divisions. This problem was compounded by operating divisions' lack of technical expertise, their suspicion of central R&D as 'corporate spies' and their resentment of the levies which financed R&D.
2 *Lack of involvement with divisional planning*. A more fundamental disadvantage of centralised R&D is that its distance from operational decision-making can easily result in its complete lack of involvement in divisional planning. As such, R&D can neither influence technology strategies beyond the corporate level, nor – even if the internal relations and communications were perfect – can it be more than *reactive* to the technological demands emanating from the divisions.
3 *Influence on technology strategy*. The directors of central R&D might be expected to take the lead in the development of an overall technology strategy for their companies. The development of technology is, after all their *raison d'être*. However, Whittington found that this had not occurred in the majority of firms he looked at. Indeed, when it had occurred R&D appears to have used the process of developing a technology strategy as a

political means of defending its budget or justifying its existence, rather than in the interests of the company as a whole:

> R&D only arranged technology strategy conferences when already clearly under threat of cutbacks or closure. Although there were widespread complaints at the lack of strategic thinking at mainboard level [in other cases], there was little evidence that the in-house laboratories had well-developed strategies of their own.[16]

This highlights our argument that the development of company technology strategy should be a company-wide activity led from the top, in which R&D plays a key role as *one* means of technology acquisition. Technology strategy is far too important to be left to R&D. Technology leadership seems to have fallen to R&D in many firms because of the absence of a technology strategy from top management.

DECENTRALISED RESEARCH AND DEVELOPMENT

Since the 1970s, many corporations have broken up their centralised R&D organisation and devolved its functions within their operating companies or divisions. Elf Aquitaine is an example of this form of R&D organisation, as described by Jacques Bodelle, Vice-President of Research and Development. The company's R&D organisation is illustrated in Figure 6.2.[17] Each large operating division has its own R&D unit with its own Vice-President (VP) of R&D under the authority of the division's President. However, these divisional VPs also report to the Senior VP of the small corporate R&D team, which has no laboratories and very few people. The role of Corporate R&D at Elf is to co-finance longer-term projects with the divisions. For this they have a budget of $70 million, which, although a large sum, represents only 8–9 per cent of the Group's total R&D expenditure. The aim of corporate R&D is to protect divisional research from short-term pressures and to provide pump-priming and start-up funding for projects which are subsequently taken over by the division once a project's prospects are clearer.

Advantages of decentralisation

Physically devolving R&D resources to operating divisions in this fashion has the potentially major advantage of making R&D more commercial. Some senior managers have found that their requirement for R&D objectives, activities and outputs to be commercially-oriented, albeit in the longer term, is not satisfied by centrally organised R&D. Physically devolving its activities to operating divisions is one method of introducing commercial pressures to research objectives and decision-making.

Disadvantages of decentralisation

Decentralisation of R&D can lead to a number of problems. First, it is possible that it can lead to short-termism. Managers in operating divisions have a tendency to look to their

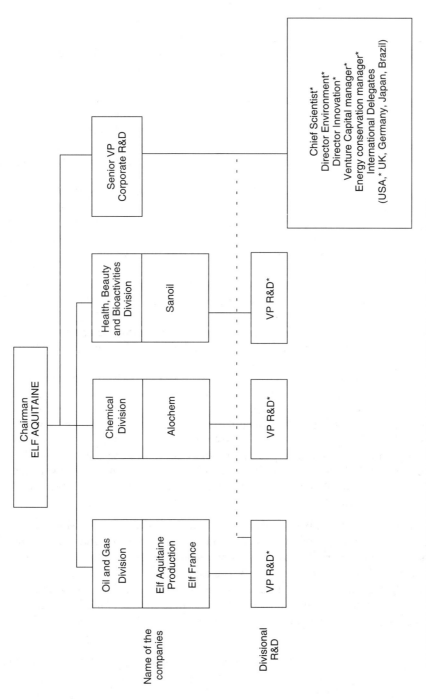

Name of the companies

Oil and Gas Division	Chemical Division	Health, Beauty and Bioactivities Division	
Elf Aquitaine Production	Alochem	Sanoil	
Elf France			

Chairman
ELF AQUITAINE

Senior VP
Corporate R&D

Chief Scientist*
Director Environment*
Director Innovation*
Venture Capital manager*
Energy conservation manager*
International Delegates
(USA,* UK, Germany, Japan, Brazil)

Divisional R&D

VP R&D*   VP R&D*   VP R&D*

* Individuals are members of the Group Reasearch Committee chaired by the senior VP Corporate R&D.
Each vice-president of R&D is under the authority of his own division's president while at the same time reporting to the senior VP of Corporate R&D.

Figure 6.2 Organisation of research and development at Elf Aquitaine
Source: Grady, D. and Fincham, T. (1990) 'Making R&D pay', *The McKinsey Quarterly*, no. 3, McKinsey & Co. Inc.

dedicated researchers to solve today's technological problems immediately while longer-term projects are discriminated against by annual profit centre accounting.

Second, decentralisation can lead to technological reactiveness because the role of R&D is to react to identified customer needs by providing technological solutions. Technological advance in decentralised companies tends to be market-driven. This is good in that it is more commercially orientated, but bad if the company aims to be a technology leader. Fiat, for example, aims to be a fast technology follower rather than a leader. After market research to determine what their key buying groups most value. Fiat's R&D concentrates on advanced engineering projects for specific models. This is technical development or 'advanced engineering', which is directed by the market rather than calculated technological opportunities.[18]

A third potential problem with decentralised R&D is that of strategic drift. With R&D split between divisions a central technology strategy is difficult to achieve. Indeed divisional technology strategies may conflict or even duplicate areas of research. The Elf solution of retaining a small core research facility may not go far enough. 'Without a coherent and consistent strategy to serve, no R&D lab can do more than just tread water.'[19]

INTERNAL RESEARCH AND DEVELOPMENT MARKET

An example of the use of an internal R&D market as a way of avoiding the break-up of the central research facility in an Australian company is described by Diane Grady and Tony Fincham of McKinsey.[20] The company had considered decentralising the R&D to its divisions, but decided that this would not work. If all of the scientists from the company's R&D staff were assigned individually to each of its six divisions, the consultants feared that a potential competitive advantage would be destroyed, since the research resources would be spread too thinly and none of the divisions would maintain the critical mass of human or investment capital. The consultants developed a solution which kept the central R&D facility intact but overcame the disadvantages of its separation from the operations. They recommended a 'contract R&D model' in which research works on a 'market-driven, fee-for-service basis'. The new role of the central unit was to provide research services on a project basis to the operating divisions:

> This involved converting research from a 'functional cost center' to a 'professional client service' mentality . . . Division clients would commission projects and be charged market rates for the research services provided. They would be free to purchase research outside should they find the internal costs or services unattractive. Achieving this new vision required defining and building new skills both within the lab and within the operating division. Operating divisions now had to *determine their technology strategies to meet business objectives rather than passively waiting for research to 'find something'* [our emphasis].[21]

The results of this change were startling and the company has since won many awards for its research:

> A number of the company's myths about how to run research have been exploded in the course of implementing the professional client concept. The structure, which some

believed would be too costly, has proven to be leaner than in the past. Cross-fertilization has happened, and has been the key to success on several important projects. Contrary to predictions, research costs have been made competitive with commercial rates. New projects have multiplied and attractive payback on the $40m pa [research] budget is no longer in question.[22]

Drawbacks with the internal market

The main problem with the internal market in R&D centres on technological and strategic reactiveness. Despite the benefits for the company in this example of an internal market form of organisation, this type of market-led approach can result in the same problems of short-termism, technological reactiveness and lack of strategic coherence and technical leadership as the decentralised model of R&D.

Example
Technology development, product development and organisation

This example illustrates how the development of new technologies can be closely linked to the development and success of the products in which they are to be applied. The example also illustrates that the eventual route for a technology's application may be different from that initially envisaged.

Westland is the only UK manufacturer of helicopters. In common with other aerospace firms, it is continually looking for new ways to solve perennial technical problems and performance limitations. One of the biggest problems with helicopters has always been the high levels of vibration produced by the complex engine, gearbox and transmission systems which drive the rotor. This has meant not only uncomfortable flights, but rapid wear of the drive-train and difficulties in operating delicate instrumentation and weapons systems.

Early approaches to the problem were 'remedial', and used passive deadening materials or devices. During the 1970s,

with interest and funding from government, the company's attention moved to 'active' systems in which vibrations would be neutralised at source or by the deliberate generation of equal and opposite vibrations. The company's technical development proceeded and contacts were expanded with specialist partners, in particular with a manufacturer of the actuation systems which would produce the neutralising signals. The key question became how the system could be convincingly demonstrated.

At the same time, another part of Westland was struggling with the development of a new aircraft. The W30 was a commercial transport derivative of the Lynx naval helicopter and was under trial by airlines in the USA. Unfortunately it was suffering from excessive vibration. W30 engineers were made aware of the ACSR project through the professional 'grapevine' and it quickly became clear that the helicopter's design made it ideal for a system demonstration. In early 1987 ACSR successfully flew on the W30.

Unfortunately the W30 aircraft was cancelled shortly afterwards for commercial reasons. This meant that the ACSR technology was now proven but had 'nowhere to go' in the firm's own helicopter range. Similar disappointments were to follow as Westland's recently established New Business Marketing group sought ways to exploit the firm's skills outside its own helicopter programmes. Possible applications were investigated on other firms' helicopters and on fixed-wing projects such as the revolutionary 'unducted fan' engine, but no firm orders emerged.

Development of the technology languished inside the company until another internal Westland project provided the opportunity for a full production implementation of the technology. The first flight of EH101, a large Anglo-Italian designed helicopter aimed at both military and civilian markets was also seen in 1987. Once again severe vibration was encountered and several solutions had been unsuccessfully tried.

The ACSR team leader successfully pressed for a feasibility study to be carried out, following which funding was granted for a prototype installation. In February 1990 an EH101 fitted with ACSR flew for the first time and met the vibration level targets set by the aircraft designers and the customers. It has now been added to the specification for production EH101s. Continued development is under way and technical collaboration with the actuation systems company has been formalised.

The ACSR technology is now being actively marketed to a range of potential customers: helicopter operators, fixed-wing aircraft and aero-engine makers and operators. The company now faces decisions as to how its development resources will be allocated between these and its 'core' helicopter programmes internally.

PROJECT SELECTION, EVALUATION AND FUNDING

However the company's R&D is organised, choices have to be made between alternative projects and programmes. How can managers who are not technically trained evaluate the appropriateness of this or that investment in R&D? The simple solution is to let the accountants do it for you! They can calculate the financial and risk factors for each project according to the sort of formula shown below:

$$\text{Project index (benefit : cost)} = \frac{S \times P \times p \times t}{100 \, C}$$

where S = peak sales volume (£ p.a.)
P = net profit on sales (%)
p = probability of R&D success (on a scale 0–impossible to 1–certain to succeed)
t = a discounting/timing factor (years)
C = future cost of R&D (£)

There are of course some types of research where it is possible to quantify these factors with a high degree of accuracy. These are usually shorter-term development projects. Most R&D investments have a longer pay-off period, a less calculable outcome and an unclear commercial prospect. We have argued in a previous chapter that the rate of return on the investment in R&D is rarely well considered and, in particular, that a clear view of the potential applications and the different means of exploitation are rarely taken. Furthermore, there are other important factors which managers should consider in selecting projects that are omitted in such simple financial formulations – particularly what the project will contribute to the company's wider technology strategy. We have used here a method for assessing individual research projects and overall programmes which was developed by Thomas Lee of the International Institute for Applied Systems Analysis and John Fisher, formerly of General Electric's (GE) R&D staff and Timothy Yeo a planning manager at the Electric Power Research Institute.[23]

The evaluation of each project is broken down into five independent issues. Three relate to individual projects and two to overall R&D programmes. The five are:

- project strength;
- project timing;
- project fit;
- programme funding profile;
- programme robustness.

Project strength

The key questions here are can the project achieve its technical goal and its market goals and, if so, what is the potential value of its success? The more achievable the goals and the greater the value, the greater the project's strength. Potential value is hard to estimate. It has a number of dimensions which concern both the pattern of exploitation of the technology and its relationship to subsequent generations of technology. We deal with these more fully in later chapters. For the moment, it is important to emphasise that the potential of a technology needs to be assessed in relation to its exploitation in all potential applications and by all internal and external means. Further, the potential of an individual technology must be related to the need for, and availability of, other technologies to support it in any application. Also important is the effect of a continuing presence in a particular technology area on the company's future strategic direction, or conversely, the effect of a cessation of activities in that area on that direction. This means that decisions on the potential of a technology are not the prerogative of a single function such as R&D, nor are to be taken in isolation from the company's overall technology strategy.

Project timing

There is a series of decisions which managers have to make about when to move on from one stage of a project to the next. Moving ahead too early – or too late – can cause problems. Both technical and economic criteria must be met before proceeding to the next stage. Figure 6.3 shows a project timing scoring system that can be used to evaluate the extent to which a project is ahead or behind schedule.

If a project at any point satisfies the technical readiness criteria for all prior stages but *not* the current one, then its technical timing is correct; i.e. its score is 0. When the remaining

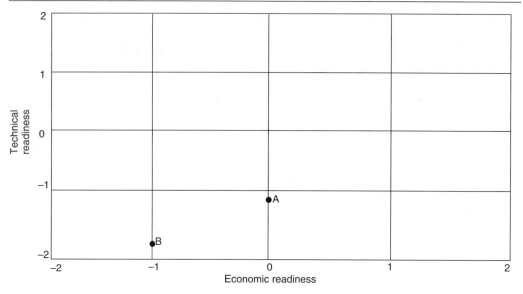

Figure 6.3 Project timing matrix

criteria for its current stage are satisfied then its score will become +1; i.e. it would be ready to go on to the next stage. If any criteria for the previous stage were still not fulfilled the score would be −1.

Project fit

This refers to how well the project fits the company's specific features and plans – its competencies, culture, technology strategy, market positioning and competitive advantage. These are necessarily qualitative considerations. The point can be illustrated by two contrasting examples of IBM and General Electric (GE).

IBM's competitive advantage has been in the supply of high-quality business equipment and services. Its R&D in electronic computers built on these strengths by also developing service-oriented software. GE had been strongest in manufacturing and selling rather than the delivery of services. It did not invest in service-based software when it began to develop its computers and did not offer the associated services which businesses really wanted, rather than computers as items of equipment in themselves. GE pulled out of computers after making increasing losses for ten years. There was a lack of fit between GE's competencies and the needs of a service-oriented business.

Programme funding profile

Policy-makers can influence the structure of an R&D programme by setting general objectives and guidelines for resource allocation and funding. For example, Figure 6.4 shows the funding profile for sixteen projects set against an index of project strength (see above).

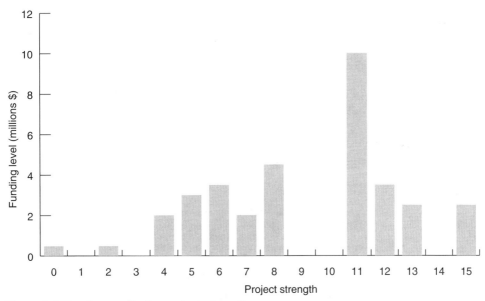

Figure 6.4 Funding profile for project strength

This profile can be used to aid resource allocation decisions within and between research programmes. For example, senior management may decide to reduce or eliminate funding on projects with a strength of less than, say, 6 on this scale and reallocate resources to those scoring over 11.

Programme robustness

Unforeseen events in the business environment may alter the potential value of any R&D project. It is likely that external circumstances will change significantly given the long time-scale before much of today's R&D will begin to pay back its investment. A measure of programme robustness estimates R&D's chances of retaining its value in the event of environmental shocks.

For any R&D programme, a forecast of potential environmental shocks can be undertaken using a number of possible forecasting techniques, which will produce probability estimates of their occurrence. Then, cross-impact analysis can be used to estimate the effect that each shock would have on each project, favourably or unfavourably, in terms of strength, timing or fit.

A diagram such as Figure 6.5 can be constructed showing a 'robustness' estimate for each project by the summing of the positive environmental effects minus the sum of the negative effects, each weighted by their probability of occurrence.

EXTERNAL TECHNOLOGY ACQUISITION

We now turn in more detail to the important, but frequently neglected, topic of external technology acquisition. This is an area where issues of technology acquisition and

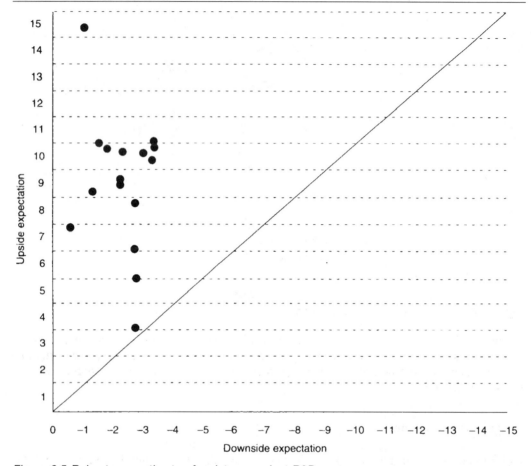

Figure 6.5 Robustness estimate of a sixteen-project R&D programme

exploitation frequently merge because the companies involved in acquisition arrangements with other companies are acquiring technology to subsequently exploit it. Also, in the case of joint ventures to acquire technology, each company brings a technology to the arrangement and the task is one of combining technology from the two or more firms. We will deal with external exploitation more fully in Chapter 7 and will concentrate on acquisition issues here.

Table 6.3 draws heavily on the work of Lei and Slocum[24] and examines the costs, benefits, critical success factors and human resource issues in different forms of external technology acquisition. For greater clarity, the table deals separately with licensing in manufacturing and service industries. An example of manufacturing industry licensing was the UK car maker Rover revolutionising its manufacturing by taking a licence to Honda's process technologies. An example in the service industries is when a hotel company takes a licence to the 'Best Western' franchise, so as to take advantage of the franchisor's expertise in branding, advertising and central reservation systems.

Table 6.3 also includes two categories of joint ventures. The first of these categories is

Table 6.3 Costs, benefits and critical success factors in external technology acquisition

Acquisition method	Benefits	Costs	Critical success factors	Human resource factors
Licensing in manufacturing industries	• Speed of acquisition • Low cost of entry • Matching with existing support technologies • Opportunity to learn from licensor	• Dependence on licensor • Deterrent to internal acquisition	• Selection of appropriate licensor • Appropriate agreement including application and area • Full transfer of knowledge	• Negotiation skills • Skills in transfer and distribution of knowledge • Managerial rotation
Licensing in services and franchises	• As above	• As above	• Selection of appropriate licensor • Appropriate agreement • Strong licensor support	• Developing and maintaining consistency in staff approach
Joint ventures – specialisation across partners	• Use of partner technologies • Acquisition of partner's skills • Economies of scale	• Dependence on partner's technology • Deterrent to internal acquisition	• Tight and specific performance criteria • Student, rather than teacher approach • Recognition that collaboration is new form of competition to learn new skills	• Management development and training • Negotiation skills • Managerial rotation
Joint ventures – shared value-adding	• Pooled strength of both parties • Upgrading of technology • Faster learning	• High switching costs • Inability to limit partner's access to information	• Decentralisation and autonomy from corporate parents • Long 'courtship' • Harmonisation of management styles	• Team building • Acculturisation • Flexible skills for implicit communication
Non-acquisition – buying final product or service	• No resource investment or commitment • Allows concentration on critical technologies	• Lost possibility to acquire technology	• Good purchasing/relationship management skills	• Maintaining motivation of own R&D staff
Consortia, keiretsus and chaebols	• Shared risks and costs • Critical mass in process technologies • Fast resource flows and skill transfers	• Skills and technologies that have no real market worth • Bureaucracy/hierachy • Loss of critical technologies	• Government encouragement • Shared values among managers • Personal relationships • Close monitoring of member company performance	• Clan cultures • Fraternal relationships • Extensive mentoring for common vision/mission
Contracted-out R&D	• Acquisition of Technology close to 'State of the Art' • Access to greater R&D resources • Broadening of technology portfolio	• Possible dependence on outside sources • Possible loss of R&D capability • No side-effects of acquisition	• Selection of best R&D house • Clear briefing • Good liaison • Technology insertion and management skills	• Maintaining motivation of own R&D staff

Developed from Lei and Slocom, Op. cit.

'specialisation' ventures, which Lei and Slocum suggest is where each party brings a distinctive competence or technology to the alliance, such as that between Thomson of France and JVC of Japan. In this venture, Thomson brings the marketing technology needed to compete in fragmented European markets and JVC contributes the process technologies involved in producing optical and compact discs, computers and semiconductors. Thus each brings technology for exploitation and has the effective use of the other company's technology in return. In contrast, 'shared value-adding' ventures are those where both parties have strong, but related competences. An example is where Boeing and a number of European aerospace companies are considering joining forces to develop new generations of large civil and supersonic aircraft. The table also deals with the alternative to acquisition in which case the company chooses not to acquire the technology but to rely on the services of another company that has the technology to provide product or service for it, while retaining the technology.

Also in Table 6.3 are consortia. These range widely in area and scale from limited agreements between a number of companies to develop a specific technology, to larger-scale groupings which involve product development and subsequent production as well as R&D. Consortia also include the more permanent multi-industry groupings which are common in the Far East. Larger-scale consortia are not well developed in the USA, despite attempts to build cross-industry groupings such as Microelectronics and Computer Technology Corporation (MCC) and Sematech. Lei and Slocum point out that these and other consortia have failed because of the problems in getting firms to pool their resources into an integrated organisation. Europe has seen a number of consortia with various degrees of success, particularly in the aerospace industry. Perhaps the best-known example is the Airbus group which brings together companies from several European countries and has been successful over many years in developing a wide range of commercial aircraft.

However, it is in the Far East that consortia have reached their most developed form. The Japanese keiretsu consist of a combination of twenty to fifty companies, probably centred on a bank and/or a trading company, which are likely to include component and final product producers as well as distributors. The links between the individual units are not those of a conventionally vertically integrated company and individual companies will deal with companies outside the consortia. Instead, the keiretsu are held together by interlocking shareholding, trading patterns and strong interpersonal ties between management. The South Korean chaebols differ in that unlike keiretsu which are financed from group banks, they are financed by the government and managed by family members, and links between constituent companies are based on blood relationships.

The final acquisition method in the table is contracted-out R&D which occurs when a company uses the services of a contract research house, another company or a university to develop a product or process technology for it.

The table outlines the benefits and costs of each means of acquisition as well as the consequent critical success factors and human resource issues. It also covers the alternative to acquisition of a technology which consists of buying a product or service from a supplier based on the technology, which is retained by the supplier.

Licensing

We have already noted that the benefits of licensing in manufacturing industry include speed of entry to different technologies and its relatively low cost compared to internal acquisition. The licensee also has the benefit of matching the acquired technology to its own support technologies and the possibility of learning from the licensor. For service and franchise licensing a particular benefit is the opportunity to enter a market without the costs, time and risk of developing the company's own offering. Against these advantages must be set the danger of dependence on the licensor. When a company takes a licence for a technology it is possible that it will neglect its own technology development in that area. This is particularly likely when the licence has occurred as a reaction to an immediate technological inadequacy and the company lacks a strategic technological direction. We have seen in Chapter 2 how common this situation is.

The critical success factors in both types of licensing can be divided into two areas. The first centres on the actual decision to license. We have seen that licensing is often used as a short-term way to overcome an urgent technological inadequacy. All too frequently, companies pay little regard to the reasons why licensing has become necessary and the implications of this for its previous technology strategy processes. Similarly, many managers do not evaluate the situations to find out if licensing is an appropriate strategic decision to take as we have discussed above. Finally, the almost audible sigh of relief which emanates from companies that have 'rescued' themselves from a technological problem through licensing may drown out any talk of the need for a longer-term strategic technology appraisal – so much so that the company will be as unprepared for its next technology requirements and will be dependent on another 'fix' of technology from outside.

The second critical success factor centres on the management task which is involved in the licensing in task itself. This task needs skills in licensor selection and most particularly in determining exactly what technology is to be transferred. Our research has shown that disagreements over exactly what is involved are common in licence deals.

In human resource terms the emphasis is first on the licensee's skills in maximising the learning of its staff in the technology which is being transferred and in the wider skills of the licensor. This demands a conscious programme of staff rotation, evaluation and internalisation if the company is to optimise the value of the licence. The licensee's organisation must also have a clear strategy for the exploitation of the licence, with market analysis, the development of appropriate support technologies and marketing programmes in exactly the same way as would be appropriate for its home-grown technology training. The acculturisation of licencees in the appropriate core values of the licensor is critical in the case of service or franchise licences.

It is easy to suggest that licensing is not a proper way of acquiring technology, perhaps because licensing implies an inadequacy in the licensee's technology. However, we would argue that licensing in is a valuable part of a company's armoury, as long as it is strategic. Therefore, it must be used in those situations requiring a support technology, a technology in a non-distinctive area, where the company does not have the resources or skills to develop its own technology or where urgency of acquisition has arisen because of an unanticipated technology or market change. This is strategic licensing and it is quite different to the unplanned reactive licensing which takes place without regard to its future implications.

Joint ventures and consortia

We deal with these two areas together as they share a number of commonalties, but are separate from the large-scale far-eastern consortia of keiretsus and chaebols. Joint ventures in which the partners each contribute a matching technology provide the obvious advantage of each company having effective use of the other's technologies without the investment which the company would otherwise have to make to acquire those technologies (even if the company had the skills or time for that acquisition). These externally acquired technologies may be necessary as overall support technologies or may be essential for a specific application. Those joint ventures based on shared value-adding do not offer this synergy but do provide the benefit of pooling the strengths of both parties and the opportunity for rapid learning in new areas.

Officially recognised R&D consortia, usually between a number of firms, have increased in number over the past ten years in both the USA and Europe. There have been more than 200 consortia registered in the USA since 1984[25] and over twenty joint R&D programmes of the European Community, one of which in information technology (Esprit) comprises 226 projects involving more than 500 separate organisations.[26] R&D consortia, in which companies share the costs and technical output of research, vary in membership, size, funding arrangements, organisational structure and technological emphasis. In the USA, consortia must be registered with the Commerce Department since the passage of the National Cooperative Research Act in 1984, in order to protect member firms from falling foul of US anti-trust laws. The 203 registered consortia involve 902 business organisations and 255 government and academic institutions. They cover a range of emerging technologies in fields such as semiconductor manufacturing, telecommunications, microelectronics, software engineering, superconductivity, biotechnology and transportation.[27]

R&D collaboration, whether by joint venture or consortia have a number of specific advantages which are outlined below.

Cost reduction

The rapid growth in collaboration between firms has occurred in part because R&D costs in some technologies have become too great for one firm to finance alone. In the UK, Rolls-Royce's aerospace expenditure on R&D averaged £225 million per year during the 1980s. Yet this budget would not be sufficient to maintain a development programme in just one of the new technologies which it may have to have in the 1990s in order to compete with larger rivals such as General Electric.

In order to remain competitive in the future, aero-engine manufacturers may have to take a stake in the new prop-fan engine technology. Engines based on this will consist of new types of gas turbines with propellers, and they will consume up to 40% less fuel whilst travelling at speeds close to those of jet-propelled aircraft. The overall consensus in the industry is that full-scale production of such engines will be achieved some time in the 1990s. There are two types of prop-fan engines that are possible: 'open-rotors' which have propellers at the rear of the aircraft and are not covered by a nacelle, and 'ducted-rotors' which are larger engines with shrouds round the propellers making them suitable for underwing installation on big aircraft.

The giant US firms appear to be ahead of Rolls Royce at least in open-rotor technology. The company may, of course, opt out of this sector of the market and invest solely in the development of ducted-rotors. But this could have adverse consequences since most airlines will require both types of engine, and aero-engine manufacturers that produce the two could manifestly have a strategic advantage. The obvious benefits of having the two types of engine in the product portfolio, together with the expense of development (the smaller open-rotor is likely to cost at least $500m) may lead to Rolls Royce collaborating with other aero-engine manufacturers.[28]

Access to technologies

Consortia are often composed of competitors in the market who are willing to co-operate to conduct mutually beneficial research. One of the first to be established in the USA was the Microelectronics and Computer Technology Corporation (MCC) in 1983 by computer and semiconductor companies. Now with 56 members they co-operate on basic research and then compete during development, production and marketing. In Japan, NEC generated a 23 per cent per year growth record in the electronics industry, during the 1980s despite having an R&D budget much smaller than either IBM or AT&T. It supplemented its R&D budget with 130 technological alliances with other companies, which all fitted within its overall technology strategy (strategic architecture).[29]

From looking at a number of studies Todd Watkins of Harvard concludes that: 'The empirical evidence suggests the most important motivation for cooperative R&D is simply access to technologies.'[30]

'This development is bigger than we are'

Companies form R&D consortia because they can achieve things that no single company can. Craig Fields, the president of MCC lists three key things that they achieve:

1 Consortia establish the standards, protocols and interfaces that will accelerate the whole market. Members will thus get a 'bigger piece of a bigger pie'.
2 They set common qualifications for suppliers.
3 They conduct multi-company market trials and 'market risk is higher than technical risk'.

Fields emphasises the infrastuctural nature of R&D consortia because they stimulate the creation of new business from them – often in unforeseen ways: 'They're like the interstate highway system begun in the 1950s . . . [along which] companies built new businesses in chains of gas stations, motels, trucking of perishable foods and many more ways.'[31]

Dan Dimancescu, head of Technologies Strategies Group, Cambridge, MA describes the effect of the electronics industry consortia in similar terms: 'They're like a used car strip where you have twenty dealers side by side . . . That creates a critical mass of businesses that feed on one another.'[32]

Reduce individual costs and risks

Other potential advantages of R&D collaboration are the collective spreading of risks, economies of scale and the avoidance of non-rival duplication of research. In an analysis of 92 firms in the USA the rate of return to R&D expenditure among co-operating firms was estimated to be nearly one and a half times more than for non-co-operating firms.[33] From another survey of 59 companies Fusfeld and Haklisch conclude that the rise in collaborative R&D is part of a general trend towards the broadening of firms' technology bases through access to external sources of technology.[34]

Learning from others

Co-operation gives firms the opportunity to track new developments, assess alternatives and monitor the technological capabilities of their competitors. A set of case studies in Sweden shows that there are considerable learning benefits for firms in long-term R&D collaboration.[35] In interviews with both Renault and Peugeot about their joint research in automobile instrumentation and control technologies it was reported that they felt that the benefits included 'a reduction in search costs, a better working relationship, and a better understanding by the research group of the needs of the automobile industry. Both firms feel that these benefits exceed [those of] a shorter-term contracting strategy.'[36]

Altering the basis of competition

Joint ventures between industry leaders can be used to effectively alter the basis of competition in an industry. An example of this is the pan-European attempts to develop and exploit high definition picture quality televisions. This could have the effect of shifting the basis of competition away from selling standard televisions on a price basis and towards competition based on relative picture quality.

Small-firm collaboration

It is not only large firms that choose to enter into joint research agreements. In the study of small and medium-sized UK firms referred to earlier, 26 per cent of the firms engaged in some form of collaborative R&D, of which 56 per cent were with other small and medium firms.[37] Forty-six per cent of collaborations were with suppliers and 34 per cent with customers, which is significant because it has been suggested that collaborative R&D arrangements will increasingly be vertical in character, as opposed to the horizontal nature of most consortia formed so far.

Vertical collaboration

For some time it has been established practice for leading technology companies to work closely with selected suppliers to achieve higher quality products and services. A significant amount of industrial product development work is already carried out jointly between supplier and user firms. Robert M. White, the US Under Secretary for Technology at the Department of Commerce, suggested that the next step that we may see emerging is towards more formalised R&D consortium arrangements of a vertical nature between suppliers, manufactures and customers. These may spin off from horizontal consortia, White suggests: 'In some cases it makes sense to share the risk and expense of generic technology and then go off down the road and form vertical consortia. Ten horizontal teams could lead to ten vertical teams.'[38]

   Both horizontal and vertical collaboration are already happening on a one-to-one basis in leading technology companies. For instance, Frank Carrubba, Director of Hewlett Packard (HP) Laboratories reported that HP have joint R&D teams with suppliers, such as Canon; competitors, such as Philips; customers, such as Ford; and non-competitors, such as DuPont.[39]

Problems with joint ventures and consortia

A main disadvantage of joint ventures and consortia is that they may lead to long-term dependence by discouraging the company from investing more widely in necessary technologies. They may also fail if the company is unable to acquire the necessary technologies to make the joint venture a success. An example of a joint venture where one of the partners was unable to acquire critical technologies is provided by Lei and Slocum – that between General Electric and Fujitsu Fanuc. This joint venture was originally established to co-design and co-produce industrial robots and flexible automation systems. GE's inability to learn the necessary process technologies from its partner had meant that it now acts simply as a distributor of the robots produced by Fujitsu. As we have already discussed, this problem is particularly acute when one company uses the time of the joint venture to acquire the technologies of the partner and then displace it with its own operations. Further problems are the company being too small, having too many conflicting interests and lacking capacity to absorb the research output.

Too small to have much impact

At present R&D consortia of all types only account for a small proportion of industrial R&D expenditure – less than 1 per cent of the total in the USA in 1991 according to the National Science Foundation.[40] IBM alone spends considerably more than this on research. It has been argued that in some industries US consortia have not been a success: '[Consortia] have been a major disappointment to their supporters' and have 'barely had an impact on the US electronics industry'.[41] This perceived failure may have much to do with a lack of commitment by the members by putting in no more than token membership fee and treating this as an insurance policy.

Too many conflicting interests

Companies are likely to participate in joint ventures for different and sometimes conflicting reasons. They can bring together highly specialised staff from radically different corporate cultures. Negotiations to set up collaborative research can be difficult and tend to focus on cost-sharing arrangements and the distribution of property rights to the (at this stage unknown) outputs. Agreements tend to be most difficult for pre-competitive basic research and generic industrial technologies such as materials, processes and standards. These difficulties have led to the government offering support in this area through the Office of Technology in the USA, the Commission of the European Community and MITI in Japan.

An even more significant problem of conflict of interests centres on the dangers of loss of technology from the company to the partner, the partner seeking long-term advantage through that technology transfer and the development of ways of supplanting the partner. Also the venture itself has a limited lifetime and is based on the acquisition of technologies which are themselves perishable. This again emphasises the importance of the management task in establishing and monitoring performance criteria and being organised for, and willing to learn from, the partner – the 'student rather than teacher approach'. Human relations issues in these joint ventures include skills in negotiation, management development and particularly in managerial rotation to maximise the learning process. Heavy dependence on a specialisation joint venture can significantly affect the strategic value of a company in the case of an acquisition or merger. British Aerospace's subsidiary Rover cars gained considerably in both product and process technologies from its long relationship with Honda. Honda had a 20 per cent stake in Rover and the two companies had developed products together and operated a complex set of production interrelationships, such as for Rover to buy engines from the UK Honda plant and for Rover to supply Honda with body panels. However, when British Aerospace sold its 80 per cent stake in Rover to BMW then Honda not only decided to sell its stake, but also threatened to cancel all its technology agreements with Rover. If implemented, such a threat would have left BMW with a purchased company of much less value and without its previous development potential.

Those joint ventures which involve shared value-adding do not have the advantage of technology matching, but may find that shared resources can assist the acquisition process and reduce each companies' risks. The corresponding disadvantages again include long-term dependency on the partner and the consequent high switching costs. A major problem is also that of controlling the transfer of the company's technology to its partner, which is a particular danger in this situation because of the closeness of contact between many members of each company in this type of venture.

Further critical success factors centre on the need to establish an appropriate culture in the venture. This may have to be quite different from that which exists in either of the two partner companies. For example, it is likely that a joint venture in a new technology area will need a faster speed of response than either of the two partner companies operating in more established areas are used to. The need for a distinctive culture leads to the requirement for autonomous operation and commonality in style between those who join the venture. The consequent human resource issues centre on the process of team-building during the long 'courtship' between the companies, which both sides must accept and work towards. Lei and Slocum contrast the success of Corning's joint venture with CIBA-GEIGY, which had a two-year gestation time, with the failure of that between AT&T and Olivetti to produce personal computers. The latter joint venture was eventually dissolved because of wide differences in management styles, corporate cultures and missions which the two companies failed to explore before they embarked on the venture. Finally, Lei and Slocum point out that one of the most difficult things for managers to remember is that joint ventures are actually just competition in another form. Many commentators have noted that Japanese companies enter into joint ventures with companies they hope to compete with after learning their technology and indeed to carry on parallel competition in other product or market areas during the time of their co-operation.

The capacity to absorb the research output

It is of little value for a company to participate in joint R&D if it does not have the means for developing, testing and exploiting the resulting technology. For this reason, collaborative research cannot be regarded as a substitute for other means of acquiring technologies which may be more appropriate in certain circumstances. The emphasis is on the complementary nature of different forms of external technology acquisition and an in-house R&D facility:

> The failure of firms of all sizes to detect and gain access to newly emerging capabilities at an early stage can rapidly result in both product and process obsolescence. Appropriately constructed strategies, based on a combination of in-house technological accumulation *complemented* by external inputs can, in contrast, enable firms technologically to update existing products and/or move to new product areas . . . This means that it is not only in-house R&D commitment that should be a prime focus of corporate technology strategies: also of extreme importance is having an external orientation directed towards creating a network of linkages plugging the firm into appropriate sources of complementary technological information and expertise.[42]

Large-scale consortia, kieretsu and chaebol

Unfortunately, many consortia are effectively 'shot-gun marriages' into which companies are forced by inadequacies in their resources or because there are no other partners, the others having already joined rival consortia. The relationship between the parties may lack the critical success factor of shared values and common mission that are necessary to reproduce the clan-culture found in far-eastern consortia, which have the advantage of long-term acculturation between the partners. Any consortia involves costs for the individual members. The skills and technologies which it develops within the consortia may have value only in that context and not in any wider market.

Perhaps even more significantly, a company in a joint venture may lose control or the lead in distinctive technologies, either by their acquisition by partners or by the fact that they do not form part of the technologies for which the company is responsible in the consortia. For example, it has been alleged that Deutsche Aerospace gained immeasurably in technological terms at the expense of British Aerospace during their membership of the consortium which developed the Tornado military aircraft. Similarly, a major issue in negotiations between the British and Italian partners in the consortium which developed the EH101 helicopter was which company would be responsible for the rotor-head, an area widely regarded as a 'manhood technology' in the helicopter world.

The far-eastern consortia avoid a number of these problems and also achieve further advantages. Lei and Slocum indicate that because member companies' stock holdings are distributed across group companies and there is little external financial pressure to achieve short-term financial results, the consortia are uniquely positioned to share the risks of investment in high-risk, high-technology projects. Their diversification also reduces risk, and the commonality of culture provides for effective transfer of technologies acquired in one application to other and seemingly distant areas. At the same time, the long-term buyer–seller relationships between constituent companies provide a measure of security, subject to long-term performance and, more importantly, an improved allocation of the technological load between buyer and seller.

Contracting out R&D

Contracting out does not involve the same level of investment as the establishment of a separate joint venture. It has the overall benefit of allowing the company to have access to technology which is close to the state-of-the-art, but with a lower level of commitment and it can broaden a company's technological portfolio through access to the technology and research skills of specialists in an area. After the growth of internal research expenditure which occurred during the 1960s and 1970s, the proportion of R&D which is conducted in-house by companies has fallen. In the UK for example, the proportion of external (extramural): internal R&D expenditure increased from a low of 2.9 per cent in 1978 to 8.2 per cent in 1986 (see Table 6.4).

Table 6.4 Extramural R&D in the UK, 1967–86

R&D expenditure £ million	1967	1972	1978	1981	1985	1986
Total industry	405	831	2,324	3,793	5,146	5,673
Extramural	20	27	68	n.a.	332	463
Extramural/Total %	3.3	3.2	2.9	n.a.	6.5	8.2

Sources: British Business, 9/12/83; 24/7/86; 5/2/88; and 1986 figures, J. Bowles, Department of Trade and Industry.
Note: Data collection on extramural R&D was curtailed in the 1981 and 1983 surveys; however, for 1981, the amount of R&D carried out by (extramural) research associations increased to £88 million, from £51 million in 1978.

The more specific benefits of contracted-out research can be outlined as shown below.

Bide your time and learn

One reason why firms choose to contract out R&D projects is that when a new technology is emerging and there is uncertainty about the future path of its development, early investment in dedicated in-house research facilities and staff are a high-risk and expensive proposition. This is illustrated by the development of the biotechnology industry since the early 1970s. In the early years of this industry, the many new small specialist firms which had been established – often by university scientists – were the dominant source of biotechnology R&D. In 1978 only three of the large pharmaceutical and chemical firms had any in-house biotechnology research programmes. Most of the other established firms did not start in-house biotechnology R&D until after 1981.[43] In the period 1976–85 the established firms funded R&D outside in the independent biotechnology firms through research contracts, joint ventures and equity investments – accounting for 56 per cent of the independents' total funds. In one of the best-known of the new biotechnology firms, Genentech, revenues from development contracts supported 70 per cent of its total R&D between 1976 and 1980. In another, Cetus, contract R&D accounted for 65 per cent of its total R&D in 1981.[44]

The main reason why the pharmaceutical and chemical firms decided to contract out so much of their biotechnology R&D to specialist research firms is explained by Sharp:

> It was very unclear what would succeed: genetic engineering techniques themselves were new; the problems of scale-up and development were untackled, and the issue of patents and safety-ethical controls a big unknown. In such circumstances it suited the major companies to bide their time. A $10 million research contract with Genentech or Cetus or one of the other companies was a good way to hedge bets. It kept their fingers in the pie, but it was a limited commitment – and it gave them time to see where biotechnology was going before building up their own internal competence.[45]

If you can't afford a cow, you have to buy milk

Of course, only the largest firms can afford to maintain a complete in-house R&D facility – even if this is the best acquisition means. Small and medium-sized firms requiring R&D work must engage in contract or collaborative research agreements. A survey of 100 UK small and medium firms found that 39 per cent contracted out R&D, of which 53 per cent were 'forced to undertake such action because of lack of skills'. For 70 per cent of those contracting out this represented less than 10 per cent of their total R&D. Eighty-five per cent of subcontracts were with other small and medium-sized firms and 47 per cent of the contractees were suppliers and 18 per cent were customers.[46]

Save on fixed costs, stay flexible

It has also been argued that some technologies have advanced to such a level of complexity that they now require a broader range of specialisms than can be maintained in-house by even the largest firms. Contracting out more R&D has also been stimulated by the general trend in business towards more contracting out of discrete activities, rather than retaining a full in-house capability. This policy is perceived as having the advantages of reduced overheads, more flexibility and greater accountability.

Against the advantages of contracting out are a number of disadvantages of which probably the greatest is the potentially negative effect on the company's own R&D of increasing dependence on external sources of technology. Once responsibility for a particular area of technology is delegated to a contractor there are often loud calls for a reduction in in-house R&D costs and, hence, capability. Unless a strategic view of technological direction is taken an unplanned loss of capability in a critical area can result. A further cost of contracted-out R&D is that it removes the chance of unplanned discovery or synergy between different internal R&D projects – the side-effects of acquisition. Finally, despite the advantages of contracting out R&D, as we explained in the previous section, this policy cannot completely obviate the need for some internal R&D capability. Certain key functions which enable the firm to make decisions about technology – and specifically, what research to contract out – can only be performed if the company has at least a minimal in-house capability.

The critical success factors in contracted-out R&D include selection of the most appropriate R&D contractor, clear briefing of the contractor and good liaison. Many companies develop long-term relationships with suitable contractors so that they can guide the development of the contractor and benefit from its wider growth. A further major success factor is skills in inserting the newly acquired technology into the company. It is at this point that the 'not-invented-here' syndrome may be a problem. In-house R&D staff may well regard a decision to use a contractor as an adverse comment on their skills and, indeed, as a threat to their future. Therefore, maintaining and motivating the company's own R&D staff is a major human resource issue in contracted-out R&D. A key aspect of this is for these staff to have a clear view of the need for contracting out and how this relates to the company's overall technology strategy and the use of different means of technology acquisition in appropriate circumstances.

The far-eastern consortia avoid a number of these problems and also achieve further advantages. Again we refer to Lei and Slocum's comments on member companies' stock holdings mentioned earlier in this chapter (p. 124). These consortia's diversification also reduces risk and the commonality of culture provides for effective transfer of technologies acquired in one application to other and seemingly distant areas. At the same time, the long-term buyer–seller relationships between constituent companies provide a measure of security, subject to long-term performance and more importantly, an improved allocation of the technological load between buyer and seller.

CONCLUSIONS: TECHNOLOGY ACQUISITION AND STRATEGY

This and the last chapter have examined the technology acquisition activity within companies. We have seen that technology acquisition can be carried out by a number of different means. A major issue facing companies is to distinguish between 'doing the right thing and doing it right'. All too often the debate about technology acquisition is narrowly focused on how R&D can be made more productive or on how R&D projects should be selected. Instead, we argue that the major decision facing a company is which technologies it should invest its resources to acquire and for which it should depend on others and not acquire. Those for which it relies on others will be the greatest in number and may indeed be the most critical to its success. The realisation of this technological dependence on others is only slowly dawning on industry and leading to the most radical changes in the nature of the purchasing function. Decisions on which technologies must be acquired are long term and strategic. The direction of technology acquisition probably has more effect on the future nature of a company than any other aspect of its operations.

Once a company is committed to an acquisition direction its future products, processes and marketing are firmly established. If this direction is indadequately thought through then the company will either fail in its markets or it will have to resort to the short-term expedient of licensing or simply acting as a distributor for the products of others. The establishment of a sound technology strategy and the setting of an acquisition direction in turn depend on a well carried out technology audit. Once direction is achieved the company can decide what are the appropriate means of acquisition, whether internal development, contracted-out R&D, strategic licensing or non-acquisition and product purchase. Only when it has decided on the 'right thing' can it concentrate on 'doing it right', which involves decisions on the organisation of its R&D and on such things as the critical success factors in licensing.

Finally, it is obvious that until the company has acquired the appropriate technologies it cannot begin to exploit them in its markets. Now we have established a sound basis for technology acquisition we move on to the task of technology exploitation and profit generation after the following example.

Example
Monitoring a distinctive external technology: Burmah Castrol

Burmah Castrol, a specialised lubricants manufacturer, faces competition from full-line multinational oil companies which have the advantage of very wide and intensive distribution channels. The company must prosper on the basis of the distinctive product technology incorporated in its oil. If this could be equalled by its competitors, their superior distribution would destroy Burmah Castrol's position.

Despite the importance of its product technology, the company decided some years ago that it would cease to develop its own oil additives, which are critical to product success. Instead it has close relationships with a number of additive manufacturers and it retains a close watching brief in additive technologies. This shadow development means that it knows the directions that additive technology is taking and what is likely to become possible in the future.

REFERENCES

1   Jankowski, J. (1991) 'Two year decline in R&D spending', *Research Technology Management*, **34**(3), May–June.
2   *White Paper on Science and Technology* (1990) US Department of Commerce, Washington, DC.

3   Chandler, A. D. (1985) 'From industrial laboratories to departments of R&D', in K. B. Clarke, R. H. Hayes and C. Lorenz (eds), *The Uneasy Alliance*, Boston: Harvard Business School Press.

4   Kenward, M. (1990) 'A dip in the R&D pool', *Financial Times*, 11 December 1990.

5   Rosenbloom, R. S. (1985) *Research on Technological Innovation, Management and Policy*, vol. 2, Greenwich, CT: JAI Press.

6   Steele, L. W. (1991) 'Needed: new paradigms for R&D', *Research Technology Management*, July–August: 14.

7   Kenward, M. (1990) 'A dip in the R&D pool', art. cit.

8   Williamson, O. E. (1981) 'The economics of organisation: the transaction cost approach', *American Journal of Sociology*, **7**(3).

9   Quoted by Wolff, M. J. (1991) in 'What does the CEO want?', *Research Technology Management*, July–August: 11.

10 Quoted by Whittington, R. (1990) in 'The changing structures of R&D, in R. Loveridge and M. Pitt (eds), *Strategic Management of Technological Innovation*, Chichester: John Wiley, p. 195.

11 Grady, D. and Fincham, T. (1991) 'Making R&D pay', *Research Technology Management*, **34**, March–April: 22, 23.

12 Marsh, P., 'A double dose of resources', *Financial Times*, 13 June 1990, p. 26.

13 Holberton, S., 'R&D deserves a strategic position', *Financial Times*, 22 January 1991.

14 Lewis, W. and Linden, L. (1990) 'A new mission for corporate technology', *The McKinsey Quarterly*, no. 4, McKinsey & Co. Inc.

15 Whittington, R. (1991) 'Changing control strategies in industrial R&D', *R&D Management*, **21**(1): 43–53.

16 Ibid.

17 Bodelle, J. (1991) 'Why corporate research? The case of Elf Aquitaine', *Research. Technology Management*, September–October: 33–37.

18 Holberton, 'R&D deserves a strategic position'.

19 Kantrow, A. M. (1986) 'Industrial R&D: looking back to look ahead', *Harvard Business Review*, July–August: 52.

20 Grady, D. and Fincham, T. (1991) 'Making R&D pay', art. cit.

21 Ibid. 23–25.

22 Ibid. 47.

23 Lee, T., Fisher, J. C. and Yau, T. (1986) 'Is your R&D on track?', *Harvard Business Review*, January–February: 34–43.

24 Lei, D. and Slocum, J. W. (1991) 'Global strategic alliances: payoffs and pitfalls', *Organizational Dynamics*, **19**, Winter: 44–62.

25 Rhea, J. (1991) 'New directions for industrial R&D consortia', *Research Technology Management*, September–October: 16–19.

26 Watkins, T. (1991) 'A technological communications costs model of industrial R&D consortia as public policy', *Research Policy*, **20**: 87–107.

27 Smilor, R. and Gibson, D. (1991) 'Accelerating technology transfer in R&D consortia', *Research Technology Management*, January–February: 44–49.

28 Littler, D. (1988) *Technological Development*, Oxford: Philip Allen, p. 84.

29 Prahalad, C. K. (1993) 'The role of core competences in the corporation', *Research. Technology Management*, November–December: 40–47.

30 Watkins, T., 'A technological communications costs model', art. cit.

31 Rhea, J. (1991) 'New directions for industrial R&D consortia', *Research Technology Management*, September–October: 18.

32 Ibid. 18–19.

33 Link, A. N. and Baur, L. L. (1989) *Cooperative Research in US Manufacturing: Assessing Policy Initiatives and Corporate Strategies*, Lexington, MA: Lexington Books.

34 Fusfeld, H. I. and Haklisch, C. S. (1985) 'Cooperative R&D for competitors', *Harvard Business Review*, November–December: 60–76.

35   Hakansson, H. (ed.) (1987) *Industrial Technological Development: a Network Approach*, London: Croom Helm.

36   Marti, P. and Smiley, R. H. (1983) 'Cooperative agreements and the organisation of industry', *Journal of Industrial Economics*, **31**: 437–51.

37   Beesley, M. and Rothwell, R. (1987) 'Small firm linkages in the United Kingdom', in R. Rothwell and J. Bessant, *Innovation, Adaptation and Growth*, Amsterdam: Elsevier.

38   Rhea, J. (1991) 'New directions for industrial R&D consortia', art. cit.

39   Ibid.

40   Jankowski, J. (1991) 'Two year decline in R&D spending', art. cit.

41   Leibowitz, M., quoted in Smilor and Gibson, 'Accelerating technology transfer', art. cit.

42   Rothwell, R. and Dodgson, M. (1991) 'External linkages and innovation in small and medium-sized enterprises', *R&D Management*, **21**(2): 128.

43   Office of Technology Assessment (1984) *Commercial Biotechnology: an International Analysis*, US Congress, Washington, DC.

44   Pisano, G. (1991) 'The governance of innovation: vertical integration and collaborative arrangements in the biotechnology industry', *Research Policy*, **20**: 237–49.

45   Sharp, M. (1985) 'The new biotechnology: European governments in search of a strategy', *Sussex European Papers*, **15**: 43, Science Policy Research Unit, Brighton.

46   Wolff, M. (ed.) (1991) 'How research affects firms' productivity', *Research Technology Management*, September–October: 2.

Chapter 7

Technology exploitation: Problems and analysis

INTRODUCTION

In the last chapter we provided a guide to the different methods of technology acquisition which are available and examined the circumstances when each might be appropriate. In this chapter, our attention turns to the process of managerial decision-making for exploitation.

The aim of technology exploitation is to achieve the best possible rate of return on the technological assets which the company has acquired with such difficulty and at such expense. The chapter starts by examining some of the reasons why companies have difficulty in effectively exploiting their technology, then presents a methodology for assessing a company's position as a basis for more complete exploitation of its technological assets and finally leads to the use of the idea of strategic technology areas as an approach to taking exploitation decisions.

Success in technology exploitation can be measured by performance in two tasks as was illustrated previously in Figure 3.1. The first of these tasks is when the company exploits its technology in its own products, processes and operations – internal exploitation. The second task is the external exploitation of technology by any other means. External exploitation can include the following methods:

- licensing out – licensing a technology to others;
- engaging in a joint venture with others to exploit a technology;
- contracting in – using the company's process technologies to manufacture the products of another firm to that firm's design;
- using the company's product technologies to design a product for another firm;
- using the company's marketing technologies to market a product for another firm;

- contracting out – arranging for another firm to design, manufacture or market products for the company.

WHY COMPANIES HAVE PROBLEMS IN TECHNOLOGY EXPLOITATION

We argue that a main problem in achieving an optimum return on technological investment is that many companies approach both the analysis and implementation of exploitation from a restricted perspective. Only the internal exploitation of technology is given anything like systematic attention in the strategy formulation of most companies. Few companies take a strategic view of external exploitation and examine how and when they should sell their technologies to others, or co-operate with others in exploiting technologies in wider applications. Even internal exploitation is often ill thought through and many exploitation opportunities are missed. There are a number of reasons for this restricted perspective on exploitation.

Senior management orientation

Senior management's attention tends to be restricted towards increasing the sales of the company's existing products and bringing new ones to the market. The development and exploitation of the company's process and marketing technologies often receives less strategic attention and, instead, are considered only as a support for the company's products. They are less commonly thought of as assets in their own right, which can form a main basis for the company's competitive advantage. Despite this, it would be equally valid for many companies to build strategy around the exploitation of their distinctive production or marketing technologies. This view would then see products as the necessary vehicles to bring these process and marketing technologies to market. Such an approach would radically change the company's approach to investment in each type of technology and to the range and timing of its product introductions.

Organisational structure

A second reason for a restricted approach to technology exploitation is organisational. Many companies are organised as strategic business units (SBUs), which are structured around products and/or markets, rather than the technologies on which they are based. Other companies adopt a product management structure, which emphasises the short-term exploitation of individual products and the manipulation of the company's existing marketing resources. Both of these entail the task of maximising the exploitation of all available technologies cutting across the normal activities and reward structures of the company. A similar point is made by Prahalad and Hamel when they discuss the problems which companies have in building on the company's core competences.[1] We will return to the interrelationships between core competences and technologies in Chapter 10.

Marketing's product orientation

A related problem in technology exploitation is that the marketing department in most companies is structured for the task of marketing products, rather than for the market exploitation of the technologies on which these products are based. This lack of attention is particularly significant in the case of the company's process strengths. Those people within a company who understand its process strengths are unlikely to be in marketing nor indeed to be involved in the company's debate on marketing strategy. More generally, marketing people are often uncomfortable or openly antagonistic to the idea of making licensing deals, which they may view as conflicting with their product sales, particularly when the licencees in those deals are their current or potential competitors.

Accounting inadequacy

Another reason for a restricted view of technology exploitation is that accounting for technological development and the assessment of rates of return on technological assets is at best primitive. Many companies treat R&D expenditure as a company overhead which is then allocated to individual departments or product areas on an arbitrary basis. In this system, the cost of acquiring individual technologies is, effectively, unknown. The costs of developing process technologies are even less likely to be adequately accounted for. Marketing technology does not appear in company financial reporting, except in so far as a press debate exists over the issue of whether the value of the consumer franchise for the brands it has developed should appear on the company's balance sheet.

Other companies allocate R&D spending more specifically to individual projects, such as each new product. This expenditure is then regarded as a cost of that project. There then remains the issue of how that expenditure should be written off against revenue and what revenue it should be written off against. Many companies take a conservative view and write off R&D spend against profits for a specific project in the year that this spend was incurred. Others will spread development costs over the anticipated life of a particular product. But, each piece of R&D spend is effectively a capital investment in a technology.

Few companies have any mechanism for assessing the rate of return which has been achieved on a technological investment or for assessing whether the company is achieving an appropriate rate of return on that investment. This is because no benchmark for such an assessment exists in most companies. The companies' attention is devoted to their products and not their technologies, and they are unable to examine the different applications in which a particular product, process or marketing technology could be exploited, whether in its initially defined area, elsewhere in the company, in other combinations with different company technologies or externally to the company.

Mechanical approach

Companies devote considerable attention to the mechanics of product development. This includes questions ranging from how to generate new-product ideas to how the company should review the development process at each stage and control its costs. Companies tend to devote rather less attention to the strategic issues of the technology on which their products are based. For example, they often do not fully address the following questions:

1 How should all of the technologies on which the company's products are based be fully exploited?
2 Should the company continue to develop successive generations of products which exploit an existing technology, or at what point should it make the switch to products which use new technology, whether product, process or marketing?
3 Can the company combine process or marketing technologies from elsewhere in the company with its existing product technologies to exploit new applications?
4 Failing this, can it develop the new support technologies or co-operate with another company which already has them?
5 What are the implications for the company as a whole of taking a particular direction in its product development?
6 Does the company have, or can it acquire, the process and marketing technologies that will be necessary to exploit this particular product technology?

Poor life-cycle planning

The concept of the product life cycle is commonly understood. Despite arguments about whether the product life cycle is valid or relevant, it is a valuable reminder of the changing character of the marketing task at different points in time. The product life cycle emphasises that the marketing task is different at each stage in the cycle and more generally, that product and process requirements change as markets and competitive characteristics evolve.

These changes in products, processes and marketing require succession planning in different technological areas and the integration of the efforts of different functions to achieve a strategy over time. This is rarely well carried out. Each function tends to see its task in terms of its own narrow functional area – process improvement, changes in marketing plans or product development.

More profoundly, the necessary changes through the life cycle of a product need to be seen as part of some overall task of exploiting the company's technologies. This exploitation may be based on the company's distinctiveness in a single technological area or more general competence over a range of technologies. Marketing is usually seen as the function with responsibility for managing through the *product* life cycle. Marketing's traditional role has been to co-ordinate the activities of product development, introduction and life-cycle management, although they are less commonly involved in process issues. All too often marketing's approach is based on a narrow promotional view of new product introduction or product management. Less frequently do they give the necessary attention to a wider view of even their traditional brief in such areas as product portfolio analysis or product deletion. Product deletion is particularly difficult to face up to because the loss of someone's job often rests on the decision.

Even less often does marketing take a coherent role in the exploitation of process technologies throughout their life cycles. More generally marketing does not, and perhaps cannot, take responsibility for a wider view of the life of a product or process as part of technology exploitation. This wider view can only occur if the company itself has a strategy for that exploitation as part of an overall strategy for the technologies themselves.

Life-cycle management for technologies is complex, not least because technology as a unit of analysis does not fit within the planning horizon of any single functional area. The exploitation of technologies over their life cycles requires the integration of the inputs of different functional areas and this may require organisational change. More importantly, effective technology exploitation also requires a change in both perspective and culture in order to raise individual and functional horizons from the short-term and the product level to the long-term and the technological.

VIEWS OF TECHNOLOGY EXPLOITATION

Technology exploitation is not a separate task from that of product development or marketing. Instead it is a wider and more fundamental interpretation of both of these activities. As well as aiming to achieve the best return possible on the company's technological assets, exploitation decisions will also impact the direction of technology acquisition because specific technologies will have to be acquired to support and facilitate current and future exploitation.

There are two common views of technology exploitation in strategy. The first sees the company as possessing certain technological assets and therefore facing the task of developing strategy to find applications and methods to exploit them – 'We've got this technology, what can we do with it?'. The second view is to see strategy as the process of looking for market opportunities and then acquiring the technologies to exploit them – 'Here's a great market, what do we need in order to get into it?' The former approach is often loosely referred to as technology push and the latter as market pull, and there is a seemingly endless debate about the implied choice which companies have to make between the two approaches.

We argue that this is an artificial choice. A more appropriate view of the exploitation task is to see it as integrating the efforts of those with an understanding of the company's technologies and those with a view of the external world it faces. In order to facilitate this integration we will use the concept of the strategic technology area (STA) in our analysis. An STA consists of a combination of product, process and marketing technologies and the specific application for which they are intended.

This integrated approach requires that the company develop strategy for both internal and external exploitation of its technologies as well as procedures and organisation for matching its abilities and opportunities; a different marketing task, which may or may not be carried out by the current or conventional marketing department. This task can be defined as: Achieving the optimum exploitation of the company's product, process and marketing technologies, both internally and externally, together with an input into decisions on the acquisition of technology in each of these areas, based on analysis of the external environment which the company faces.

ANALYSIS FOR TECHNOLOGY EXPLOITATION

The task of fully exploiting the company's product, process and marketing technologies is a microcosm of the whole technology strategy task. It involves internal analysis of the company's current position, a clear definition of the problems it faces and the technologies which the company has. It also involves external analysis of existing and potential opportunities, and the organizational skills needed to bring technologies from different sources together and to tailor them to a particular application. This analysis task is listed below:

1 Internal company evaluation:
   - Technology position;
   - Technology investments;
   - Technology applications.
2 External company evaluation:
   - Market application trends;
   - Technology trends and trajectories.

INTERNAL COMPANY EVALUATION

This is an appropriate starting-point as it re-emphasises the importance of the technology audit. A one-off, major audit may be appropriate in the first stages of developing technology strategy. It may show that the company has significant technological inadequacies in some areas or assets which are underexploited in others, or which are capable of being used in some new application. This can lead to major strategic moves by the company. But from the point of view of technology exploitation, a continuing technology evaluation within the company is probably more important as a way of maintaining an awareness of current technology position and relating this to technology investment and application.

Technology position

The evaluation of technology position for the purposes of exploitation is a deceptively easy notion. Many annual strategy reviews incorporate such an evaluation which categorises the company's position in terms of whether it is the leader or a follower in different areas. These areas are often confined to product areas and are usually restricted to discussion of the products themselves and not the technologies on which the products are based. We should be cautious about simple, straightforward categorisations for at least two reasons.

First, they tend to concentrate on the most obvious technologies and usually those which can be readily associated with specific product areas. The full range of technologies is rarely assessed. Our research has shown how difficult it is for companies to identify their exploitable technology assets when compared with the relative ease with which they can spot an inadequacy in the technologies which they are currently using. The reason for this appears to be that a technology inadequacy will readily show up as a marketing problem and lead to urgent action to acquire the appropriate technology either internally or externally. In contrast, an underutilised technological asset may remain hidden inside the company. Often the hidden asset's value is only realised when a similar technology is exploited by a competitor or if the company is approached by another firm wanting to use one of the company's technologies. In either case the company is likely to be galvanised into action, but often this is after the best opportunities have passed. For example, the international consumer group, Unilever was successful with its early, frequent-use shampoo, Timotei. It subsequently exploited this product through a series of brand extensions into conditioners and skin preparations. At about the time it originally developed the frequent-use technology it also developed a *combined* shampoo and conditioner. However, because of the success of Timotei, it chose not to introduce a product based on the other technology. Approximately ten years later this technology was used by its arch-rival Procter and Gamble to introduce Wash and Go, which rapidly acquired a 30 per cent share of the market leaving Unilever in a catch-up situation, from which it has not recovered.

Second, many companies have found that leadership in a particular product technology is no guarantee of competitive success. Companies need a viable bundle of product, process and marketing technologies for success in any particular application. Therefore, we need to know the company's competitive position in significant individual technologies, and that the company has the appropriate bundle of technologies for each application or group of applications.

Technology investments and technology applications

A sound analysis of technology position enables a review of the company's technology investments to take place. The first point to emphasise here is that the review is of investment in all three areas; product, process and marketing technologies. Second, the analysis is at the level of technology rather than, for example, a consideration of spending on a new product or change in a production method. This review of technology investment provides a clear idea of potential problems or opportunities in a number of areas through answering the following questions:

1 Is the scale and direction of technology investment realistic when set against the company's exploitation plans?
2 Does the company need to invest more in other technologies in order to support exploitation either internally or externally?
3 Is the company investing disproportionately in one technology area to a level or in a direction which does not relate to current or planned exploitation methods or applications?
4 Does technology investment relate to competitor or environmental changes or to technology trends and trajectories?

More generally, the review may highlight problems in the ways in which investment decisions are taken. Common problems include decision-making in each technology area which is unrelated to other areas, such as product technology investment without appropriate process or marketing investment. Other problems include a failure to involve process personnel in exploitation analysis, so that consideration is confined to the product area and a failure to take potential external exploitation into account when making investment decisions.

Strategic technology areas

An approach which deals with the complexity of technology analysis has been provided by Graham Mitchell as Director of Planning for GTE Laboratories.[2] He uses an extended unit of analysis on which to assess a company's position which he refers to as the 'Strategic Technological Area' (STA). An STA is the combination of a bundle of technologies and the specific application for which they are designated. He gives the example of an STA involved in integrated circuit processing, which he describes as follows:

Skills or disciplines:
The principal skills include lithographic techniques (photo, X-ray, electron beam) for defining fine geometries on semiconductors, as well as high-temperature solid state chemistry and thin film processing.
Which are applied to:
The fabrication of semiconductor integrated circuits, i.e. which form the basis of a set of process technologies for the company.
Which are used:
In a wide range of switching and transmission products (which are also based on the company's product technologies).
Which address:
Specific market needs throughout the telecommunications industry (based on the company's marketing technologies).

Advantages of Strategic Technology Area Analysis

Strategic Technology Area Analysis is based on the idea that a bundle of technologies is required for any particular application, which in the example is a wide one in the telecommunications industry. The analysis can be used at different levels of aggregation. At the corporate level, an assessment can be made of the company's respective strength in different areas of the necessary bundle, when compared to actual or potential competition in a range of STAs. This can be useful in the development of strategic vision. Thus, such an analysis would show the relative inadequacy of Sony's marketing technologies when compared to those of Matsushita, but that Sony had significant advantages in the product technology areas and in some aspects of process technology which had contributed to its innovativeness. Matsushita did not match Sony for product technology and had consistently been a product technology follower, but had process strength in achieving low-cost production. This analysis can be seen in the long-term strategies of the two companies. Sony traditionally emphasised a vision of innovativeness and speed of response based on these technological strengths and weaknesses.

More recently, Sony has attempted to address its relative weakness in marketing technology through the acquisition of companies in the entertainment software industry as a way of speeding its product innovations to market. Matsushita traditionally emphasised its ability to capitalise on its process strength and low production costs, and its marketing skills that enable it to penetrate markets for its follower products. More recently, it too has moved to address inadequacies in its overall situation by seeking to improve its innovativeness.

STA Analysis can also be used at the more detailed tactical level in the long-term management and control of the company's operation. We will see that STAs can form the basis of the company's organisation and strategy, and programmes can be developed for each STA. The use of STA approach requires a thorough analysis of the company's technologies, but it does have two important advantages. First, it is carried out at a level of aggregation which reflects the complexity of the bundles of technology for each area of application and relates closely to those applications and to the strategic task facing the company. Second, STA Analysis brings each of the three different technology areas – product, process and marketing – into discussion. A particularly important aspect of this is that the analysis can show which of these technology areas acts as a limiting factor in the company's development. In the integrated circuit processing example, it may be that the company's abilities to cash-in on its process technological strength may have been constrained by inadequate product technology or by problems in producing products to quality and cost constraints. Alternatively, the company's performance in meeting the requirements of some of its applications may be reduced by problems in its sales operation and relationships with customers, or it may have succeeded in some areas despite the inadequacy of its logistics or other aspects of marketing technology.

We will return to the use of STA Analysis in Chapter 8 when we examine how it can be used to develop programmes for technology exploitation.

EXTERNAL COMPANY EVALUATION

The assessment task outside the company is of both markets and technologies.

Market application trends

The evaluation of current and emerging markets is part of the development of conventional marketing strategy. The difference is that analysis for technology exploitation must be much wider and deeper. If a company is to effectively exploit its technological assets, it must look for potential applications outside its current or conventional product/market areas. It must look at market trends further into the future and at consumer requirements which may be unrecognised or unarticulated by potential customers. The importance of this scanning is emphasised because research suggests that 60–80 per cent of successful technological innovations seem to have been initiated in response to a perceived need or demand.[3]

There is a danger that an uncontrolled emphasis on market scanning could lead to the company simply chasing after market opportunities which do not relate to its technological strengths or current market position. This danger can only be avoided if those carrying out the assessment are fully aware of the company's technological position. Similarly if this assessment is to be translated into effective exploitation decisions, it must be shared with those in a position to bring the company's existing technology to bear, to modify that technology or to develop or acquire further technologies.

Technology trends and trajectories

Even for a company which believes that it has the most restricted range of technological assets and a weak technological position in each of its STAs, there will be a wide range of possible applications for its technologies and means of reaching them. For example, we have in the past encountered the example of a company which has successfully exploited its process technology in the manufacture of school desks by selling this technology 'whole' to a country in the Middle East. A technology bundle can be assembled from existing unexploited technologies in the company by developing new technologies or in combination with the technologies of others on an external basis.

Spotting technological opportunities can lead to fanciful moves into different application areas which may require high levels of investment, risky alliances or which depend on an exaggerated assessment of technological strength. It is necessary for those involved in exploitation to keep their corporate feet on the ground. This can be achieved by having people involved in decision-making who know the reality of the company's current and potential technological position across an STA, the real costs of development in each area, the potential in each application, the probabilities of success of alliance formation and the long-run strategic implications of any move. External assessment cannot be carried out by a single function. Instead, it requires co-ordination between marketing and technical departments, such as R&D and production.

TECHNOLOGY-WATCHING

In order to develop strategic decision-making regarding the exploitation of their own technologies, managers require a substantial amount of information about current and future developments in the potential technological outputs. There are several systematic techniques which the company can employ to survey and forecast technological developments outside the firm. Technology surveillance involves the passive observation of events in the technological environment, whereas technology forecasting seeks to predict future changes in technologies. Surveillance techniques can be categorised according to the degree of focus involved in the process of information search and interpretation. A number of techniques are outlined below.

Environmental scanning

This is the least focused of the surveillance techniques. It aims to identify general developments in the technological, socio-economic and political environments that may produce changes that will affect the firm technologically. Scanning procedures are particularly useful in identifying new uses for present or emerging technologies and in suggesting socio-political factors which may impede or accelerate the acceptance of new technologies.

Research indicates very mixed results when a dedicated environmental scanning department has been established. A study by Lenz and Engledow[4] found that many scanning units had a wide role including responsiblity for public policy issues, and many were staffed by outsiders newly recruited to the companies, sometimes academics, who were vulnerable to corporate reorganisation or the departure of a sponsoring senior manager. They conclude that the use of a centralised unit for scanning the environment is, unlikely to facilitate critical and pertinant thinking about the organisational environment. Perhaps significantly, the longest surviving example in their sample was of a department whose role was narrowly focused on maintaining the technological leadership of a company.

Technology monitoring

This is a more focused and disciplined activity than scanning. Technology areas are explicitly selected for monitoring, and criteria for 'levels of importance' to the firm are assigned. A database of changes in these technologies and their degree of importance is built up, reviewed and updated in a formal, ongoing monitoring procedure.

Technology tracking

This is the most intensive and detailed technique. It is a highly concentrated effort to follow detailed developments in technologies that are of major significance to the firm. Technologies that are tracked might be those which are involved in the firm's new products that are nearing market launch or they may be potential breakthroughs in which the firm must become established.

Technology forecasts can help managers to develop and formalise their views of future technologies. There are several techniques which can be used and these vary widely in their complexity, cost and reliability. Overall, they take one of two approaches. The first is based on the projection of past experience or trends, known as 'exploratory' forecasting. The second is based on future objectives or requirements and investigates the technological means by which they are likely to be achieved – these are called 'normative' forecasts. Some of the techniques of technological forecasting are discussed next.

Trend extrapolation

The historical trend in the key parameters of a specific technology are projected into the future. These projections can be helpful in setting R&D goals, assessing technological progress which other firms may make and identifying new possibilities for exploitation.

Lead-lag predictions

Over a period of time developments in one area of technology may follow developments in other fields in a predictable manner. Where such relationships have been identified it is possible to forecast the 'lagging' technology by observing the state of development in the 'leading' technologies.

Delphi technique

This method gathers experts' opinions about future developments in a formal, structured procedure. This procedure goes through several rounds or iterations in which experts in the technology reassess their estimates about the nature and timing of future developments. The mean value of their estimates gives a projection of when a specific technical development is likely to occur and the spread of values provides an indication of the degree of consensus among the members of the forecasting panel.

Scenario development

This combines projections of a number of technical and non-technical factors into an integrated picture of the future. It allows for more breadth and depth in managers' consideration of the future technological environment as a whole and enables them to compare alternative scenarios which may emerge.

Relevance trees

This methodology divides the relevant elements of a technology decision (such as which technology to exploit, and how) into its component parts and specifies criteria for judging the relative importance of each part. Quantitative values are then assigned to all of the components and the criteria and different technical solutions are scored according to the resulting combination of criterion and component values. Those with the highest scores show the best combination of technological solutions.

Morphological analysis

Most new technologies emanate from the need to perform some technical function more effectively, efficiently or economically than at present. However, often many subordinate functions are involved in the achievement of the overall function. In morphological analysis the methods used to perform these contributory functions are identified and different ways of combining these subordinate technologies are studied in order to identify new approaches to carry out the basic functions of the overall technology. This technique is useful for producing ideas for new technological means of meeting existing and future requirements.

CONCLUSIONS

This chapter has introduced some of the issues and problems facing companies in the task of exploiting their technology. In particular we have emphasised that many companies start from a position of disadvantage because of an organisational form, a reward system and a corporate culture which militates against effective exploitation either internally or externally. Much of this disadvantage is because companies operate and, indeed, think at the level of products rather than the technologies of product and process which underlie them. We have suggested that technology exploitation requires a continuous process of analysis inside the company which goes beyond the single analysis which forms a technology audit. Technology exploitation also requires an external analysis which extends beyond a view of market trends and must rest on an understanding of technological trends in close and more distant application areas. In the next chapter we consider the ways in which the tasks of analysis and exploitation can be carried out.

REFERENCES

1   Prahalad, C. K. and Hamel, G. (1990) 'The core competence of the corporation', *Harvard Business Review*, May–June: 79–91.
2   Mitchell, G. (1986) 'New approaches to the strategic management of technology', *Technology in Society*, **7**(2–3): 136.
3   Roberts, E. B. (1988) 'Managing invention and innovation', *Research Technology Management*, January–February: 11–29.
4   Lenz, R. T. and Engledow, F. (1986) 'Environmental analysis units and strategic decision-making: a field study of selected "leading-edge" corporations', *Strategic Management Journal*, **7**: 69–86.

Chapter 8

The technology exploitation task

INTRODUCTION

In this chapter we examine the tasks involved in the internal and external exploitation of technology. We first examine the different ways in which a company can exploit a technology and the circumstances under which each might be appropriate. The chapter then turns to the factors which are critical for success in technology exploitation, irrespective of the method used, and finally leads to the tasks which must be accomplished by the marketing function in technology exploitation.

The integration of different methods of exploitation is critical if a company is to achieve anything like the optimum rate of return on its technological assets. But this does not mean that any single technology can or should be exploited by all available methods. Various methods may be appropriate under different circumstances and at successive stages in the life of a single technology. Also, as we have noted earlier, competitive advantage for a company is not achieved by having a single technology, but by putting together an appropriate bundle of product, process and marketing technologies for a particular application.

We have already referred to this combination of technologies and application as a strategic technology area (STA) and we will describe how the company's task is to develop programmes which combine product, process and marketing technologies to exploit and develop opportunities. These opportunities may be based on a perceived strength in a single technology, a skill in speedily and effectively putting together a bundle of technologies, or on spotting a market opportunity. It is important to emphasise that the unit of analysis for building these programmes is the STA, which has two dimensions, the market or application in question as well as the technologies used to satisfy it. It is not sufficient to emphasise either one of these dimensions in the exploitation planning process.

However, the above does not mean that decisions about the exploitation of an individual technology or individual application are unimportant, particularly when that technology is distinctive for the company, or the application is critical to its survival. For this reason we first consider decisions about the choice of exploitation methods for individual technologies.

CHOICE OF EXPLOITATION METHODS

The choice of which methods of exploitation should be used and when they should be used are the key decisions in individual technology exploitation. We can examine some of the different ways in which technology can be exploited and the factors which may affect the choice of exploitation method by referring to Table 8.1.

The first row in the table is of internal exploitation, using a technology in the company's own products, processes or marketing. This can be contrasted with the four different external methods which are also listed. The first external method is whereby the technology holder contracts another firm to manufacture products for it, based on the company's own product technology or design, or when someone else carries out the marketing of products which the company has designed and produced. The second method of external exploitation is contracting-in whereby the company uses its own product, process or marketing technologies at the service of another firm. Thus the company could design product for that other firm, produce product to the firm's design or market the products which the other firm had produced. The third method is that of joint venture. With this method two or more companies combine their respective technologies to serve a particular application. The joint venture can either take the form of a separate company established for the purpose or be carried out within the existing organisations. The final method listed is that of conventional licensing of one or more technologies to another company.

We have already used the concepts of technology standing and category when discussing technology acquisition. A company's standing in a technology refers to an objective measure of its technology when compared to others. The category into which a technology falls depends on whether that standing is a source of competitive advantage to it. When standing is low it is likely that the company's version of the technology will have to be exploited internally as it will have little value in external exploitation. Such a technology will not be a source of competitive advantage for the company – it will be basic. When the company has a high standing in a technology it will still wish to exploit the technology internally and the technology may also be a source of competitive advantage – it will be distinctive.

A high standing in a product technology may form the basis for external exploitation by contracting out the manufacturing or marketing to someone else. This strategy may be appropriate as a way of reaching other applications where the company's technology has some distinctiveness or where such distinctiveness could be built. By contracting out, the necessary process and marketing technologies become external. Contracting out may be appropriate if the company has no distinctiveness in these technologies, lacks the financial resources to acquire them or the exploitation is particularly urgent. Exploitation by contracting in or licensing out both require the technology to be distinctive if it is to be of value to the other party. This may also be the case in a joint venture which is based on technological specialisation between partners. However, in those joint ventures which are

Table 8.1 Choices in technology exploitation

Exploitation methods	Company's relative standing	Categories of technology	Urgency of exploitation	Need for support technologies	Commitment/ investment	Technology life-cycle position	Potential application
Internal exploitation • Employ in own products/processes/marketing	All levels	Distinctive/basic	Lowest	Lowest	Highest	Earliest	Narrowest
External exploitation • Contract out manufacture or marketing to others	Product technology High Process/marketing technologies Low	Distinctive product technology (Manufacturing/marketing becomes external technology)	High	High	High	Early	Narrow
• Contract in manufacture marketing or product design for others	High	Distinctive	High	High	High	Later	Wider
• Joint venture	High or Low	Distinctive/basic	Higher	Higher	Low (because you are not going to develop own)	Early	Wide
• License out	High	Distinctive	Low	Low	Lowest	Later	Widest

based on shared value-added, both partners are seeking to build their technologies together and in this situation their initial standing can be low and their technologies basic.

The urgency with which technologies must be exploited will vary considerably depending on the strength of competitive technologies and the rate of technological development in other companies. If the company has sufficient standing in a technology then licensing to a number of other companies is likely to offer rapid exploitation. Other methods of external exploitation are also likely to be more rapid than reliance on the internal method, particularly if other companies already have the support technologies necessary to assemble the appropriate bundle. However, the financial return to the technology holder per unit of sales is likely to be lower via the external route.

The need for other support technologies will have a strong effect on exploitation decisions. Where this need is lowest then internal exploitation is more feasible. But where significant support technologies are required this may delay internal exploitation and render it uneconomic. An appropriate bundle of technologies for any specific application can be assembled by a joint venture, or the technology holder can use the technologies of other companies on a contract basis or offer the single technology it possesses as a service to others by contracting in. The need for support technologies may sometimes restrict the chance of licensing. This is because the technology holder may not be able to license a single technology to others, but may need to offer a bundle of technologies to suit a particular application for the licensee.

The fourth column in Table 8.1 refers to the company's commitment to a technology. This can be measured by the importance of the technology to the company's strategic future or by the level of investment made into it. Where the company is highly committed to a technology, it may wish to restrict itself to internal exploitation even though the immediate returns from this may be less than from wider exploitation. The company can accept this restriction on exploitation for at least two reasons. The first is to lessen the risks of passing technology to potential competitors. The second is so that the internal exploitation can serve to enhance the company's standing in the technology area for future market advantage, or because use of the technology will assist further development in that area.

The next column on the technology exploitation table introduces the idea of sequencing exploitation methods. We have already noted how valuable it is to initially exploit a technology internally in order to prove it and how important it is to control the loss of a technology to other companies. Loss is likely to be less of a concern as the technology ages and a whole series of other, perhaps geographically distant applications can be exploited, for example by licensing.

The width of potential applications for a technology will affect exploitation decisions at all life-cycle stages. Wide potential applications will suggest the need for support technologies, particularly in the marketing area when little is known of the wider applications for a technology. For example, a UK components company developed a product technology in ceramics which had tensile properties. This had wide applications in areas ranging from machine tools, where the component company had neither the necessary process or marketing technology, to aerospace components, where it had both. The company exploited the technology internally in areas where it had the necessary support technology and externally, by a combination of joint ventures and licensing deals, where it did not.

CRITICAL SUCCESS FACTORS IN TECHNOLOGY EXPLOITATION

We now deal with some of the critical success factors in the exploitation of technology. All technology exploitation issues relate to the acquisition of technology and some of the things in our check-list are covered in more detail in the chapters on technology acquisition.

SPEED OF EXPLOITATION

Speed in technology exploitation is important for a number of reasons including the difficulties which companies have in protecting their technologies by legal means, the R&D capabilities of competitors or the presence of low-cost producers with up-to-date process technologies who can reverse-engineer the company's offerings and bring a low-priced product quickly to market. Whatever the reason, the time in which a company has to exploit a new technology before competitive pressure outweighs any advantage decreases with each successive generation of product. This is illustrated by Kotabe who quotes a Sony executive as saying that Sony's technological lead time over competitors is six months at best.[1] Unless the need for speed in technology exploitation is accepted, all attempts to achieve an optimum return on technology investment will fail.

WELL-DEVELOPED EXPLOITATION PROGRAMMES FOR EACH STRATEGIC TECHNOLOGY AREA

A critical factor in successful technology exploitation is the development of coherent programmes for that exploitation. Sometimes one of the bundle of technologies which a company assembles for a particular application will be distinctive, such as if it has a reputation for consistency of product quality, based on its process technology. In this case the company's other technologies act to support that distinctive technology. In other instances the company may not have a single distinctive technology, but the company's ability to combine a range of technologies may be the key competitive advantage. We found this to be the case in a leading food ingredients company. A technology audit revealed little in the way of distinctive technologies but a well-developed ability to bring together a variety of basic product technologies with the appropriate, and equally basic, process technologies to meet those market requirements which were well communicated by an active marketing function.

The same individual technologies are likely to be used in a variety of combinations across a number of divisions or operating companies to comprise the bundles for specific applications.[2] Therefore, programmes must be developed for each strategic technology area (STA). In this way, each programme manager can give appropriate attention to all the technologies which comprise the bundle and to the area of their application. An approach based on STAs also enables the company to systemise the informal development of its technologies. Mitchell suggests that there is likely to be an informal network among technical staff:

> which often cuts across the formal management and organisation structure. While this linkage and synergy may be understood by the technical specialists it is unlikely to be

widely recognised at all management levels. This network provides insight and power to drive the businesses in new technical directions, some of which may challenge the conventional wisdom as articulated by the formal business plans.[3]

STA programmes and technologies

Figure 8.1 illustrates a matrix of technologies and applications and gives examples of STA programmes. The diagram is simplified for illustration purposes, and in practice each STA will consist of more than one product, process and marketing technology. Also, some of these technologies may be external to the company. It is important to determine which technologies should be included in the analysis, for clarity, and which can be excluded for simplicity.

STA 1 consists of a bundle of product process and marketing technologies (a), (b) and (c) which are directed to a particular Application 1. The strategy for this STA over the next three years is to change from product technology (a) in year 2 to a newly developed

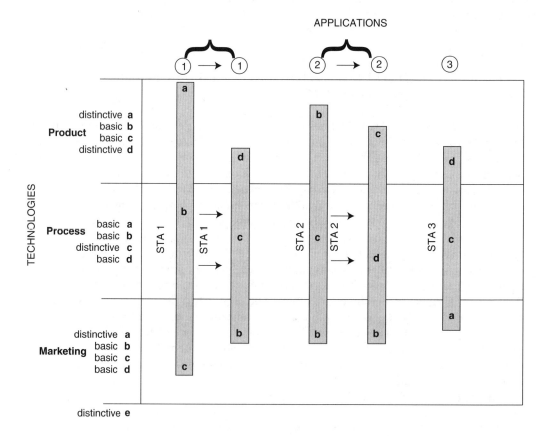

Figure 8.1 Strategic technology area programmes

product (d). At that time the company will switch to process technology (c), which is suitable for the new product technology and which is currently being used for the product in STA 2. The new technology will be marketed differently, using the sales force currently being used for STA 2 in marketing technology (b).

The same new product technology (d), together with process technology (c) will also be directed at a different application (Application 3), comprising a new STA. This new STA will also include the use of a direct marketing operation, based on a recently developed database, that is, marketing technology (a).

In the meantime, STA 2 will go through much more modest changes. A new generation of product technology (c) will be introduced, but the bundle of technologies will still be directed at the same application, using the same marketing skills, although in year 3 the company will make a shift to automated assembly, (d). This new (to the company) technology will subsequently be applied to other STAs.

The company's task is to manage the transitions in each of the three technology areas and their application into different markets. It may be that each technology combination can be the basis of a succession of products for a particular application. The company's management will still be involved in planning, introducing and marketing these products in the conventional manner. Therefore, STA programmes are an additional dimension to the company's activities, not a replacement for conventional market or product management.

As well as providing for the development of programmes to manage the integrated exploitation of a company's technologies, STA programmes also provide the basis of monitoring the company's exploitation activity and technological position. To the left-hand side of Figure 8.1, the technologies are characterised as either basic or distinctive. A horizontal scan across the different programmes allows analysis of the extent of exploitation that has been achieved and conversely the level of the company's dependence on each technology. For example, product technology (a), in which the company is seen to be distinctive is only used in one STA (STA 1). This can lead to questions about whether this technology could be used elsewhere in other applications and what support technologies would be needed to achieve that exploitation. Similarly, the company is planning to continue to use marketing technology (b), which is perceived as basic in Application 2 and it is proposing to convert from marketing technology (c) to (b) in the evolution of STA 1. The scope for distinctiveness in technology (b) may be limited. However, it may also be that the introduction of a new technology in that area could transform the company's success in that STA.

The use of STA programmes allows the company to manage the exploitation of all its technologies across a variety of applications. Analysis of the companies' programmes will also have a number of other benefits, for example, by

- enabling the company to question the appropriateness of individual technologies in its portfolio;
- highlighting the implications of whether technologies are distinctive or basic;
- showing the company's level of dependence on each technology and the width of exploitation it has achieved in each area.

EFFECTIVE INTERNAL TRANSFER OF TECHNOLOGY IN THE COMPANY

The optimum internal exploitation of technology in any large company cannot be achieved if that technology remains solely within the location in which it was developed because, first, the division which developed the technology may not have the necessary support technologies in other areas so that it can exploit all the potential applications for the technology. For example in the case of a newly developed product technology, the division which developed it may not have the necessary sales force (marketing technology) to exploit the technology in important potential applications. Similarly, it may not be able to produce at the right volumes or costs to penetrate new markets.

Second, the company may find it valuable to move the technology round in the organisation at different stages in its development or exploitation,[4] because different applications may have been identified or different support technologies may be required.

Third, unless the company has the mechanisms to inform others of the technological assets and developments of each division, it runs the risk·of the same technology being developed more than once in different parts of the company. This occurs to a great extent in the area of marketing technology where different divisions are very likely to acquire similar skills and resources to tackle different market segments, which actually have closely related requirements. In this way the company neglects the opportunities to use joint facilities or to learn from its previous experience. The same can also happen in the process and product areas. Here the incidence is perhaps rarer, but the cost effects are more dramatic.

Fourth, the developers of a technology may not know about the potential for its external exploitation. This may make it a good idea to transfer the technology to a dedicated technology exploitation unit or to a division which has either the contacts with partners or the knowledge of applications which can be addressed in co-operation with others. We discuss the issues of internal transfer of technology more fully in Chapter 10 when we deal with the management of technology.

PRODUCTIVE INTERNAL RESEARCH AND DEVELOPMENT FOR PRODUCT, PROCESS AND MARKETING TECHNOLOGIES

This critical success factor includes the conventional activities of product research and development which we have discussed in the chapters on technology acquisition. Only two points need to be made here. The first is that product development is not solely an R&D activity which can be carried out in a sequential way by R&D personnel, following a marketing specification. Others have pointed out that development decisions are often taken with a view of costs which extends only as far as the narrow direct costs of the R&D itself and which do not fully reflect the (often much greater) costs of getting a product into production and to market. Many things can change during the development time including the specification itself, the application to which it is directed and the available process and marketing technologies with which it must integrate. This emphasises again the importance of what Takeuchi and Nonaka call the 'rugby scrum' approach to development with good functional integration as opposed to the traditional sequential 'relay race' approach where different stages and skills are separated and not integrated.[5]

The second point is that the same approach as for product development needs to be taken to the other two technology areas – process and marketing – if a coherent view of technology strategy is taken. For example, this approach involves the same priority in the allocation of budgets for process R&D and the same professionalism in organisation for research and development in marketing.

EFFECTIVE INTEGRATION BETWEEN THE THREE AREAS OF TECHNOLOGY

Successful exploitation of any one technology depends on effective integration of development in each of the three areas, so that development in any one technology area takes place in a direction which capitalises on strengths in the other two areas. For example, the company must relate the areas in which it is developing new products to its process strengths or marketing skills. A strong case is needed before product development takes place in areas which are outside the company's marketing capabilities, require major changes in production or lead to disruption in that area. The failure to integrate process issues into product technology development has long been argued to be a major failing in US industry.[6]

EFFECTIVE MARKETING

Effective marketing is probably the most critical factor in the successful exploitation of a company's existing technological assets. Marketing usually takes the responsibility for the development of programmes for specific markets or applications, but this task is often based on an inadequate appreciation by marketing people of technological possibilities. For the company to be able to effectively integrate its technologies and their possible applications a change in marketing thinking is required. We have already noted that marketing is usually more concerned with products than with the technologies on which those products are based. Additionally, marketing tends to concentrate on what Shanklin and Ryans call 'demand-side marketing'.[7] This means that the prevailing culture of marketing is oriented towards the outside of the company and the opportunities which marketing people can recognise in the markets they know. Indeed, many marketers view technology as a service function that simply supplies their requirements of suitable product to an acceptable quality, or that comes up with product ideas which marketing can then evaluate.

Shanklin and Ryans also discuss the idea of 'supply-side' marketing, which consists of marketing strategies built on the theme of exploiting the company's existing assets. Both they and we argue for an integration of demand and supply side marketing. To achieve this, marketing must integrate closely with other functional areas to evaluate the company's technological possibilities and relate the exploitation of these to the applications which exist in the market. This cross-functional involvement is less concerned with the simple question: 'Have we got a technology in-house which is unexploited?' It is more concerned with the deeper questions: 'Have we got a particular strength or capacity in a product or process areas? Can this be added to by development or by acquiring other technologies and directed by marketing to a specific application?' and 'Have we got a product, process or marketing technology which could be used in a different application, perhaps in conjunction with technologies existing elsewhere in the company or in another company?'

Both of these deeper questions require interfunctional debate about the interplay between current and potential technologies. More significantly, they require the development of explicit programmes at the level of the individual STA and for multiples of STAs. Marketing's responsibilities still include market analysis, the development of the company's marketing skills (marketing technology) and the management of these in particular applications. But they also include an input into the development of overall programmes for each STA and this, in turn, requires a greater appreciation of the interplay between different technologies and their application.

We now consider some of the more detailed aspects of the importance of effective marketing in technology exploitation.

Links between marketing and R&D

One aspect of the need for the marketing function to be more involved with issues of technology concerns its links with R&D. The role of the marketing function is not only relevant in technology exploitation once the product has been developed, but it also plays a critical role in communicating user needs to R&D staff involved in the internal acquisition of technology. Market information and research should ideally act as a gatekeeper, providing a description of key performance and technical variables which are associated with customer response. However there are major difficulties in managing this gatekeeper role.

Often, customers do not become aware of a feature of a product which is essential for their approval until that feature changes or disappears. It is therefore difficult for market research to identify beforehand all the key variables.

Marketing must also successfully describe and communicate to the scientists and technologists in R&D the market research data which can be compiled. Organisational and professional divisions between marketing and R&D staff can make this communication task difficult. Staff in these two areas tend to speak different languages; commercial v. technical vocabularies. The orientations of their interests are different between the world of business and the world of science and technology. Formidable communication barriers can result, thus mitigating against effective technology exploitation which takes place in the absence of sufficient market information.

There are a number of ways in which companies can improve the communications process between the marketing and R&D functions to ensure that customer-based factors do provide an input to technology exploitation. These include:

1 *Involvement of marketing in R&D projects.* If marketing people are involved earlier in a project, not only can market information be more easily communicated, but also potential marketing problems can be identified and resolved at an earlier stage of technical development. Proposals for new or spin-off offerings can be suggested and, indeed,

stimulated directly to the scientists and technologists involved in the project by marketing staff. In this way, market criteria can be applied to potential new products and processes at an early stage in their development.

2 *Involvement of marketing in company R&D decisions.* Decisions regarding the exploitation of technology in many companies are dominated by R&D personnel and their considerations. A formal role for marketing in the decision-making process ensures that customer considerations are also taken into account. Despite the potential for political battles in some cases, there are considerable, offsetting benefits which result from the exchange of information, open communication of difficulties and interfunctional commitment to projects which are agreed.

3 *Greater use of market information for technology.* Marketing should use their customer contact and research facilities to gather data regarding technological aspects of existing and potential new products, customer satisfaction ratings and requirements, and competitors' activities. The non-technical orientation of marketing people often means that in the absence of an explicit remit to gather technology-based market data, they will commission research which focuses on non-technical factors in customer decision-making. This occurrence can be compounded by customers' own lack of technology awareness or knowledge in the area. Information requirements for market research regarding technology should be also sought from R&D by the marketing department.

4 *Utilising R&D as a marketing resource.* The links between marketing and R&D should not be regarded as 'one-way traffic'. Research and Development can assist in developing the exploitation programmes for products which exploit their technologies. Many customer firms engaged in their own R&D for equipment, materials and processes necessary for their operating procedures. Marketing can use its R&D function's contacts with customer firms for identifying early adopters of its new products. The supplier's capacity to demonstrate and guarantee customer support and servicing through its R&D function can be an important factor for potential buyers. Strong R&D can also be used as a marketing tool in persuading customers to adopt a new technology.

Thus, the key to making R&D more productive in technology exploitation is the improvement of communication links between it and the marketing function at all levels.

Match between technology and market success

The presentation of a new product, whether or not based on innovative technologies, is no guarantee of market success even if that product meets an obvious customer requirement. Shanklin and Ryans,[8] drawing on the experience of Sony and many others, have shown that the more innovative a new product is, the more likely it is that potential purchasers initially will not see its benefits. Therefore, less reliance can be placed on conventional market research in the case of innovative products, simply because customers cannot want what they cannot conceive of. For example, there were no demonstrations in the streets thirty years ago under the slogan, 'We want microwave ovens!'

The extent to which useful information is available from the market is a function of the characteristics of the application and particularly of the specific expertise of potential users.

In those cases where users have high expertise then much innovation comes from them. The specific problem for the technology-based marketer is that users are often unable to articulate their requirements, or to imagine the possible uses of a new technology: 'Their (users) insights into new product (and process and service) needs and potential solutions are constrained by their own real-world experience. Users steeped in the present are thus unlikely to generate novel product concepts which conflict with the familiar.'[9]

Common examples of this problem and the success of those companies which have disregarded conventional market research are the reported refusal of Hewlett Packard to accept a McKinsey analysis that demonstrated an absence of demand for their calculator, and Sony's founders who did not believe the research that showed that consumers would not buy a tape recorder that didn't record – 'You can't research a market for a product that doesn't exist.'[10]

Johansson and Nonaka[11] however, have suggested improvements to conventional market research in their discussion of Japanese approaches. They described how the search for context-specific information can be carried out by interviewing those who are close to, or who have made, recent purchases or, where this is not possible, by the collection of 'soft-data' through conversations with distributors and dealers.

Many industrial companies underestimate the considerable costs involved in creating demand for even minor technological breakthroughs. This is particularly critical for small companies that have invested heavily in product and process technologies or, indeed, for large firms which do not have the necessary marketing technology.

Relationship marketing

Business marketing is a relationship management task. The exploitation of product or process innovation involves clear decisions about relationships with user companies and distributors. It may be that certain relationships will be built to gain access to a geographical market, or to add to the user's technology so that another down-stream market can be penetrated. Similarly, relationships with some customers may preclude relationships with others. For many companies, the management of their portfolio of relationships is a critical success factor. The addition of a new market offering which involves a change or addition to this portfolio can have a dramatic effect on corporate well-being. Almost all relationships involve adaptations for either or both parties. These adaptations are not just in their respective products and processes, but in their marketing, administration and, even, culture. Business marketing relationships tend to be close, complex and long term.

Lead users

The technology-based marketer who relies on his or her own vision of a technology, its direction and its application can face disaster, either because a product based on a new technology may have a fundamental flaw or because of some minor technological detail which if addressed could radically alter its prospects. Von Hippel has suggested that the thoughtful use of lead users can help to address the problem of market research in areas of new technology. Lead users are those who have real-life experience with novel product or process concepts. He defines lead users as facing needs that will be general in a market-place, but who face them much earlier than the bulk of the marketplace and are positioned to benefit significantly by obtaining a solution to those needs.[12]

The critical issue in this approach is to identify the lead users! Von Hippel suggests that an essential precursor to finding them is the identification and description of trends. These trends can range from technical trends of importance in industrial markets and which might be identified informally or through formal Delphi methods to the trend analysis and projection in the consumer markets carried out by such authors as Popcorn.[13] Identification of users at the leading edge of a trend is likely to be easier in industrial markets because the position of companies on a range of trends is likely to be predictable from its activities and performance and to be known to industry experts. Consumer lead users are only likely to be identified through field study as a preliminary to detailed market research. In neither the industrial or consumer contexts should the search for lead users be confined to the existing customers of the company.

All these factors show that the planning of the company's relationships is a critical element in developing strategy for exploitation of technology. Not only can failure to do this mean failure for the technology, but it can produce much more wide-ranging failure in the company's interrelated activities which depend on those same relationships.[14]

Product success and technology success

Success in exploiting a technology must not be defined narrowly in terms of the sales and profits of a particular product which uses that technology. Each product is simply the means by which a technology is being exploited at that time. Each must be managed to maximise its contribution to the return on that technological investment. For example, it is common in the early stages of a product market for a dominant design to emerge. If that dominant design becomes defined in terms of the technology of a particular company then that company is likely to gain not only product sales, but also credibility for subsequent generations of product, as well as royalty payments from licences. In such circumstances, the marketing strategy for the early products based on the technology must be to achieve standardisation. This may involve quite different pricing and distribution decisions to those required to maximise profits on the individual product. A well-known example which illustrates the issues in product sales and longer-term technology exploitation is the deal by Microsoft to have IBM use the MS DOS operating system and the stipulation by Microsoft that IBM would not have exclusivity on the software. This ensured standardisa-tion of MS DOS, probably at the expense of price achievement on the original deal. A similar challenge of trying to achieve standardisation was faced by Sony and Matsushita when initially marketing products based on rival Betamax and VHS systems for video recorders, and currently in the battle between the new formats of mini-CDs from Sony and digital audio-tape players from Philips.

Decisions on the life of a particular product must include whether it is appropriate to replace the product with another which is based on the same technology, in order to more fully exploit that technology, or whether it makes strategic sense to replace the technology itself. Problems often occur because managers do not distinguish between, on the one hand, their personal stake in the existing product and the strength of its current market position and, on the other hand, what may be the underlying weakness of the technologies on which the product is based. These problems are illustrated by Foster:

> When R&D concentrates on extracting marginal improvements from old technology, windows of opportunity open up for competitors. And, when a competitor does move in with a new technology, the company's response is typically to increase its investment in the old. But, in choosing to defend an existing technology, rather than displace it with a new one, management only increases the inherent economic advantage of the attacker by enabling him to develop his product or processes unhampered by entrenched competition (quoted by Morone).[15]

Bases of competition and market life

The bases of competition in a market change through the life of that market. These changes are driven by movements in customer requirements and changes in product, process and marketing technologies in all competing companies. For example, Japanese companies made reliability a main basis of competition in the auto industry, based on the superiority of their process technology and the product and process technologies of their component suppliers. Product reliability is a less important basis for competition, now that most manufacturers have achieved acceptable levels of build quality. Japanese manufacturers currently are using changes in their process technologies and advances in product and marketing technologies to compete on a basis of technological and design innovation, and to fill previously unavailable market positions such as those for Lexus or Infiniti. Further, their process and product technologies have allowed them to follow a strategy of driving down both the product development and change time, and the break-even point. This enabled them to offer different cars for different national markets and specialised segments, until the slowing down of the world car market led them to revert to a more restricted model range.

The marketers' task through the life of a series of products must relate to a wider STA Analysis and to developments in all three technology areas, in order to achieve marketing success for each individual product and for each product to contribute to overall technology exploitation.

Product deletion

Finally, an important aspect of effective marketing in technology exploitation is the analysis and timing of product deletion decisions. Most of the marketing literature assumes that product deletion is something which occurs at the maturity and decline stages of the life of a product. It is also taken as self-evident that a product is deleted because of its poor performance in terms of sales, profits or market share. Yet a technology-based view of product policy and the use of STA Analysis can provide the opportunity for the reinvention, rejuvenation and repositioning of products at any stage of their life. Decline and deletion are not pre-ordained or inevitable processes. Furthermore, product deletion can occur for many other reasons than poor market or financial performance. One study found eight basic problem situations which can lead to the withdrawal of a product from the market:[16]

1 Government policies and regulations.
2 Changes in third-party specifications.
3 Decline in future market potential.
4 Parent organisation decisions.
5 Poor technical performance.
6 Development of new products.
7 Rationalisation due to merger or acquisition.
8 Variety reduction policy.

It is often unclear in particular cases why a product was deleted. Often, several of these problem situations may overlap, which further complicates and may delay a deletion decision. The urgency of deletion decisions depends on the importance to the company in terms of sales or resources consumed, whether or not a new product is available to replace the one under consideration, the intensity of competition in the market from other firms' products and the number and roles of the 'stakeholders' in the decision. Because product deletion affects the balance of resources between functional areas and individuals in the company, it becomes a highly political process, and involves conflict and bargaining between interest groups inside and, perhaps, outside the company. There is often considerable resistance to deletion and several aspects of the decision may be disputed, such as measures of performance, the other options available, the relative performance of the product, the market forecasts, the revenue or profit accounting and the impact on customers and distributors.

Of the various criteria which are used to make deletion decisions, the impact of the decision on the technology base and strategy of the company is rarely taken into account. Analysis tends to be at the level of the product itself and not its underlying technologies. The withdrawal of a product can mean that a distinctive technology of the firm is no longer used and effectively lost, investment in technologies on which the product is based and which support other products can no longer be justified and that the technology balance in the firm as a whole is adversely affected. Conversely, a deletion decision can free up resources to be invested in the acquisition of new product, process or marketing technologies.

Product deletion can alter the technology bases of suppliers and customers, and it can speed up the rate of technological change in the external environment by stimulating developments in the partners for new products. Product deletion can even require the acquisition of new technologies. For example, offshore operators of oil platforms are having to develop new technologies to de-commission them. A company also needs to consider how the old technologies used to support a deleted product can be used in other applications. For example, Fiat very successfully licensed the product and process technologies for deleted model cars to eastern European manufacturers and this pattern has also been followed by Citroen and Volkswagen. However, technologies may have to be retained after products have been deleted in order to fulfil service and maintenance agreements with previous customers (British Aerospace still supplies spare parts for Spitfire aeroplanes) or to develop and produce other products in their range.

Example
BP 'Super-Wetters' technology

This example shows how complex organisations face particular difficulties in ensuring that the technologies they have acquired are exploited in the applications where they are needed. It also shows that exploitation can be driven in unexpected ways. In this case the key role in achieving exploitation has been undertaken by technical specialists who normally operate at some distance from the 'market', but who demonstrated skills in internal and external analysis.

As a large and diverse organisation BP has long maintained a central research establishment. Generally this has contained sections aligned to the needs of operating divisions, e.g. Chemicals and Catalysis, Oil refining and retailing, Exploration together with a section looking at more basic R&D, known as Physical Sciences and Engineering (PSE). Typically PSE performs work both for the group as a whole on long-term fundamental research and skills maintenance and for individual divisions and businesses on shorter-term work aimed at specific product or process development. BP, like many similar firms, is trying to ensure that the divisions provide an increasing proportion of the funding for central R&D activity. Colloid and Interface Science (CIS) is one of seven specialist groups in PSE and is concerned with the behaviour of fluids and their interface with surfaces.

During the early 1980s one group in CIS had been involved, together with many other research groups, in the development of techniques allowing recovery of residual oil from mature oil fields in the North Sea. The group's work had focused on the formulation of fluids which, if pumped into the porous rock of such fields, would release oil from the rock surfaces, hold it in suspension and allow its subsequent extraction. Corporate and divisional funding was involved, the latter from the Exploration division as the potential 'customer' and the Chemicals division as the potential supplier of the fluids. Considerable knowledge of surface acting, or 'surfactant' chemicals had been gained, but the collapse of oil prices made the cost of such techniques uneconomical. Work on surfactants faded into the background.

No obvious uses for these skills were apparent within BP, though the members of the group could envisage a number of potential applications. At this time however, CIS was approached by a client within BP Specialty Chemicals with an unusual request: He would provide limited funding for a wide-ranging exploration of possible new product concepts, with the expectation that focus would narrow down to a single area within two years. Around the half-way point of this search, it appeared that a natural focus had been provided for the work. BP became interested in ways of cleaning metal surfaces and inhibiting corrosion; the surfactant team was confident that it could develop a formulation which could do both. Work continued with the expectation of a clearly defined end product. However, outside factors ended this promising project. A key ingredient of the formulation, developed on the basis of the original planned application in oil recovery, was not economical when produced in low 'speciality' volumes and once again full development was halted.

A third possible application emerged as a result of government environmental concerns over oil production methods. Drill bits were typically lubricated by oil-based fluids which produced contaminated mineral waste. BP Exploration, expecting legislation restricting these methods, began an urgent search for solutions. The possibility of 'cleaning' waste with surfactant fluids was attractive both to them and to BP Chemicals, which could profitably supply the finished formulation. A programme was agreed and in 1986 development commenced. Two years later, with trials completed, an effectively proven technology was transferred to a BP Chemicals plant for the run up to production. Even at this late stage however, hopes were dashed. The anticipated legislation was indeed passed, but with draconian contamination limits beyond the capabilities of this technology. Production and launch plans were abandoned.

By this point however, the technical staff in CIS were increasingly confident of their ability to produce workable product applications. Pursuing literature searches and development funding vigorously, they isolated another promising use. The soldering process involved in printed-circuit board production left behind residues which were removed using CFC-based cleaning agents. With environmental sensitivity growing, such agents were expected to come under legislative threat, while surfactant-based cleaners provided a 'green' option. Corporate, and subsequently Chemicals divisional funding was obtained, market appraisals were commissioned and potential customers contacted directly. A successful transfer of the technology to a production unit was completed. Since then distribution agreements have been signed with a solder specialist and initial orders have been won from a commercial aircraft manufacturer.

The group is now actively investigating a range of further applications, including oil-spill clearing and the rehabilitation of industrial sites contaminated by oil.

Example
Carneau-Metal Box: Exploiting technology with partners

This example illustrates the importance of seeking partnership with other companies in the surrounding network in order to exploit a new technology. It also shows how organisational issues can frustrate success.

Carneau-Metal Box (CMB) produces a range of metal and plastic packaging for consumer and industrial products, including paints, cosmetics and foods. The firm was formed in 1989 by the merger of two European packaging manufacturers. Following the merger, the combined company was reorganised by materials type so that separate businesses were established based on materials – 'plastics food' and 'metals food'.

Well before this reorganisation, one of the main technical thrusts of each of the companies was the search for innovative products to offset the steadily declining prices obtainable for standard products such as drinks cans. In 1978 an R&D team conceived of a three-piece food container using a plastic body and metal ends similar to those of beverage cans. Attractive and convenient, it seemed to have considerable potential. However the lack of an obvious market, and the likely complexity of the manufacturing process, kept it as a 'shoestring' development project.

In 1981, however, another firm approached Metal Box with a proposal of a joint venture to produce a similar product: a two-piece plastic drink can with a metal top. Although it was more complex and expensive to produce, it led to a revival of interest in the existing project. Driven by the partner's enthusiasm, Metal Box commenced a crash programme to fully develop the three-piece 'STEP' can. Samples were test marketed to a major food retailer on the initiative of the company's chief executive who was now a 'champion' of the project. A very positive response was received and a trial production system was established with similar success.

With all the signs encouraging, plant for the new product was established in surplus space at an existing metal can factory and a marketing programme set up. This programme emphasised to potential customers STEP's applicability for exotic seasonal products. At the same time the firm invested in the development of other applications such as a substitute for wine bottles and also a 'heat-treatable' version for perishable foods. Costs were high, but this seemed a unique product which could receive patent protection and which was capable of generating premium prices.

Underlying problems with the project were exposed with the 1989 reorganisation. Because STEP was both plastic and metal, it had no clear home in the new system. Moreover, the high development and manufacturing costs made it unattractive to each individual business, which under the new structure would have to bear the capital depreciation of investment in the project. For the group, there seemed no option but to close the plant, to the fury of the main customer for whom this pack now supported some highly profitable food products.

CONCLUSIONS

In this chapter we have examined some of the tasks and problems which companies face in exploiting their technology. We have chosen not to take a conventional view of this task or to look in detail at what is often called 'High Technology Marketing' or the marketing of technological products. Although marketing people must be involved in technology exploitation because of their skills in analysing customer requirements and programme building and management, it is important to separate the task of technology exploitation from the narrower conventional activity of product marketing which may form part of it. Some of the issues which we believe to be important in this area are summarised below:

The technology exploitation task cannot be separated from the acquisition task. It is a short-term view to think of exploiting the technological assets which the company has acquired in the past without thinking sufficiently of future acquisition. This means that those (typically marketing people) who understand the company's current applications must be involved in long-term acquisition decisions as well as the more detailed questions of new product development.

Irrespective of the distinctiveness of a particular technology, a bundle of a number of product, process and marketing technologies is necessary to meet the requirements of any application. The company's exploitation task is more to do with the assembly of that bundle, using both internal and external technologies, than it is about selling the products which are based on the technologies.

The unit of analysis in technology exploitation is not the product, nor the individual technology but the strategic technology area. This consists of the technology bundle *and* its application. The company must manage the evolution of each STA over time as well as the detailed implementation of each STA programme. Marketing personnel may well be involved or responsible for STA programmes, but an exclusive marketing orientation may lead to problems of short-termism and underexploitation.

Technology exploitation is the task of achieving the optimum exploitation of all the company's product, process and marketing technologies by choosing from a number of different means which may be more or less appropriate at different times. The strategic exploitation of a company's technologies may conflict with the short-term sales of some of its products and may require co-operation with some competitor companies.

Effective technology exploitation requires a level of interaction between those who understand its different product, process and marketing technologies, that goes well beyond that which is needed for conventional new product development and introduction. To achieve effective exploitation requires a level of debate, a language and a technological literacy which involves a major change in culture and attitude and the breakdown of conventional demarcations and reward structures.

Finally, effective technology exploitation requires a new attitude to co-operation with other companies for external exploitation to take place and it is to this issue that we now turn.

REFERENCES

1   Kotabe, M. (1992) *Global Sourcing Strategy*, New York: Quorum, p. 207.
2   Mitchell, G. (1986) 'New approaches to the strategic management of technology', *Technology in Society*, **7**(2–3): 132–44.
3   Ibid. 136.
4   Grandstrand, O. and Sjolander, S. (1990) 'Managing innovation in multi-technology corporations', *Research Policy*, **19**: 35–60.
5   Takeuchi, H. and Nonaka, I. (1986) 'The new new product development game', *Harvard Business Review*, January–February: 137–46.
6   Wheelwright, S. C. (1985) 'Restoring the competitive edge in US manufacturing', *California Management Review*, **XXVII**(3), Spring: 26–41.
7   Shanklin, W. and Ryans, J. K. (1984) *Marketing High Technology*, Lexington, MA: Lexington Books.
8   Ibid.
9   Ford, D. (ed.) (1991) *Understanding Business Markets*, London: Academic Press.
10 Morone, J. (1989) 'Strategic use of technology', *California Management Review*, Summer: 91–110.
11 Johansson, J. K. and Nonaka, I. (1987) 'Market research the Japanese way', *Harvard Business Review*, May–June: 20.
12 Von Hippel, E. (1986) 'Lead users: a source of novel product concepts', *Management Science*, **32**(7): 791–805.
13 Popcorn, F. (1991) *The Popcorn Report*, London: Arrow Books.
14 Von Hippel, E. (1986) 'Lead users', art. cit.
15 Morone, J., 'Strategic use of technology', 93.
16 Morone, J., 'Strategic use of technology', 103.

Chapter 9

The special case of external exploitation

INTRODUCTION

In this chapter we concentrate on the particular issues which a company faces in exploiting its technology outside its own products and production. The external exploitation of technology is an emotive issue in companies; it is commonly argued that technology is the heart of a company's current operations and the seed-corn for its future. Therefore, so the argument continues, the transfer of current technology to other firms must inevitably weaken the company's current market position and reduce its long-term competitiveness, so no technology should be transferred to others while it still has value in the business. This argument oversimplifies the case, but it does emphasise the central fact that external exploitation involves the transfer of a company's hard-earned technologies to others.

We start by looking at some of the implications of the external exploitation of technology for national policy. Having established this context, we move to some of the critical success factors in external exploitation. This analysis leads to examination of the costs and benefits of different methods of external exploitation and, finally, we look at the issue of acquiring technology for external exploitation.

EXTERNAL EXPLOITATION OF TECHNOLOGY AND NATIONAL POLICY

Technology transfer provokes powerful issues of national policy, particularly in terms of relationships between companies in the West and those from Japan. The argument about the dangers of technology transfer for both western companies and countries was strongly developed by Reich and Mankin.[1] They believe that joint ventures between US and Japanese companies are, 'part of a continuing, implicit Japanese strategy to keep the higher paying, higher value-added jobs in Japan and to gain the project engineering and production process skills that underlie competitive success'. They further suggest that the US 'strategy' is 'dangerously shortsighted' by exchanging its competitiveness for a few low-skilled, low-paid jobs and for access to the Japanese high-quality, low-cost products. Essentially the argument is that licensing is an easy way to generate short-term revenue, but unless it is carried out on the basis of clear analysis it can lead to a fatal leakage of technology to competitors who have a long-term view of the technologies they need to retain and acquire for strategic dominance. Similarly, if the licenser does not have a strategy for the continuing development and exploitation of its technology then the transfer will not only cause immediate loss of market, but also long-term loss of technological position.

Joint ventures pose similar dangers. All too often, US companies enter joint ventures on the basis of use of their product styling and market and distribution knowledge (marketing technology). The contribution of the Japanese partner is in its product design and production skills (product and process technology). The US company effectively degenerates into the role of assembler of Japanese parts and distributor of Japanese finished products. Reich and Mankin cite the case of the IBM PC as an example which at their time of writing had manufacturing costs of about $860, of which roughly $625 worth, or 73 per cent, of the components were made overseas. Over two-thirds of the joint ventures between US and Japanese companies that they studied were agreements by which the US company would sell and distribute Japanese products.

Similar conclusions were drawn in a study by Hamel, Doz and Prahalad[2] of European–Japanese joint ventures. These authors suggest that a critical difference between the joint venture partners was that the Europeans viewed the ventures as continuing activities in which they were happy to be dependent on Japanese product and process technologies. In contrast, the Japanese saw the ventures as temporary devices which were necessitated by a specific technological inadequacy which they hoped to rectify by acquiring their partners technology or through their own development efforts. Hamel *et al.* quote one Japanese manager as follows:

> When it is necessary to collaborate, I go to my employees and say, 'This is bad, I wish we had these skills ourselves. Collaboration is second best. But I will feel worse if after four years we do not know how to do what our partner knows how to do'. We must digest their skills.[3]

Reich and Mankin[4] argue that there are important cultural and organisational differences which militate against US companies' investment in their process technologies, of which the prime difference is the higher rates of job turnover and the consequent loss of training investment. They suggest that there is an important role for government in addressing the problem of technological loss. Government could subsidise investment in process technologies and build mechanisms to transfer technologies to smaller firms.

The question of government policy towards technology transfer is important, but any policy will not remove the responsibility of managers for planning the strategic exploitation of their technology.

SUCCESS FACTORS IN THE EXTERNAL EXPLOITATION OF TECHNOLOGY

The short-term external exploitation of technology can affect overall technology strategy in several ways. Ill-considered licensing can cause a company's core technologies to become available to a number of emerging competitors in its main application areas. The technology itself can also be devalued because of poor exploitation by those licensees. Badly chosen joint-venture partners or poorly managed ventures may lead to the company being displaced from the venture, from the technology itself or from particular applications, all because of the uncontrolled leakage of technology to another company. Such poor exploitation pro-motes the argument for a strategic approach to external exploitation. Some of the factors which make up this type of strategic approach and which are critical factors in its success are described next.

An appropriate locus of decision-making

The scale of the issues involved in the external exploitation of technology through such mechanisms as strategic alliances means that decision-making for these is often seen as being the monopoly of top management. On some occasions the involvement of top management can bring both a strategic focus and a visionary insight to matching and exploiting the respective technologies of the two or more companies in an alliance. However, perhaps more frequently, the top management approach is either opportunistic or reactive. In whichever case, the basis of the top-management's vision or approach must be effectively communicated downwards so that it can be used in other lower-level exploitation decisions.

Senior management's decisions on external exploitation may also not be well grounded in the reality of the company's technology position; a position which is probably better understood by those in touch with day-to-day technology issues. This reinforces the need for continuing analysis, both internal and external for technology exploitation, so that the basis for taking individual exploitation decisions can be made explicit and the company can seek out and evaluate opportunities, rather than react to those which are thrust at the company.

An organisation which addresses wider exploitation opportunities

This is an important issue because it centres on the key attitudinal problem which often affects technology exploitation. We have already noted some of the reasons why the exploitation of technology may be restricted. For example, many managers feel fully occupied with their day-to-day responsibilities and have little time for wider issues. This is particularly the case for those managers in charge of the company's process technologies. Few companies have a clear view of the technological assets which they possess and so have problems thinking about the rational exploitation of these assets. Even if companies do have a clear view of the exploitation task, they are more likely to restrict their analysis to internal exploitation because external exploitation does not fit easily into anyone's job remit. We have seen in Chapter 2 that the lack of a strategic view of external exploitation means that it is the acquirer who tends to take the initiative in many technology deals. External exploitation is often reduced to an *ad hoc* reactive process where the only professional involvement is likely to be of those with a legal background who are responsible for drawing up a licence agreement.

Managers must be alert to the necessity for external technology exploitation if an appropriate return is to be achieved on an ever-increasing level of technology investments. A realisation of this necessity is particularly important in what appears to be the prevailing business culture, which seems to stress that companies should 'stick to the knitting' by concentrating on their core activities and not venturing into the diversifications which were so much a part of corporate culture during the 1980s.[5] It should be emphasised that the critical difference between diversification and external exploitation of technology centres precisely on the critique of diversification which has been advanced so frequently; that it involves companies in chasing opportunities in high potential markets by ventures which do not capitalise on their abilities or technologies. External technology exploitation builds on the technologies which the company possesses. In its licensing form it offers incremental returns, and in its joint-venture form it offers the opportunity for synergies with the technologies of others and the chance to acquire those technologies for the company.

Use of Strategic Technology Area Analysis

One way in which managers' thinking can be directed towards external exploitation is by re-emphasising the importance of continuous analysis as we have described in Chapter 8 and by determining that individual technologies and the STAs built on them become the unit of analysis in strategy formation. A shift away from a product–market approach allows managers to interrogate their operations to look for wider exploitation opportunities, either by 'hands-off' licensing deals, or by co-operation with others. Specifically, STA Analysis can alter managerial reward mechanisms to those which focus on the company's overall return on its technology.

We can illustrate the value of the STA approach to external exploitation by examining Figure 9.1. This is the same figure showing STA Analysis that we used in the previous chapter, but we have now added STA 4. The company in our example was planning to introduce the new product technology (c) into STA 2. Suppose that its continuing analysis indicated a possible use for this technology in another area, however, in order to satisfy the requirements of this application the product would have to be produced in much larger quantities and at a very low cost using an automated production line, as illustrated by process technology (a). Further, suppose that the investment required in order to achieve these production requirements was considerable and that the company had little similar production experience in the past. Additionally, success in this application would require the development of a channel of distribution and a promotional activity which was entirely new to the company, illustrated by marketing technology (e). The company would have to decide whether the STA was worthwhile and what investment could be justified.

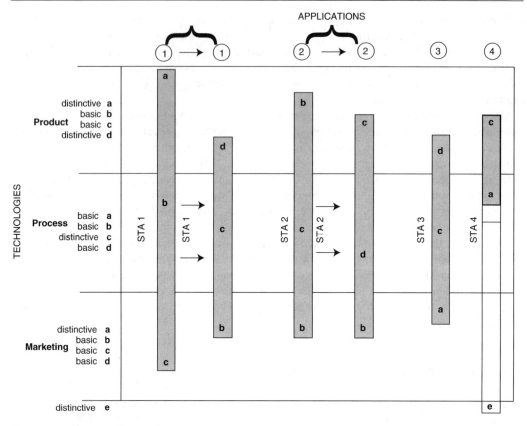

Figure 9.1 Strategic Technology Area Analysis

It could well be the case that investment in the process technology was worthwhile, despite its cost. For example, the technology perhaps could also be employed in refined form in another planned STA and it has the capability to be a distinctive technology for the company. However, suppose that the marketing technology investment could not be justified, because its cost would render the whole STA unviable. More importantly, there were no other potential applications for this technology in the company's strategy and it involved a learning curve which meant that there was little chance of the company achieving distinctiveness in the near future. For this reason the company could choose to construct an STA using marketing technology (e) as an external technology. This would involve either contracting out the marketing to another company or establishing a joint venture with that company for the STA.

Appropriate allocation of responsibility for external exploitation decisions

External exploitation decisions are often beyond the normal experience and responsibilities of the managers who have charge of a company's products, processes and marketing. In fact, external exploitation may often appear to conflict with internal activities. For example, a decision to licence a product technology may lead to greater returns than restricting its application to the company's own products, but that decision could restrict the sales or life of those products and may adversely affect the career of those responsible for them.

Many companies have established a licensing office to handle outward and inward licensing deals. The basis for such an office is frequently the need to centralise expensive legal expertise and to avoid pitfalls in licensing deals. There are two related problems in such an arrangement. First, the licensing office may have little idea of the strategic thrust of any particular technology deal, so decisions may be taken on narrow cost or revenue grounds, rather than to support an overall strategy. It is also possible that the office will operate too much in a reactive mode and without either the resources or abilities to positively market the company's technology. Second, any delegation of decisions about the external exploitation of technology to a service department detracts from the overview and involvement of those responsible for a technology. It is vital that exploitation decisions are taken by those with strategic responsibility for a technology, and a licensing office must then operate in a service mode within that strategic context.

Some companies realise the potential value of the technologies which they have developed and establish a technology marketing department to proactively exploit these technologies. We can illustrate the advantages and problems of such an approach by looking again at the example of the Anglo-French packaging company Carneau-Metal Box.

Example
External exploitation of technology:
Carneau-Metal Box

This example illustrates how a company can develop the external exploitation of its technology. It also shows how a company must be careful to examine the interrelationships between different means of exploitation and how, if not careful, it can actually end up competing against itself!

The Anglo-French packaging group Carneau-Metal Box (CMB) is organised into a large number of profit centres targeting specific product/market combinations. Each is responsible for initiating and funding technical development projects, drawing on the resources of the main group R&D centre in the UK. During the 1980s this well-funded centre generated more exploitable technology than the operating companies could absorb. As a result, some licensing activity was undertaken and technology was used to support subsidiary and affiliated companies in developing countries. By 1988 this external exploitation of technology was producing approximately 13 per cent of group profits.

In 1989 the company's Technology Sales and Licensing unit was transformed into a profit centre in its own right. It was now free to exploit technology wherever it could. Moreover, it was able to fund its own development projects within R&D (or indeed with outside agencies such as universities). In addition, it could take over projects sponsored by operating companies when the latter chose not to take them to the market. Its 'products' range from routine development work to genuinely new technologies. In essence the large group R&D database is presented as a menu, with levels of access priced between £25,000 and £1.8 million. Marketing of the technology is handled by five regional managers and customers range from local packagers to American and Japanese multinationals. Where appropriate, the unit can commission dedicated research projects on behalf of its customers, buying R&D time in the same way as operating companies.

At times this free market in technology can mean that CMB operating companies, having declined to take up new products or processes, can find themselves competing against firms which have bought licenses for these very technologies from the Technology Sales and Licensing unit. Some managers believe that a high-level co-ordination and communication mechanism is needed to resolve such situations.

Correct timing of external exploitation

Another main question about external exploitation is, 'When might it be appropriate to externally exploit a particular technology?' A useful way to answer this question is to start by noting the four obvious reasons for a company to decide to exploit a technology externally:

1 To enter a specific new application area for which it does not have the appropriate bundle of technologies.
2 To seek additional revenue from a technology in areas beyond its control.
3 Because of an approach from another company that wishes to use the technology in its operations.
4 Because of a wish to exercise a measure of control over the use of technology or of the pattern of innovation in a particular application.

In an ideal situation, a company could plan the roll-out of a technology through successive application areas by internal or external exploitation according to the following factors:

1 The potential or strategic importance of the application area.
2 The appropriateness of the bundle of technologies for each application that the company has available or can easily assemble.
3 Whether the support technologies it needs to acquire could later be used in other applications or have some overall strategic significance.
4 The ease of access to the application area – for example whether entry is made difficult by restrictive agreements between other players or where other barriers to entry are high.
5 The urgency of the exploitation of the area because of competitive activity or technological replacement, and according to whether the company has the relevant support technologies, can easily acquire them or has use for them elsewhere.

In this ideal case, the internal or external exploitation decision is based on which approach is suitable for the successive applications that the technology-holder chooses. This of course presupposes that the company has worked out an exploitation strategy in advance and has the continuous tracking and evaluation mechanisms we have referred to in order to spot emerging opportunities.

However, it is not sufficient to take decisions on internal or external exploitation on an application by application basis. There are a number of additional factors which affect whether external exploitation should be considered early or late in the life cycle of a technology and these are illustrated in Table 9.1.

The first factors for and against early external exploitation centre on the complicated issue of R&D recovery. Briefly, early external exploitation is likely to be appropriate when the company is in a situation where the speed of pay-back on its technology investment is more important than the overall amount of return which is achieved. This could occur if the company was in a situation of cash shortage, or if funds were urgently needed to finance a new project. In this case, a company is likely to seek licence or joint-venture partners early to maximise the return it could achieve before the, possibly greater, amount from its own product sales.

Standardisation is a common issue in technology exploitation, and refers to the situation where the initiator of a new technology believes that the potential for licence revenue from other users of the technology or the chance of its own product sales will be affected by whether or not the technology becomes the standard used by one or more applications. Perhaps the best-known example occurred with the different video formats, Betamax and VHS. The success of VHS owed less to any technical differences between the formats, but more to the fact that Matsushita achieved good distribution for its products based on its superior marketing technology and through licensing the technology to Sanyo, Sharp and Toshiba, and supplying VHS format video recorders to RCA, Magnavox and GTE Sylvania for resale under their respective brand names.[6] The subsequent standardisation of VHS led to the demise of the Betamax format. Similar examples have occurred in a variety of electronic componentry, such as the way in which Intel has achieved near standardisation of its 386 and 486 chips for personal computer applications and Philips achieved standardisation via licensing for its audio-cassette technology. However, it is important to emphasise that the issue of standardisation is not confined to major markets. Very often a company

Table 9.1 The critical timing of external exploitation

Early	Later
←	→
Need to recover R&D spend quickly	Need to maximise return on R&D spend
Need to achieve standardisation	Technology is distinctive
Need to pre-empt competitive R&D	Need to achieve full exploitation of an application
Short life-cycle prediction for the technology	Lack of suitable recipients for the technology

will seek to license the use of its technology widely to ensure that the resulting standardisation causes potential users to write specifications in terms of its product.

Other reasons for early external exploitation relate to the need to pre-empt competitive R&D or application entry. In this way, if a technology is seen by competitors to have been proved through licence use or to have thoroughly penetrated a particular application, then it is possible that potential competitors will direct their development efforts in other directions. In turn this can mean that competitors are unable to develop their own versions of subsequent generations of the technology and hence may be dependent on the originator. Because of this danger of long-term technological dependence, competitors are more likely to choose not to develop their own version of a technology or to take a licence for the originator's technology when the technology itself has a short life cycle. In that case, if the initiator has succeeded in achieving a major share of the likely application then its attractiveness is considerably reduced for any other entry.

In contrast, there are a number of factors which argue for later external exploitation, or indeed against external exploitation completely. If a technology is of major distinctiveness for a company or suitable for an application which is central to its strategy, there is a strong case for delaying any external application until that technology has degraded in order not to transfer competitive advantage to others. Unfortunately, this may mean that by the time the technology is externally exploited it will have little value and may only be exploitable in lower technology countries. In some cases a company may wish to concentrate on exploiting a technology in a particular application. If the application is an important source of profit to the company then it may wish to, at least initially, allow the application exclusivity. For example, many consumer goods manufacturers now give exclusive distributions rights in the early stages of introduction of their most innovative new products to one or other of their major retailers. This is as a way of improving their relationships with a critical customer. External application may have to be delayed if there are few suitable recipients. It is not simply that incompetent users may not fulfil the potential of the technology, but they may reduce its value if they cause it to acquire an unfavourable reputation.

There is a tendency among many managers to delay the external exploitation of technology because of concerns about 'selling the seed-corn'. It is worth emphasising that although the value of a technology may follow a curve which approximates to the shape of the technology life cycle, it tends to decline much faster than the slope of the use curve. This is because a technology in the later stages of its life cycle will have become widely known and a number of competitors are likely to have their own versions. Also, potential users of a technology late in its life cycle will appreciate that the technology's useful life is limited and they will be less inclined to spend money to acquire it.

COSTS AND BENEFITS OF DIFFERENT METHODS OF EXTERNAL EXPLOITATION

Earlier in this chapter we examined the circumstances when it would be appropriate to exploit a technology internally or by different methods of external exploitation. We now look in more detail at some of the costs and benefits of each method of external exploitation and the critical success factors in their use. Many of the relationships which companies form with each other are nominally formed to exploit the respective and complementary technologies of the partners. But they may also have a long-term motivation of acquiring technology from the partner or filling a gap until that technology can be acquired internally. Other relationships are formed for the overt purpose of joint technology acquisition, whether or not the companies are planning to operate by using the acquired technology in separate or the same applications. We confine our discussions here to the former case of alliances which are at least nominally intended for the exploitation of technology. Acquisition-based technology alliances are discussed in Chapter 6.

Table 9.2 follows on from the analysis of different exploitation choices described in the previous chapter. It uses similar categories of exploitation methods to those we have considered in earlier chapters for discussing technology acquisition, and draws heavily on the work of Lei and Slocum.[7]

As earlier, the table separates licensing in manufacturing industries from licensing in the service and franchise sectors. The table also includes the same two categories of joint ventures which we have used previously; specialisation ventures, in which each party brings a distinctive competence or technology to the alliance, and shared value-adding ventures in which both parties have strong but related competences. An example which Lei and Slocum cite is of USX Corporation which invested $400 million in a 50/50 venture with Pohang Iron and Steel Company of South Korea to update and build a modern, integrated facility to produce metal sheets, coils, and rolled steel for the automotive, hardware and appliance markets. Both sorts of joint venture involve setting up a separate company.

Table 9.2 also includes contracting out, which refers to the situation where a company contracts with a partner to use the latter's technologies to complement its own. An example would be using the partner to manufacture a product to the company's design or to distribute or design a product for it. Table 9.2 outlines the benefits and costs of each external exploitation method as well as the consequent critical success factors and human resource issues.

Licensing

We have noted that the benefits of licensing in manufacturing industry include speed of entry to different applications and the chance to use the support technologies of the licensee. For service and franchise licensing a particular benefit is the low level of capital expenditure which is involved when compared to conventional expansion. Against these advantages must be set the dangers of loss of control of the technology which is being licensed through the establishment of potential competition in the form of previous licencees. Perhaps the best-known example of this danger is RCA's licensing to Japanese companies, the product technologies on which colour televisions are based. The Japanese companies then developed the technologies further and combined them with their process skills to the eventual exclusion of RCA from the market.

Technology can also be devalued by inappropriate use by a licensee. This often shows up as a loss of quality control in franchise licensing. Such a quality problem led the Kentucky Fried Chicken franchise to drastically reduce the number of its franchisees in the UK. The corresponding critical success factors in both types of licensing centre on the management

Table 9.2 Costs, benefits and critical sucess factors in external technology exploitation

Exploitation method	Benefits	Costs	Critical success factors	Human resource issues
Licensing out manufacturing industries	• standardisation • speed of entry • width of applications • use of licensees' support techniques	• possible new competitors • loss of control over technology use • dependence on licensee • possible eventual exit from industry	• selection of non-competitor licensee • enforcement of patents • sound licence agreements	• technical knowledge • local training of managers on site
Licensing out services and franchises	• speed of market entry • low capital costs	• quality control problem • trademark protection	• partners compatible in philosophies/values • tight performance standards	• socialisation of franchisees and licensees with core values
Joint ventures specialisation across partners	• use of partner's support technologies • economies of scale • speedier/wider application	• dependence on partner's support technology • deterrent to internal inquisition	• tight and specific performance criteria • recognition that collaboration is new form of competition in technology acquisition • clarity of strategy • market technology	• negotiation skills • management development training for new technologies and applications
Joint ventures shared value-adding	• pooled strength of both partners • upgrading of technology • use of other's resources	• high switching costs • loss of independence • shared exploitation benefits	• decentralisation and autonomy from corporate parents • harmonisation of management styles • strong marketing technology	• team-building • acculturisation • entrepreneurial approach

	Benefits	Risks	Success factors
Contracting out manufacturing or marketing or product design	• use of partner's technology • economies of scale • avoids development or capital investment • speed of application	• possible dependence on partner, lower recovery on investment • deterrent to internal acquisition	• selection of reliable partners • good control mechanisms • good bundling skills • distinctiveness in other technologies • development of partnership culture • communication/negotiation skills
Keiretus/chaebols	• shared risks and costs • critical mass in technologies • ready availability of support technologies	• skills and technologies that have no real market worth • bureacracy/hierarchy • loss of critical technologies	• government encouragement • shared values • good internal technology transfer • clan culture • fraternal relationships • extensive mentoring for common vision/mission
Contracting in manufacture, marketing or product design for others	• fuller exploitation of distinctive technology • incentive for further development in contracted technology	• possible neglect of other technologies and other applications/bundles	• close communication with partner • good negotiation skill • service culture in those responsible for contracted technology • development of entrepreneurial culture in contracted technology • sound overall strategy formulation • good control mechanisms

task involved. This task needs skills in licensee selection and patent enforcement to avoid problems of subsequent competition, and in the establishment of sound performance standards to avoid misuse of the technology. In human resource terms the emphasis is on training, particularly for service or franchise licences for which the acculturisation of licencees in the appropriate core values of the licensor is critical.

Joint ventures

Joint ventures in which the partners each contribute a matching technology provide the obvious advantage of each company having the effective use of the other company's technologies without the investment which the company would otherwise have to make to acquire them (even if the company had the skills or time for that acquisition). These technologies may be necessary as overall support technologies or may be essential for a specific application. Joint ventures between industry leaders can be used to effectively alter the basis of competition in an industry. An example of this is the pan-European attempts to develop and exploit high-definition picture quality televisions. This could have the effect of shifting the basis of competition away from selling standard televisions on a price basis and towards competition based on relative picture quality.

Against the advantages of joint ventures must be set the problem that joint exploitation may only provide a short-term benefit and may lead to long-term dependence by discouraging the company from investing more widely in necessary technologies. An example of a joint venture where one of the partners was unable to acquire critical technologies provided by Lei and Slocum is that between General Electric and Fujitsu Fanuc. This joint venture was originally established to co-design and co-produce industrial robots and flexible automation systems. General Electric's inability to learn the necessary process technologies from its partner has resulted in it now acting simply as a distributor of the robots produced by Fujitsu. As we have also noted, this problem is particularly acute when the other company uses the period of the joint venture to acquire the technologies of the partner. Therefore, a critical success factor in these joint ventures is the recognition that the venture must in part be regarded as but another form of competition in the acquisition of new technologies. Also the venture itself has a limited lifetime and is based on technologies which are themselves perishable. This again emphasises the importance of the management task in establishing and monitoring performance criteria and being organised for and willing to learn from the partner – the 'student rather than teacher approach'.

Human relations issues in joint ventures include skills in negotiation, but also in management development and particularly in managerial rotation to maximise the learning process. Heavy dependence on a specialisation joint venture can significantly affect the strategic value of a company in the case of an acquisition or merger, as in the case of Rover cars' acquisition by BMW as we discussed earlier.

Those joint-ventures which involve shared value-adding do not have the advantage of technology matching, but find that shared resources can assist overall exploitation, the penetration of specific applications or the joint acquisition of support or next generation technologies. The corresponding disadvantages again include long-term dependency on the partner and the consequent high switching costs. A major problem is also that of controlling the transfer of the company's technology to its partner, which is a particular danger in this situation because of the closeness of contact between many members of each company in this type of venture.

Further critical success factors centre on the need to establish an appropriate culture in the venture. This may have to be quite different from that which already exists in either of the two partner companies. For example, it is likely that a joint venture in a new application area will need a faster speed of response than either of the two partner companies operating in more established areas are used to. The need for a distinctive culture leads to the requirement for autonomous operation and commonality in style between those who join the venture from either of the companies or, indeed, from outside. The consequent human resource issues centre on the process of team-building during the long 'courtship' between the companies, which both sides must accept and work towards.

Lei and Slocum contrast the success of Corning's joint venture with CIBA-GEIGY, which had a two-year gestation time, with the failure of the joint venture between AT&T and Olivetti to produce personal computers which was eventually dissolved because of wide differences in management styles, corporate cultures and missions which the two companies failed to explore before they started it. Finally, they point out that one of the most difficult things for managers to remember is that joint ventures are actually just competition in another form. Many commentators have noted that Japanese companies enter into joint ventures with companies they hope to compete with after learning their technology, and to carry on parallel competition in other product or market areas during the time of their co-operation.

Contracting out

Contracting out does not involve the same level of investment as the establishment of a separate joint venture. It offers the advantages for the technology exploiter of being able to use the support technologies of the other company or its knowledge of a specific application, and the possible economies of production, design or marketing scale which the other company can achieve. In many cases, a technology may be developed by a company specifically for exploitation in its own operations. This exploitation may well require the involvement of suppliers of supporting products using other technologies. For example, a company faced with a process technology inadequacy in its own operations may not be able to find a ready-made solution in the products available from equipment suppliers. Faced with this situation the company may develop new process technology and then contract with a manufacturer to produce equipment for it based on that technology. Subsequently, the manufacturer may go on to exploit this technology more widely by incorporating it in production equipment which the manufacturer markets. In this case the entrepreneurial activity is confined solely to the equipment supplier and the originator of the technology restricts itself to internal exploitation.

Foxall et al.,[8] drawing on earlier work by Von Hippel,[9] distinguish between this approach and that of a more entrepreneurial originating company. The entrepreneurial approach involves the company in seeking patent protection for its technology and conducting market surveys to determine the technology's wider application. If the outcome is positive the company may negotiate licence deals with potential users of the technology or incorporate the technology into equipment which they either manufacture themselves or subcontract to others.

However, there are costs of contracting out which must be set against its more short-term benefits. These costs are that the exploiting company is less likely to invest in developing its own technologies in the contracted-out areas. It may be a sound strategy to rely on the technologies of others, but the effect can be a long-term dependence on the contractor and the loss of future opportunities. These costs highlight the need for a strategic approach to external exploitation and are further emphasised because expedient contracting out in one area can mean that a company fails to achieve economies of scale in the use of its own support technologies. The 'domino effect' can lead to further restriction of the company's investment in those areas. This problem is often seen in the area of process technology. If a company starts to use contracted manufacture, this can lead in stages to withdrawal from all manufacture as each remaining manufacturing process is seen to be less viable because of reduced scale and, more importantly, because of reduced investment. In this way, the company can lose its core process technology and through strategic drift simply become a distributor of other companies' products.

If it is strategically appropriate to enter into a contracted-out method of technology exploitation, this decision should be taken after a clear audit of the company's technologies and subsequent decisions about which areas of technology it is appropriate to invest in. Because of this, any decision to contract out the use of a technology is likely to be long term. In this case the human resource issues centre on the development of a partnership culture between the companies as opposed to a short-term antagonistic relationship.

Example
Contracting out and entrepreneurship:
British Aerospace

British Aerospace set up a Business Development Group charged with the external exploitation of new technology generated within the business. The responsibilities of the group include:

- the identification of internally-generated processes and products which have potential for successful commercialisation;
- the protection of the company's intellectual property in these items through patents and copyrights;
- the identification and evaluation of firms which are capable of co-developing,

manufacturing and marketing the resulting products;

- the assessment of potential markets, in conjunction with those responsible for the invention and application of the technology as a process innovation so that any unique qualities and/or user benefits can be speedily identified, adding to the possibility of successfully concluding a profitable licensing deal with an equipment manufacturer;
- the negotiation of licensing arrangements on the basis of market knowledge gained through the preceding stage and the administration of agreements concluded with outside companies.

Among the examples which Foxall *et al.* give of the system in practice are of an ultrasonic test probe developed to identify structural flaws in such materials as carbon fibre composites and a two-tool robot used in aircraft manufacture. This robot combines the tasks of drilling a hole and inserting a rivet, thereby increasing the accuracy of construction which had previously been easily lost when the operation was carried out by two machines. In both cases the British Aerospace engineers identified their own need for the equipment and suggested a possible solution to the company's suppliers. The company financed and shared development of the equipment by the suppliers and both are named on the patents as co-inventors. The suppliers market the equipment under formal licence agreements with British Aerospace.

A third example is of a computer programme used in the operation of numerically controlled machines. This software was initially purchased by the company, but drastically altered by its engineers. The company has obtained the rights to the marketing of this altered programme which has been purchased by a number of aircraft manufacturers. The Business Development Group has concluded agreements with a computer bureau and a software firm for the wider dissemination of the programme. The bureau pays royalties to the company, based on clients' use of the programme and the software company pays royalties based on the sales of sub-licences.

(Taken fom Foxall et al.[10])

Consortia

Consortia represent an approach to strategic external exploitation on a much greater scale. For example, the planned consortium between Boeing and the companies which comprise Airbus Industries, for a stretched version of the Boeing 747 owes its origin to the fact that the required scale of investment is beyond the resources of either of the two companies or their supporting governments. Unfortunately, many consortia are effectively 'shot-gun marriages' into which companies are forced by inadequacies in their resources or because there are no other partners, all other potential partners having already joined rival consortia. Therefore, the relationship between the parties may lack the critical success factor of shared values and common mission that are necessary to reproduce the 'clan-culture' found in far-eastern consortia, which have the advantage of long-term acculturisation between the partners. Any consortia involves costs for the individual members. The skills and technologies which are developed within the consortia may have value only in that context and not in any wider market. Perhaps even more significantly, the company may lose control or lead in distinctive technologies, either by their acquisition by partners or by the fact that they do not form part of the technologies for which the company is responsible in the consortia.

The far-eastern consortia avoid a number of these problems and also achieve further advantages. As Lei and Slocum point out,[11] member companies' stock holdings are distributed across group companies. Therefore, there is little external financial pressure to achieve short-term financial results and so the consortia are uniquely positioned to share the risks of investment in high-risk, high-technology projects. Their diversification also reduces risk and the commonality of culture provides for effective transfer of technologies acquired in one application to other and seemingly distant areas. At the same time, the long-term buyer–seller relationships between constituent companies provide a measure of security, subject to long-term performance and, more importantly, an improved allocation of the technological load between buyer and seller.

ACQUISITION OF TECHNOLOGY FOR EXTERNAL EXPLOITATION

A logical development of the external exploitation of technologies which a company develops for its own internal use is to develop technologies specifically for external exploitation. Yet, this is a relatively rare occurrence. The obvious questions are 'Why?' and following from this, 'Are there occasions when development specifically for external exploitation might be appropriate?'

In order to make sense of these questions we need to revisit the technology life cycle (Chapter 4). We have noted how important and difficult it is to make sure that the right long-term factors are brought into play when decisions are taken to continue the development of a technology and to target it at specific applications. We have said that these decisions are not the prerogative of R&D staff alone, but must also involve those who have responsibility for exploiting the companies technologies and those responsible for the other technologies which form part of the bundle for any application. All organisations face increasing difficulty in funding the growing acquisition costs for those technologies which have been identified as critical to their future. This problem is compounded by the strong tendency in many companies to spread their acquisition activity too broadly and not to take advantage of external methods of acquisition, including close co-operation with others. In circumstances where there is a restricted voice for those with a wider view of technology exploitation and a shortage of funds, it is not surprising that companies rarely develop technologies solely for external exploitation.

Another issue also argues against development for external exploitation. We have noted that in the early stages of its life cycle a technology will have little external value until it has been proved in application and unless the necessary support technologies are available. Therefore, unless a technology has internal use it is unlikely to be developed. Those technologies with immediately apparent external value are often sold early and for little reward, certainly when compared to their value if proved and packaged with appropriate support technologies.

The above calls for an evaluation of the external value of a technology early in its development. This evaluation should include the prospects for its exploitation if it were further developed, packaged or proved in application. Only if such a wider view is taken can the external exploitation alternatives of direct sale, licence or joint venture be considered. Finally, irrespective of which functions are involved in this evaluation, it should not be carried out in narrow financial terms. Externally exploiting a new technology with no apparent internal value may be a risky way of tying up large amounts of financial and managerial resources. It may also provide the opportunity for new strategic direction for the company. If such a technology were exploited externally, perhaps in co-operation with a partner, it may lead to the acquisition of new skills and market opportunities which could transform a company having only a narrow view of its direction.

CONCLUSIONS

In this chapter we have dealt with the constituents of technology strategy, before turning to the issue of overall management, organisation and strategy formulation in the next chapter. The external exploitation of technology is no different to internal exploitation, or to acquisition, in requiring a strategic approach if the company is to avoid the dangers of short-termism, technological 'leakage' to a partner, loss of control or devaluation of technology through misuse. The time during which a company is able to exploit a technology externally is limited. Its external value will decline rapidly as other companies devote themselves to reverse engineering its innovative products, low-cost producers copy its process skills and marketers seek to emulate its customer appeal. External exploitation should not be regarded as just the source of windfall profits on top of the internal use of a technology. Instead, it is an intrinsic, part of the company's task to fully exploit its expensively acquired technological assets, even though it is frequently undervalued, mis-understood and neglected.

External exploitation provides a window of time during which a company can use the revenue it generates to acquire and develop subsequent generations of technologies and the necessary support technologies for its future. Unconsidered and opportunistic external exploitation can mean that the company is selling its seed-corn. Well thought out external exploitation can be a major source of revenue and an opportunity to acquire far more than is lost, through well-managed relationships with other companies.

Example
External technology exploitation: American Airlines

American Airlines faces major competitive problems which have led to large-scale redundancies and financial losses. As well as the conventional problems caused by low or negative growth rates brought about by the recession, passengers now require low, long-distance fares and the convenience of interconnecting flights. Only global mega-carriers will be able to provide these and this has led to a rash of strategic alliances between companies. US airlines are at a disadvantage in this new environment because foreign competitors already have a network of international routes and many also have the advantage of highly regulated and protected home markets.

American Airlines strategy in this situation is not to follow competition in the race to achieve globalisation. Instead, it has assessed its technological position and is seeking to externally exploit a number of its technologies. Already its computer-reservations system, SABRE is the world's most successful and is used by travel agents in sixty-four countries and has been sold as a tool for internal scheduling to fifty other airlines. American Airlines has now begun to externally exploit a number of the other process technologies in which it has achieved distinctiveness: its expertise in handling busy telephone switchboards is being sold to telemarketing businesses; a huge clerical operation which can punch the data from 95 million tickets a year into computers is being customised for use in the healthcare industry; yield management systems, designed to maximise the revenues from every flight by American are being sold to new customers, from France's state-owned railways to Club Meditérranée.

This external exploitation is achieving growth rates of 20–40 per cent per annum and Michael Durham, AMR's treasurer says that average profit margins for these services are 15–20 per cent, on total 1992 revenues of $300–400 million. This excludes $700 million from SABRE's sales to the travel trade on which margins are thought to be higher. These revenues are tiny compared to those generated by the airline business, although the profits they produce are not. Passenger and cargo revenue accounted for 90 per cent of the group's $10.8 billion in sales during the first nine months of 1992. Analysts at Goldman Sachs forecast that American Airlines could earn nearly $500 million from service business in 1993.

However, despite the apparent oddity of running $12 billion worth of assets as a loss-leader for its external sales of technology, the company has no plans to cut back on its airline operations. Without the continuing technological investment in its own operations, the company would be unlikely to retain its lead in the systems and technologies on which its external sales are based.

(Developed from *The Economist*, 70–71, 19 December 1992)

REFERENCES

1   Reich, R. and Mankin, E. D. (1986) 'Joint-ventures with Japan give away our future', *Harvard Business Review*, March–April: 78–86.
2   Hamel, G., Doz, Y. and Prahalad, C. K. (1989) 'Collaborate with your competitors and win', *Harvard Business Review*, January–February: 133–39.
3   Ibid.
4   Reich and Mankin, 'Joint-ventures with Japan'.
5   Peters, T. and Waterman, R. (1982) *In Search of Excellence*, New York: Harper & Row.
6   Kiotabe, M. (1992) *Global Sourcing Strategy*, New York: Quorum Books, p. 205.
7   Lei, D. and Slocum, J. W. (1991) 'Global strategic alliances: payoffs and pitfalls', *Organizational Dynamics*, **19**, Winter: 44–62.
8   Foxall, G., Murphy, F. S. and Tierney, J. (1985) 'Market development in practice: a case study of user-initiated product innovation', *Journal of Marketing Management*, **1**(3): 201–11.
9   Von Hippel, E. (1977) 'Transferring process equipment from user-innovators to equipment manufacturing firms', *R&D Management* **8**(1): 13–22; Von Hippel, E. (1982) 'Get new products from customers', *Harvard Business Review*, **60**(2): 117–22.
10 Foxall, G., Murphy, F. S. and Tierney, J., 'Market development in practice'.
11 Lei, D. and Slocum, J. W., 'Global strategic alliances', art. cit.

Chapter 10

The management of technology

INTRODUCTION

This chapter looks at the third element of technology strategy; the management of technology. Throughout this book when examining the acquisition and exploitation of technology we have looked at individual aspects of this management task. We have also emphasised the importance of a strategic approach to the acquisition and exploitation of technology. The need to analytically separate acquisition and exploitation does not mean that they are separate in practice and our examples illustrate the interrelationship between the two. But if an integrated approach is to occur, a company needs a culture, organisation and procedures to facilitate it. This chapter looks at some of the key ingredients in creating such a company:

1 How a strategic vision can be developed for a company on the basis of its human and technological assets, the world in which it operates and the opportunities which it faces.
2 How an organisation can be created which can achieve long-term innovation.
3 The procedures for integrating a technological perspective into a company's decision-making and for developing a strategy for technology itself.
4 The methods of transferring technologies acquired in any one area of a company's operations to other areas where they can contribute to success.

CORPORATE VISION AND TECHNOLOGY STRATEGY

The term 'corporate vision' is used widely and often synonomously with terms such as 'mission', 'objectives', 'purpose', 'values', 'strategic intent', etc.[1] It has many elements, of which three are critical for the management of a company's technology: the first is a clarity of understanding of the company's identity and direction which includes an understanding of its technological assets as well as its market and financial position, and that this understanding is spread widely throughout the business; the second is a coherent approach to the encouragement and management of innovation inside the company, and the translation of that innovation into new business; the third is that the company must have the will and backing to adhere to, or to modify that vision over the long term.

Clarity of identity and direction

The concept of strategic intent was introduced into the literature by Hamel and Prahalad[2] to describe a characteristic of some companies that had achieved results which would have seemed beyond their resources and capabilities when their goals were initially set.[3] Clarity of intent and approach in corporate direction cuts across conventional formulas for strategic success and sound strategic vision can outweigh the advantages of competitors with what appears to be a technological headstart.

This has been well illustrated by Joseph Morone.[4] He has pointed out that in the development of the modern consumer electronics industry, companies with inferior technological abilities succeeded in using technology for strategic advantage. In the decades after the Second World War, General Electric and RCA were technological leaders, yet it was Sony, Matsushita and JVC who used technology to achieve market leadership. Morone takes the same view as that of Rosenbloom and Abernathy[5] who suggest that part of the reason for this stems from a fundamental divergence in how the different companies viewed their businesses. To firms like Sony, consumer electronics was a high-technology, consumer-oriented business, whereas to RCA and others in the USA it was a mature business for which technology no longer offered much leverage. As one US executive put it, 'The standing orders from the television division were to offer them "any new technology available, as long as it gets cost out of the product".'[6]

The successful firms in video recording perceived the opportunity which the technology represented, '15 years before the market could be tapped' and persisted despite near-term failures to develop a technology 'whose commercial benefits were distant in time and highly uncertain'.[7] In contrast, RCA became preoccupied instead by more immediate challenges from firms such as Zenith, Texas Instruments and IBM in businesses far more important to the company's short-term competitive position at the time. Clarity of vision was apparent at Sony where, 'top managers explicitly and consistently guided the direction of (video technology) development efforts. At Ampex, top management direction was sporadic and inconsistent over time; engineers on their own failed to develop a fruitful direction for technical development.'[8]

However, a strategic vision for technology is unlikely to either develop through a conventional planning process or be codified in financial documentation. According to Bela Gold, decisions on strategic technological investments are more often rooted in basic philosophical commitments rather than analytical procedures. This is illustrated by the following enlightening anecdote from a research project.

The director of manufacturing technology supported a proposal for major new facilities with comprehensive estimates of investment requirements, operating costs and projected revenues. This was dismissed by the capital allocations official as, 'nothing more than unreliable guesses which could not justify the large investments involved'. But he then added, 'tell me why the company needs to make such an investment in order to safeguard its future competitiveness'. This company consistently allocates 15–20 per cent of its capital expenditures to projects which are too new to permit realistic analysis of prospective returns, but which seem to be of major future promise.[9]

THE MANAGEMENT OF INNOVATION

We should emphasise that this process of speculative investment is not something which is intended to bring comfort to a half-serious senior management which in the mean time concentrates on the 'real job' of current activities. Instead, the evaluation of and commitment to innovation must be part of a coherent approach to the encouragement and management of innovation inside the company and the translation of that innovation into new business. One view of the ingredients of this approach comes from the work of Burgelman[10] and are summarised as follows.

A company must reconcile the two issues of diversity and order in its activities. Diversity is the product of autonomous strategic initiatives from managers at the operational level. Middle-level managers play a role in supporting these initiatives; developing strategies for them and combining them with supporting capabilities which may exist elsewhere in the organisation. Order comes about by the company imposing a concept of strategy on the organisation. Top management's contribution consists of recognising how initiatives may fit into strategic direction, rather than in detailed planning, and controlling the emphasis on diversity, order and the rate of change over time.

Burgelman makes the important distinction between autonomous and induced strategic behaviour. Autonomous strategic behaviour arises from within the company, is untidy and produces diversity which does not fit easily into a formalised strategy development process. Induced strategic behaviour results from a conventional strategy process. Induced behaviour is likely to produce incremental change and may be appropriate for those situations where a company is seeking innovation around a single core technology. It is unlikely to produce corporate entrepreneurship. Indeed the structural context of conventional strategic planning is likely to reduce the prospect of true diversity by eliminating 'errors' in induced strategic behaviour so that it conforms with the company's current strategy.

The process of corporate innovation requires not only the commitment of the operational initiator, but also the contribution of strategic management to promote the internal and external momentum for an innovative venture. Strategic management must provide for the development of an administrative framework for the innovation. This framework will need to involve an approach which diverges from the sequential, ordered problem-solving[11] which breaks down problems to their constituent parts, and analyses and solves them sequentially.

Instead, the company must learn from Japanese experience to use a form of organisational chaos to generate problems and additional (or redundant) information.[12] This is as a precursor to an interactive approach to development by groups which cut across conventional functions and hierarchies.[13]

> The organisation that has thoroughly eliminated chaos is a bureaucracy. For an organisation to evolve constantly, chaos must be actively generated to expand the possibility of taking in chance information. And at the same time, diverse systems and modes of behaviour that will inevitably connect these must be allowed to exist.[14]

Strategic management must also integrate different operational initiatives and build bridges between specific ventures and general corporate interests in an area. Finally, strategic management can avoid the proliferation of a growing number of unrelated ventures and provide a focus of attention on critical major fields in which innovative ventures can be expanded or grouped together.[15] None of this means that the responsibility for innovation can be abrogated by senior management. It is their task to develop vision, establish direction and strategic intent or aspiration level.[16,17]

Example
Top management roles in technology strategy: Burmah Castrol

The complexity of technologies, products and markets faced by many firms requires structures and management arrangements that are able to cope with rapid change. A major lubricants manufacturer has created new roles and structures with this aim foremost.

Burmah Castrol see themselves as quite different from other oil companies in terms of their strategic approach to technology and the entrepreneurial slant of their personnel. As evidence they cite their ability to respond rapidly to new customer requirements for individual products or combinations of products and services. In senior managers' opinions, a central enabling factor is the web of relationships between operating firms and central supporting functions. A largely devolved structure is used, with a matrix of supporting services. Their global markets are grouped into four regions to which the many individual operating companies report, each headed by a regional line director.

The other axis of the matrix is the central support infrastructure, whose role is characterised as 'co-ordination, advise, consent'. The two key functions are Marketing, which handles brand policy, image identification, corporate publicity, etc., together with guidance on operations and distribution. In order to enable a constant stream of new products and processes there is also a Technology function, with resources based at a Group Technology Centre (actually using three locations in the UK, Germany and the USA).

With no illusions about the potential co-ordination problems, Burmah Castrol have adopted an unusual managerial approach. A single main board director is responsible for both of these portfolios. Knowing that the development of new technology and its effective exploitation cannot be separated, they have at the same time formally linked the two areas and signalled their importance at the highest level.

VISION AND LONG-TERM INNOVATION

A particularly difficult issue for many companies to overcome is the time horizon needed to acquire and exploit major new technologies. Eight or ten years is common before radical innovations generate accounting profits and smaller innovations typically take two to five years from initiation to first cash flow. This inevitably causes problems for managers whose pay is linked to reported profits and for whom job rotation is perhaps every two years. It also causes problems for companies attempting long-term innovation and which face the tyranny of quarterly reports. In a UK study of 246 managers, two-thirds believed that the capital market values companies by reference to the current year's prospective earnings.[18] Similarly, Thurow has argued that these short-term pressures to have ever-rising quarterly profits are more intense in the USA than elsewhere. He notes that R&D spending in the USA is, for example, cyclical – falling in recessions and rising in booms. This is a pattern which he says is not observed elsewhere.[19]

But accounting practices themselves can also affect managers' decisions. The problem is that research and development and investments in advertising and training, which have been incurred at least partly to enhance future profits, are charged to the profit and loss account. Pressure for this in the UK probably followed the collapse in the 1970s of Rolls-Royce whose profits were inflated through the capitalisation of the R&D costs of its major investments in the RB 211 engine for use in the new generation of wide-bodied airliners. Although it may be prudent to write off research expenditure, company managers are so cautious that innovation is restricted.[20] The same survey found that 80 per cent of UK finance managers look for profit from investment in innovative projects within three years and only 4 per cent would be prepared to wait more than five years for a return. The study also concludes that this cautious approach to investment is not unrelated to corporate willingness to acquire companies instead of building them.

Quinn's large-scale study of large innovative firms concluded that all of them had found ways of overcoming the problem of short-term pressures.[21] In some of the firms the nature of their products creates a long-term view, such as in the case of aircraft manufacture, pharmaceuticals, public utilities, etc. However, Quinn indicates that not all companies with a long-time horizon are innovative and long-time horizons alone do not lead to innovativeness. He suggests that success comes from the fact that a few key individuals have a broad vision of what their organisations can accomplish for the world, that they have a strong market orientation at the top of the organisation and explicit mechanisms to force market-technical interactions lower down. It is the clarity of approach and focus, and the ability to communicate this to institutions, which can help to obtain the 'patient money' required for long-term success in acquiring and exploiting technology.[22]

TECHNOLOGICAL PERSPECTIVE, TECHNOLOGY STRATEGY AND BUSINESS STRATEGY

Throughout this book we have taken the view that the core of a company is its technologies; what it knows and what it can do rather than its products and its markets. The firm is an 'intellectual holding company'[23] so a prime management task is the development and full use of those intellectual or technological resources – often expressed as the core competencies or capabilities of the company. We have emphasised that technologies form the basis of core competencies, but they are in themselves simply passive resources until they are activated by the company. This activation of technological resources often occurs through interaction with other companies to satisfy the requirements of those companies or of a final market. Therefore, it is the ability to activate particular resources as well as the resources themselves which constitute core competencies for a company.[24]

In the short term, the task of technology strategy is to recognise the technological resources of the company – product, process and marketing – and to identify those which are basic and distinctive, when compared to those of other companies in the network that surrounds it. The technology strategy task is also to understand the requirements of different markets or applications for the company's technologies. The task is then to exploit these resources through assembling and directing a bundle of internal technologies with external technologies and to direct these technologies to chosen applications. If the company achieves these tasks then it will have built a core competency based on those technologies. Making the choice of which core competencies the company will seek to build is the point at which overall business strategy meets technology strategy.

In the longer term, the task of technology strategy is to build the company's technological base through the acquisition of appropriate technologies. The important issue here is that the company must have for this technology strategy a framework which sets an overall direction for the long-term acquisition and exploitation of its technologies. The acquisition of technologies and the skills in exploiting them will not be sufficient for corporate success. The second point at which business strategy meets technology strategy occurs because business strategy is concerned with the establishment of the objectives for competence-building through the development of what has been referred to as 'strategic focus' or 'strategic architecture'. Morone points out that in the three companies in his study which had used technology successfully, a strategic focus has been articulated consistently and applied for decades:

> This consistently pursued and explicitly articulated business focus had a dramatic effect on technology development . . . It created a context for technology development so that opportunities that fit the focus tend to be pursued with vigor, while those that fall outside are usually ignored.[25]

Morone's examples of focus include Corning's $100 million, 15-years pursuit of optical fibre business as a major opportunity to exploit its glass and ceramics technology and Motorola's $150 million over the same time-frame to develop cellular phones as part of its specific focus on, 'communications with people and machines on the move'. Prahalad and Hamel argue that the development of strategic architecture should make resource allocation clearer, by identifying which core competencies the company must build and what are their constituent technologies.[26] Nor does this process end at the stage of technology development. These technologies in turn form the generic basis or 'platforms' for the successive generations of products which are the final implementation of corporate strategy.[27]

The argument as to whether strategic focus is, or should be, led by the market, driven by the company's technology or simply be the result of corporate ambition is somewhat sterile and we leave it to others. What is clear is that technology strategy cannot be developed in a vacuum away from overall strategic direction nor can technologies themselves provide corporate salvation. The example below shows how the development of technologies and their management must take place within the context of an understanding of the core competence that the company has and wishes to extend.

Example
Customer-focused technology strategy

This example illustrates how a fundamental concern in the strategic management of technology is to effectively apply the company's technologies to customers' problems and to efficiently and effectively transfer resources inside the company to solve those problems.

The company manufactures and markets consumable products used by the engineering industry. It was previously organised in regional divisions which had the freedom to develop product plans separately. This led to diversification into some surprising areas such as coal-mining consumables and artificial coals for gas fires. It also led to duplication of technical effort. For example, the North American and European divisions at one point sold quite different products fulfilling an identical role in one end-use market. The European product was developed by company's UK technical centre, while the American operations licensed in an equivalent product designed by a competitor.

Recently, a more global approach to organisation has been adopted, with Technical and Marketing Directors fulfilling worldwide co-ordinating roles for the national operating companies. The company has identified its strategic focus as:

The key to continued success is the company's marketing network worldwide, in particular the profound knowledge of customer operations and requirements gained through relationships developed over many years. As new customer requirements are identified a search for relevant technologies is undertaken. Whether this technology comes from internal sources, from suppliers or partners is seen as a secondary consideration compared to the company's ability to bundle together products and services to uniquely meet the requirement. In order to gain access to others' relevant technologies, the company can use its strong market position as leverage. However, it must also retain strong technological capabilities in certain areas to allow the 'trading' of technologies and products with other major manufacturers.

In order to protect the uniqueness of offerings while streamlining the bundling process, the company is putting significant resources into the development of software tools for the definition of individual requirements using standard elements (which in some cases are effectively commodities). An internal debate continues as to whether such tools constitute 'technology or marketing'.

How far this overall approach can be applied depends in part upon national and individual customer characteristics. For example, US customers are keen to minimise fixed plant costs; as a result the company can take on a 'facilities management' role, effectively running aspects of the customers' operations and building the costs into the prices of the consumables used. In contrast, Japanese customers prefer to buy on a 'jobbing shop' basis, as they are technically advanced and see no need for such value-added service bundles. Because of these variations, further changes in structure are under consideration. For example, should applications areas be managed through an international product management structure, or centralised within the technical function?

These national differences also strongly affect the management and internal transfer of individual technologies. In the mid-1980s, a key company product was a large, but replaceable component used in an industrial process and for which the company was the European market-leader. This product had to be constructed at the customer's site and labour costs were high.

In 1989, however, a competitor launched a new product which had much lower production costs and which also eliminated on-site installation costs. (The company itself had already developed an equivalent product but had withheld it from the market, because of the threat it posed both to margins and to its investment in its manufacturing plant.) The new product was initially launched in Germany at a 20 per cent lower price and it decimated the company's sales there and subsequently in other European markets. In response, the company's German operations launched its own version of the new product. While the initial intention in the UK market was to defend its existing product 'to the hilt' it soon became clear that significant sales would be lost to the new competitor and that the new technology would have to be transferred from Germany to the UK.

Two problems quickly became apparent. The first was the conventional problem that the company found the new technology needed more development if it was to successfully penetrate the market. However, the unsuccessful trials also exposed a more fundamental difficulty. The structure of the firm at that time meant that the 'donor' company had no incentive to transfer its technology effectively. Indeed, the performance measures used encouraged it to maximise its profit on the transaction by marking up materials and machinery prices. Only in this way could it gain a return on its initial development costs. Thus costs were obscured and the recipient's margins were heavily eroded.

The lessons of this episode were taken on board when other markets required the transfer of the now fully developed technology. Transfer mechanisms are being developed centrally. Most importantly, the 'tension' between operating companies has been removed by no longer including technical development costs in performance measurement within regions. Incentives are now in place to encourage managers to think regionally rather than nationally. Work continues on the development of 'global' co-ordination mechanisms which will encourage local creativity while ensuring that individual innovations are applied wherever they will bring benefits.

MANAGING INTERNAL TECHNOLOGY TRANSFER

All companies face the problem of acquiring new technologies. They also face the problem of making the best use of those technologies which they have acquired inside their organisations. In a typical large company, a new technology may be developed internally or acquired by a wide range of operating units, but that single technology is unlikely to lead to commercial success unless it can be bundled together with the necessary support technologies. Additionally, the originating unit may be unaware of the potential applications for the technology if these lie outside its normal sphere of operations. The company could also use up resources and time in developing these necessary support technologies or go to market with a total offering which is inferior because the necessary technologies are not included, even if they exist elsewhere in the company, simply because the originators didn't know of their existence. These problems are all manifestations of the more general difficulty that companies have in internal technology transfer.

We have earlier described the technology exploitation task as that of maximising the return on the company's technological assets and relating these to its market opportunities. Internal transfer means that the company is able to bring to bear all of the appropriate resources it can command, from wherever they exist in the company, to address an identified opportunity. Second, internal transfer can mean that the company will be able to address an opportunity which otherwise it would have to ignore because the necessary technology was not immediately available.

Improvement in the management of the internal transfer of a company's technology may require changes in the company's organisation, reward systems and procedures. The example indicates how current reward systems can emphasise exploitation of a technology within a single national market and within an originator's narrow applications, rather than more broadly across other markets or company units. Prahalad and Hamel have also emphasised that the common strategic business unit (SBU) form of organisation tends to 'lock-in' competences in individual units. Competencies are corporate assets and must be used wherever required.[28] They cite the example of when Canon identified an opportunity in digital laser printers, the managers involved were given the right to raid other SBUs for the staff who had the technologies required to build an offering.

More generally, the use of the strategic technology area (STA) approach which we have advocated in this book can assist the process of internal transfer of technology. You will recall that the STA approach means that the unit of analysis in the planning process is the combination of a bundle of technologies and their application. The managers responsible for each STA are likely to be closely aware of the current position of their technologies and the technological dynamics in the rest of the company. This is because they are charged with managing the evolution of the technologies they employ and with searching both inside and outside the company for appropriate new ones. An initial and continuing technology audit in the company and an STA approach will enable the company's technological stock and its standing to be made explicit, approximating to a technological library.

Finally, a serious impediment to internal technology transfer is difficulty in communication. This seems to be particularly acute during the technology development process. In Kodak's Imaging Group organisation, the core technology development work is carried out at a central laboratory. It serves as a base from which all business units may draw technology. Specific product development is then carried out at each business unit. But the additional capabilities that these units develop may not be fed back to the centre.[29] Grandstrand and Sjolander[30] found similar problems in a division of Saab-Scania which was established in part to capitalise on and exploit new technologies from inside and outside the group. They plotted a dramatic increase in the communication patterns between various operating units and between them and the centre after the introduction of a spectrum of technology transfer policies and routines. These included:

- the formulation, communication and implementation of technology transfer routes;
- the appointment of 'lead houses' and 'lead individuals' in prioritised key technology areas;
- implementing incentive schemes for group and company management as well as for lead engineers;
- creating a strategic intercompany joint technology development fund managed by the chief executive and the technology transfer manager;
- focused seminars in key technology areas;
- establishing payment routines for internal consultation and the transfer of key technologists between companies in the group;
- creating and communicating an internal policy guide aimed at facilitating a common language and culture.

MANAGING PROCESS TECHNOLOGY

Throughout this book we have emphasised the similarity in importance and mutual dependence of the three areas of technology; product, process and marketing. We have included marketing as a technology partially to stress that it is a set of resources which require long-term development and which are capable of wide exploitation in the same way as the other two technologies, and partly because of the vital element which marketing forms in the bundle of technologies necessary for any application. On many occasions we have used product technologies for illustration and this may have further fuelled the common belief that product technologies are what really count and that process technology is merely an enabling factor in their commercialisation. In contrast, we wish to emphasise the fact that each of the ideas we have discussed in the acquisition and exploitation of technology is equally applicable to all of the three areas of technology. Failure to have a coherent strategy for the acquisition of process technology can be at least as damaging as a similar failure in the area of product technology. Likewise, failure to fully exploit a company's process (or marketing) technologies is just as much a loss of return on capital expenditure as is a missed opportunity to exploit a product technology in a new application.

As long ago as 1969 Wickham Skinner argued that process choice was a key element in competitive strategy.[31] Because no factory is able to cope equally effectively with different production processes – whether large or small batch or continuous process, limited line and low-cost or a wide variety of tailored products – it should not passively receive the instructions from those who develop products or identify market requirements and simply throw these requirements 'over the wall' to manufacturing, irrespective of how they fit with the company's installed abilities. If it does then the company will pay the penalty in higher costs, reduced flexibility or reduced quality. However, this approach to manufacturing is widespread and is described by Steven Wheelwright as 'static optimization':

process evolution in many firms and industries is considered of secondary importance . . . Processes are developed, not in anticipation of new product opportunities, but only as required by the pricing realities of the marketplace (costs must be lowered) or the product characteristics as defined by R&D (the existing process can't be used to make the new product) . . . Because little advance thought has been given to process evolution, manufacturing naturally turns to the 'experts' – the equipment suppliers . . . Thus, the expertise for process technology resides outside the organisation.'[32]

Thus, in our terms manufacturing becomes an external technology. In this situation the company has effectively contracted out of any chance of a long-term position of distinctiveness in a key area of its operations. On one level this is an argument for the involvement of process technologists in the strategy development programme so that product and market plans can be related to process capabilities. Although this involvement is important and serves the goals of shorter product development and introduction times, it still consigns process technology to a passive box where it is at the service of other supposedly more strategic or creative functions. At a second level, if the company is conscious of the distinctiveness it (still) has in its process technologies then it can build its strategy so that its product and marketing technologies and programmes are constructed to exploit this process distinctiveness. Even more importantly, at a third level, investment in process technology can form the basis of future strategic architecture for the company. Instead of being entirely in the short-term reactive mode, the long-term development of process technology can lead to major core competence for the company.

Example
Developing process distinctiveness: Lucas Industries

A fascinating example of the long-term development of process distinctiveness as part of overall strategy is provided by Lucas Industries a UK aerospace and automotive components manufacturer.

In the 1970s Lucas faced unions with a fearsome reputation for militancy and the recession of 1980–81 caused the company to react by slashing its investment in development. This meant that when recovery came it had lost its position in markets where product innovation and process quality had become paramount. Major factors in the company's subsequent rebuilding have been its strong development in a number of product technologies. In aerospace it supplies the flaps which guide the Patriot missile and the engine management systems for Rolls-Royce. In automotive components it

produces the world's first electronically controlled diesel engine management system.

But Lucas has also built distinctiveness in its process technologies under its director of manufacturing technology, Dr John Parnaby. This manufacturing technology is now partially embodied in its Engineering and Systems business which employs 400 people. It's director, David Friday says that the company decided in the early 1980s that it needed to make a fundamental study of Japanese markets. His reasoning provides a striking similarity to that of Steven Wheelwright's and suggests that using external manufacturing technology and simply buying new machinery is doomed to failure when the real problem is that of developing internal distinctiveness in manufacturing technology: 'We didn't understand then that the Japanese were concentrated on the methodology of manufacturing – we were spending just as much.

There was a lot of hoo-hah about robots – by and large it was much simpler.'

Lucas still regularly sends engineering systems experts to Japan on study tours: 'The Japanese are very free and open about the process. They've learned that no matter what they tell us, we don't do it. Brits coming back fixated on quality circles, uniforms and PE – the trouble is, its all the other things as well.'

The company's success in building distinctiveness in its process technologies is illustrated by the fact that not only does Engineering and Systems carry out internal process consulting, but 25 per cent of its work is now from consultancy assignments outside the company and the business generates a sales volume of £23 million. However, the acquisition of distinctive process technology is not in itself the basis for success. Lucas has faced major difficulties in transferring those technologies around inside its operations and in dealing with customers who themselves have not adopted innovative ideas on scheduling.

As in the case of product technology, the quest for process distinctiveness must be long term and requires the same commitment and strategic intent.[33,34]

CONCLUSIONS

This chapter has opened the wide door of corporate strategic vision and barely ventured inside. It has omitted a wide range of issues that could very properly be considered as part of the management of technology. Thus, we have not dealt with the impact of globalisation of business, the arguments as to whether markets can or should be treated as global entities and the implications of this for the development of technology strategy, for R&D location and for product sourcing. We have not examined the impact of the sum total of technology change on the environment and on employment practices. We have not considered the impact of government policy on the development of technology strategy, nor indeed what that policy should be. All of these are important topics, all are beyond the bounds of a single volume and a book which has been too long in gestation.

What we have tried to do in this chapter is to emphasise that the acquisition and exploitation of technology must take place within a strategic framework if it is to succeed. Technology strategy is one of the outcomes of overall strategy and is dependent for its direction and successful implementation on a strategic vision. Technology strategy is one of the ways in which overall strategy can be carried out, but it requires an organisation and a culture which encourages innovation and allows it to be transferred within the company. Technologies themselves are resources. Without them no distinctive competence can be built. They are not in themselves competences but can be translated into competences through activation by the company in interaction with others. Technology change is a social process which occurs through countless interactions within and outside the company. Manufacturing and marketing technologies in particular, even more than product technology, consist of the patterns of work, thinking, beliefs, attitudes and ideas of many people engaged in the company. Both are equally as vital as product technology to corporate success, and distinctiveness in all three can only be built over time.

REFERENCES

1 Collins, J. C. and Porras, J. I. (1991) 'Organisational vision and visionary organisations', *California Management Review*, Fall.

2 Hamel, G. and Prahalad, C. K. (1989) 'Strategic intent', *Harvard Business Review*, May–June: 63–76.

3 Przybylowicz, E. and Faulkner, T. W. (1993) 'Kodak supplies strategic intent to the management of technology', *Research Technology Management*, January–February: 31–38.

4 Morone, J. (1989) 'Strategic use of technology', *California Management Review*, Summer: 91–110.

5 Rosenbloom, R. S. and Abernathy, W. J. (1982) 'The climate for innovation in industry', *Research Policy*, **11**: 218.

6 Morone, J., 'Strategic use of technology', 100.

7 Rosenbloom and Abernathy, 'The climate for innovation in industry', 281.

8 Rosenbloom, R. S. and Cusumano, M. A. (1987) 'Technological pioneering and competitive advantage: the birth of the VCR industry', *California Management Review*, Summer: 68.

9 Gold, B. (1983) 'Strengthening managerial approaches to improving technological capabilities', *Strategic Management Journal*, **4**: 209–20.

10 Burgelman, R. (1983) 'Corporate entrepreneurship and strategic management: insights from a process study', *Management Science*, **29**(12), December: 1349–64.

11 Allen, T. J. (1966) 'Study of the problem-solving process in engineering design', *IEEE Transactions on Engineering Management*, June, cited by Nonaka, I. (1990) 'Redundant, overlapping organisation: a Japanese approach to managing the innovation process', *California Management Review*, Spring: 27–28.

12 Quinn, J. B. (1986) 'Innovation and corporate strategy, managed chaos', in M. Horwich (ed.), *Technology in the Modern Corporation*, New York: Pergamon.

13 Nonaka, I. (1990) 'Redundant, overlapping organization: a Japanese approach to managing the innovation process' *California Management Review*, Spring: 27–38.

14 Nonaka, I. and Yamanouchi, T. (1989) 'Managing as a self renewing process', *Journal for Business Venturing*, **4**: 307.

15 Burgelman, R. (1988) 'Strategy making as a social learning process: the case of internal corporate venturing', *Interfaces*, **18**(3): 74–85.

16 Prahalad, C. K. (1993) 'The role of core competences in the corporation', *Research Technology Management*, November–December: 40–47.

17 Przybylowicz, E. and Faulkner, T. W. (1993) 'Kodak supplies strategic intent', art. cit.

18 Collison, D., Grinyer, J. and Russell, A. (1993) *Management Economic Decisions and Financial Reporting*, London: Research Board, Institute of Chartered Accountants in England and Wales.

19 Thurow, L. C. (1987) 'A weakness in process technology', *Science*, 18 December: 1662.

20 *The Independent* (London), 1 March 1994.

21 Quinn, J. B. (1986) 'Innovation and corporate strategy', op. cit.

22 Morone, J. (1993) 'Technology and competitive advantage – the role of general management', *California Management Review*, March–April.

23 Quinn, J. B., Doorley, T. L. and Paquette, P. C. (1990) 'Technology in services: rethinking strategic focus', *Sloan Management Review*, Winter: 79–87.

24 Prahalad, C. K. (1993) 'The role of core competences in the corporation', art. cit.

25 Morone, 'Technology and competitive advantage', 24.

26 Prahalad, C. K. and Hamel, G. (1990) 'The core competences of the corporation', *Harvard Business Review*, May–June: 79–91.

27 Meyer, M. H. and Utterback, J. M. (1993) 'The product family and the dynamics of core capability', *Sloan Management Review*, Spring: 29–47.

28 Prahalad, C. K. and Hamel, G. (1990) 'The core competences of the corporation', art. cit.

29 Przybylowicz, E. and Faulkner, T. W. (1993) 'Kodak supplies strategic intent', art. cit.

30   Skinner, W. (1969) 'Manufacturing – missing link in corporate strategy', *Harvard Business Review*, May–June.
31   Ibid.
32   Wheelwright, S. C. (1985) 'Restoring the competitive edge in US manufacturing', *California Management Review*, **XXIV**(3), Spring: 30.
33   *Financial Times*, 26 May 1993.
34   Womack, J. P. and Jones, D. T. (1994) 'From lean production to the lean enterprise', *Harvard Business Review*, March–April: 93–103.

Chapter 11

Identifying and evaluating the options for technology strategy in specific situations

INTRODUCTION

Earlier chapters of this book are concerned with the overall analysis of a company's technology through use of a technology audit. The analysis has emphasised the importance of a strategic approach that recognises the interrelationships and inter-dependencies between different types of technologies; product, process and marketing and between the three activities of acquiring, managing and exploiting technology. In this overall analysis, customers' perceptions were expressed in terms of their view of the *distinctiveness* of a technology. Similarly, a company's markets were discussed in general terms as the *applications* of that technology.

This chapter complements this overall analysis by providing a procedure for analysing the *specific* product/service offerings based on a technology and their *position* in the minds of customers. It also examines the applications of a technology by looking at the *attractiveness* of *specific* markets and customers. The procedure relates ideas of product position and market and customer attractiveness to a company's technological *strength*. We believe that the overall analysis we have described in earlier chapters is a vital element in the development of technology strategy. But it needs to be complemented by analysis and planning at the level of specific technologies, products and applications. This is for at least two reasons: First, it is our experience that some companies find it intimidating or difficult to make an initial, comprehensive analysis of their technologies. Second, many companies have only a few technologies on which they depend or which are distinctive. This is particularly the case in many small and medium-sized firms and the analysis of specific technologies, products and markets described in this chapter will be appropriate to these companies and also to those embarking on the development of technology strategy for the first time.

The approach which is outlined here is developed from a methodology[1] which identifies the strategic options for each significant technology by evaluating their relative *strengths* in relation to the strengths of the product/service offerings that are based on them; the attractiveness of the customers to which these offerings are applied and the position of these offerings when compared with those of competitors.

CONSTRUCTING THE KEY POSITIONING MATRICES

Four key matrices form the basis of this analysis:

- Product positioning: This relates the *strength* of a product/service offering to the *attractiveness* of the market or application to which it is currently addressed.
- Customer positioning: This relates the *attractiveness* of individually significant supplier/customer relationships to market *attractiveness*.
- Technology positioning: This relates the *strength* of the company's technologies to customer *attractiveness*.
- Technology market positioning: This relates the *strength* of the company's technologies to market *attractiveness*.

The analysis starts by identifying the company's most important product offerings (or groups of products) and customers (or groups of customers) and then assesses the strength of those products and attractiveness of both significant individual customers and markets as a whole.[2] This process simplifies the task of identifying the technologies on which the company's operations depend and the overall strength of those technologies. The four steps leading to the construction of the matrices are described in more detail below.

Step 1 – Product Positioning

The *product positioning matrix* is designed to plot key product or service offerings on a two dimensional matrix of *product strength* against *market attractiveness*. The factors that comprise product strength will depend on a number of product, process and marketing technologies. The factors are shown in Table 11.1. The factors that comprise market attractiveness are shown in Table 11.2. The resulting product/market matrix will position each product in relation to its strength and the attractiveness of the market in which the product competes. The completed matrix will help to identify product strengths and weak-

Table 11.1 Product strength factors

• The product's market share	• Market experience/knowledge
• The product's stage of development or maturity	• Quality control
• Range of products of a particular type	• Product development skill
• Product adaptability to customer demand	• Company image
• Production costs	• Level of additional service & personnel
• Relationship management	• Additional product features
• Skills	
• Effective advertising/promotion	• Other company specified factors
• Production capacity	

Table 11.2 Market attractiveness factors

● Market size	● Socio-cultural considerations
● Market growth/maturity	● Political-legal considerations
● Market price structure	
● Competitive structure & entry/exit barriers	● Other company specified factors
● Macro-economic factors	

nesses, ultimately helping to determine the appropriate product marketing strategies. This analysis will need to be carried out for each major product group within a company.

Step 2 – Customer Positioning Matrix

The *customer positioning matrix* is designed to plot key customers or customer groups, on a two dimensional matrix of *customer attractiveness* against the already defined *market attractiveness*. The factors that comprise customer attractiveness are listed in Table 11.3. The customers to be considered here are primarily those of the products or services considered in Step 1. In order to limit the time involved in this analysis, it is useful to restrict the number of customers that are plotted. This can either be done on the basis of customers that are representative of different parts of the company's portfolio of relationships, or those that are significant relationships in themselves, in terms of sales or profit contribution or on other dimensions. This analysis can make a major contribution to the company's individual and overall relationship management strategy. For a detailed discussion of the issues of customer relationship management, see Ford *et al.*[3] The analysis of particular, named customers or types of customers also means that technology strategies can be developed with customers closely in mind.

Step 3 – Technology Positioning Matrix

The two previous steps will enable the company to document the conditions under which the various technologies it exploits relate to specific customers, markets and products. The third step is to assess the company's *technology strength* against the already defined *customer attractiveness*. Technology strength is an umbrella term describing each of the company's portfolio of technologies. It comprises a number of factors that have been discussed in earlier chapters. These factors are listed in Table 11.4. The *technology positioning matrix* will enable the user to see which technologies are strong and which are weak, clearly displaying this information in relation to the customers that each technology supports. The

Table 11.3 Customer attractiveness factors

● Contribution to profit/margins	● Long-term prospects of relationship
● Contribution to company technology development	● Relationship specific investments
	● Financial stability/reliability of customer/payment history
● Closeness of customer relationship	
● Potential effect of this relationship on development of others	
	● Other company specified factors

Table 11.4 Technology strength factors

• Category of technologies – basic, distinctive, external, internal	• Customers supported
• Company standing in this technology	• Strategic technology areas of which it is a constituent
• Technology life-cycle position	
• Products supported	• Other user specified factors

user should then be able to determine which technologies require increased effort in their exploitation or increased investment in their development. The company should also be in a position to form a strategy to decide which customer groups should be targeted and which technologies should be used. The analysis of technology strength involves the steps developed in the *technology audit* in Chapter 4 of this book for each significant product, process and marketing technologies of the company.

Step 4 – Technology Market Positioning

The three previous steps will have ensured that the user now has a clear picture of what technologies the organisation possesses or uses, what products and customers these technologies support and the strength of these technologies in the marketplace. The matrices developed in these steps are valuable in developing an overall understanding of technology/ product/market position and can assist the organisation to develop specific strategies for technology exploitation. The final step is to incorporate these into a market-technology positioning matrix as shown in Figure 11.4.

Figures 11.1–11.3 show the matrices of product strength against market attractiveness, customer attractiveness against market attractiveness and technology strength against customer attractiveness. The matrices are scored from high to low on each dimension. The matrices represent a direct link between the company's significant technologies and the associated markets in which they are applied, with products and customers acting as 'intermediaries' in that process. The logic of this approach has been developed earlier in this book and is that strategies for exploiting technologies should not be narrowly based on single products or customers, nor indeed on wholly internal exploitation in the company's own products or services. Instead, the company should consider the full range of strategic options for exploiting (and acquiring) each technology/product/market position identified by the matrices in Step 4.

This book has also emphasised that success in any market application depends on a bundle of product, process and marketing technologies, some of which will be held by the company itself (internal technologies) and some that will be held by others (external technologies). We have referred to this combination of technologies and market application as a *strategic technology area* (STA). Applying the framework developed here will most likely result in different strategies being adopted for each bundle of technologies and each market application. This is why it is important firstly to identify the *individually significant* technologies in the preceding stage of the analysis and to analyse each bundle separately, along with the existing products and markets that they support.

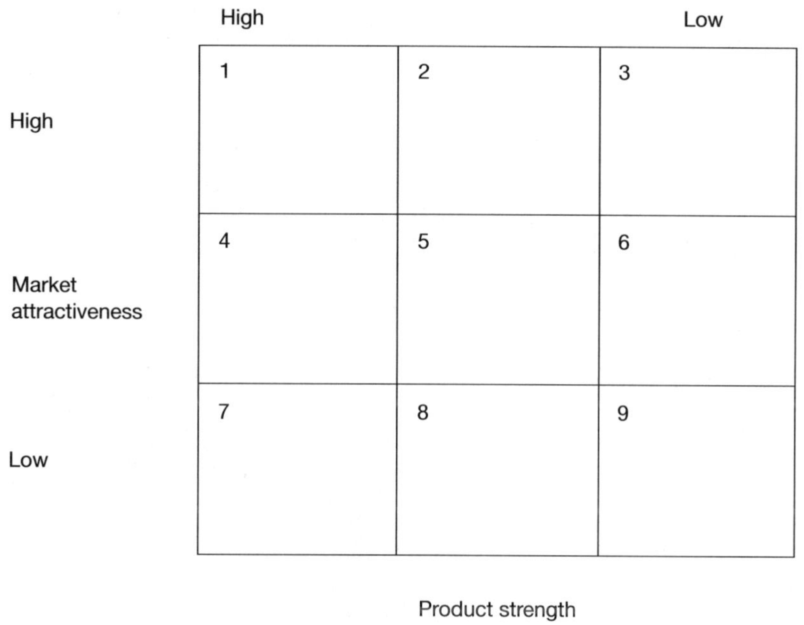

High   Low

1	2	3
4	5	6
7	8	9

High

Market
attractiveness

Low

Product strength

Figure 11.1 Product positioning

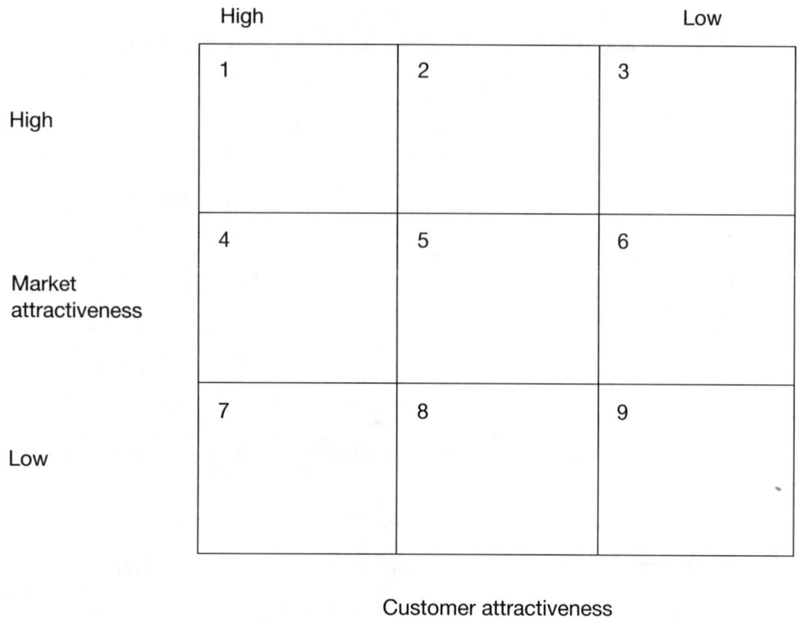

High   Low

1	2	3
4	5	6
7	8	9

High

Market
attractiveness

Low

Customer attractiveness

Figure 11.2 Customer positioning

High		Low
1	2	3
4	5	6
7	8	9

High

Technology
strength

Low

Customer attractiveness

Figure 11.3 Technology positioning

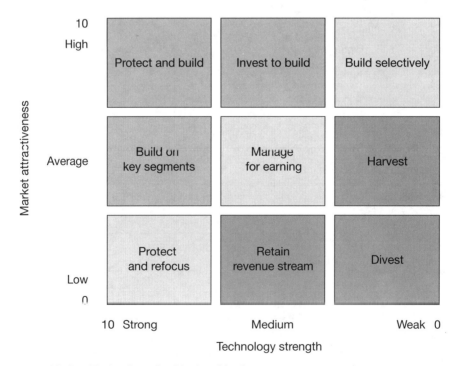

Figure 11.4 Market–Technology Positioning Matrix

THE GENERAL STRATEGIC OPTIONS

In the following sections the generic strategy indicated by each position in Figure 11.4 is outlined, followed by a checklist of key action points that are required to implement the strategic option.

Strategy 1: Protect and Build

In many respects this is an ideal position to be in. The technology in the analysis is strong, measured both in terms of the company's objective standing in it and in terms of its distinctiveness in the minds of customers. The market in which the technology is applied is also attractive. A key issue facing a company in this situation is how to defend its position. Obviously, this defence will include continued attention to the technology itself. The extent of investment in the technology cannot be considered in isolation and must relate to the life cycle position of the technology, the technological position of other companies in the surrounding network and the potential for exploitation of the technology in this and other applications. Market success is unlikely to be based on a single technology. The technology in the analysis will be supported by other technologies. For example, if it is a product technology then continued success in this or other applications will depend on the availability of appropriate process technologies, either from within the company or externally. Similarly, strength in both product and process technologies will be nullified if the company does not have access to the requisite marketing technology to complete the necessary 'bundle' for this application. It is our experience that companies with strength in a single technology often fail to capitalise on that strength by initial inadequacies in support technologies or by failing to manage the continued availability and development of that technology. A company in this cell must also consider defensive moves. These may involve the creation of market entry barriers, including technological ones and the utilisation of the firm's experience and learning to obtain efficiency in its operations.

The premium positions occupied by companies in cell one cannot warrant long-term success, since the more they develop and market their technologies, the less risky they become, thus enhancing customers' confidence to seek the technologies from companies offering more attractive financial packages. The wide use of a technology by a company and by others exploiting their versions of it can lead to the 'commodification' of that technology, so that it ceases to be distinctive. This means that the company itself must *manage* the distinctiveness of its technologies. The company must invest resources towards projecting a technology-leading or distinctive 'image' in the minds of customers. One aspect of this is for companies to collaborate closely with lead users who can play a significant role in whether or not their technologies would become the standard in the industry.

Finally, the technology strength represented by this cell is a prime asset for the company and it faces the task of maximising its rate of return on that asset. This is unlikely to be achieved within a single market application. The company must therefore plan the exploitation of the technology in other applications and assemble the necessary bundle of technologies to achieve success in these applications. In other words, to create new strategic technology areas.

Action Points

✓ Invest to grow
✓ Maintain and develop technology's strengths
✓ Go for technology leadership
✓ Build market entry barriers: technological, price, service, geography, customer knowledge, etc. Promote image of technological leader
✓ Seek alternative methods for commercialising technology
✓ Seek opportunities for technology exploitation in new applications or industries
✓ Look for other problem-solving opportunities e.g. benefit segmentation

Strategy 2: Invest to build

This strategy option comes to play when a firm finds itself in a highly attractive market offering many opportunities for growth, but which cannot be fully exploited because its technological base is only of 'medium' strength (the example which follows will provide an explanation of this term). In this position significant investments in marketing are likely to be required for the firm to keep up with the rapid growth rates that are typical of highly attractive markets. The customer attractiveness matrix (see previous section) will provide insight as to whether investments should by pursued in an aggressive or non-aggressive manner.

Aggressive actions may involve challenging for technological leadership. However, becoming or attempting to become a technological leader is not always the most appropriate move. Decisions on technological investment aimed at achieving leadership will depend on such factors as the life-cycle position of the technology, its potential in other applications and the feasibility of acquiring the technology by different means (see Chapter 6). In many cases it may make more sense to closely follow the technology leader and differentiate the company's overall offering based on strong understanding of the market and customer relationships. In this way, a loyal customer base and strong customer relationships can be used by the company to alleviate some of the effects of its technological weaknesses.

Action Points

✓ Challenge for technology leadership
✓ Build selectively on strengths
✓ Follow closely the leader
✓ Reinforce vulnerable technology areas
✓ Look for joint ventures/collaborative opportunities with technology leaders or innovators

✓ Develop customer relationships and service provision to supplement technology offering

✓ Enhance customer value of your total offer

Strategy 3: Build selectively

In this situation the firm is faced with a weak technology in an attractive market. The choices facing the company relate to both the technology and the market application. The weakness of the company's technology may make it seem attractive to invest to improve this position. However, this is likely to be expensive, even if the company has the capability to accomplish it. It is unlikely to be worthwhile to invest in the development of a technology if it is in the later stages of its life-cycle. Instead, it may make sense to acquire an up-dated technology through licensing or through a joint venture based on the company's market strength. However, any joint venture based on a company's market position but lack of technology may make that company vulnerable to being displaced from its market position by the partner providing technology. Alternatively, the company may be able to cope with its technological weakness by seeking protected market niches in which to specialise. If neither of these alternatives is feasible or the costs or risks are excessive, then an exit should be considered.

It is important when considering these alternatives to realise that highly attractive markets with rapid growth rates may offer strategic opportunity windows for brief time periods. Although the identification of these windows is a matter of the firm's ability to sense the key opportunities of the market, their utilisation depends upon a clear understanding of the firm's strengths in the product, customer and technology areas which will have been identified using the analysis that we have described above.

Action Points

✓ Specialise around limited strengths

✓ Seek ways to overcome technology weaknesses

✓ Consider bringing in new technologies

✓ Consider technological partnerships

✓ Withdraw if technology position cannot be improved

✓ Diversify based on customer relationships

Strategy 4: Build on key segments

This cell represents a company in a strong technological position in markets of only average attractiveness. Managers will be disappointed by the fact that the results of their technological leadership and capacity to innovate are not followed by premium benefits in the market place. This creates a chasm in the revenue stream of these firms that can have dramatic implications in the ability of the firm to continue investing in developing and maintaining their technology lead.

One market-based way of solving this conundrum is to identify the relative strengths and weaknesses of the firm against the different segments of customers in the market. Through this, key segments with sufficiently different characteristics can be identified and more effort put into adding value appropriate to their specific needs, independent of the market as a whole. The firm is presented with a number of options after the assessment of its current and potential customer segments and the fit with its strengths. If they decide to compete in cost-sensitive segments they should augment their profitability by increasing productivity in their operations by means of process innovations.

However, a company in this cell has a strong technological asset. Gaining an enhanced return on the investment that this represents could involve an attempt to 'shake-up' the existing market application by innovation on the basis of the technology. Alternatively, the company could seek to change the characteristics of the market and reduce its costs by joint development work with suitable companies in the market. If these actions are not feasible then the company will need to seek new applications for its technology and that may well involve investments in the technology itself, in support technologies or in customer relationship building.

Action Points

✓ Emphasise profitability by increasing productivity
✓ Consider process innovations to increase productivity
✓ Build up ability to counter competition
✓ Identify new opportunities in existing markets for technology applications
✓ Concentrate on profitable segments in existing markets
✓ Consider new technology applications in new markets
✓ Consider transferring existing technology applications to new markets

Strategy 5: Manage for earnings

Companies that find themselves in this 'middle' position possess medium technology strength in a market of average attractiveness. The situation does not justify heavy investment in order to boost the technology, because the market potential as a whole does not warrant it.

Paradoxically, however, both 'bold moves' and 'incremental adjustments' are required in order to develop a strategy aimed at managing the position to maximise earnings. Incremental adjustments will require a clear identification of the technological and market strengths that can be maintained, enhanced and protected through existing barriers of competitive entry and selective investment. Identification of these strengths can help the firm in strengthening its position in segments where there is a close fit between customer demands and its technology. However, bold moves are required to allow its position to erode in segments where costs exceed benefits and the probability of defence against competitive entry is low. Similarly, it may well be necessary to cease development in the technology and then perhaps buy in offerings based on other companies' technologies. A decision of this sort can only be made after the value of the technology in other applications has been considered and the prospects for successful development have been evaluated.

It should be remembered here that managing for earnings through administrative and organisational means does not mean surrendering growth. Instead it may lead to identification of competitive advantage in areas overlooked by the technological leaders in these segments. In addition by withdrawing from some unprofitable segments and unproductive technologies, the firm could free resources that can be invested in strengthening its position further.

Action Points

✓ Invest to improve position only in areas where risk is low
✓ Consider low-cost applications of existing technology
✓ Concentrate on most valuable customer groups
✓ Protect existing strengths and position
✓ Consider administrative/organisational methods to reduce cost and increase efficiency of operations
✓ Consider withdrawal from the technology

Strategy 6: Harvest

The weak technology of a firm in this position indicates that it should consider managing the technology for cash by minimum investment and rationalisation of operations. Modest harvesting is typical of firms in maturing or declining markets/sectors in which competitive technological efforts cannot be matched. Harvesting can be rewarding because it contributes short-term cash flows, which can be invested elsewhere. It is wrong to equate harvest with surrender because it allows the competitive position of the firm to erode rapidly. On the contrary, a conscious managerial decision of placing bets where the chances of success are higher can rejuvenate the viability of the firm in the long run.

To this end, a careful assessment of the company's technologies is required in order to determine their effective re-direction with the aim of exploiting opportunities that may appear in markets with average attractiveness.

Action Points

✓ Minimise investments and focus operations
✓ Exploit people's skills and technologies to develop markets
✓ Consider joint ventures to bring in technologies in order to protect existing customer base
✓ Consider slow phase out of technology to maximise revenue

Strategy 7: Protect and refocus

The combination of a strong technology and low market attractiveness allows management to utilise their technology-based competitive advantage as cash generation mechanism. This will require, however, careful identification of attractive segments of customers within the overall market and a sensible pricing policy to eliminate the competition or to protect share in the market whilst reaping the rewards of its technological strength. The long-term viability of the firm is ensured only if the additional cash generated is invested to defend the strengths of the firm and refocus its directions towards the more attractive segments and new market applications.

In addition, the analysis of customer attractiveness results will allow management to determine whether or not the combination of a strong technological basis and close customer relationship can give rise to new business opportunities that can create customer accounts with increasing demand in the long run.

Additionally, the company faces the task of exploiting a valuable and probably expensively acquired technology in more conducive applications. This may require new marketing skills or the addition of support technologies. If this is not possible, then the company will have to consider external exploitation such as licensing-out or joint ventures.

Action Points

✓ Defend strengths
✓ Seek ways to increase earnings without speeding market's decline
✓ Look for new markets and new applications
✓ Consider low-cost application of technology
✓ Exploit technology through licensing or joint venture
✓ Capitalise on customer relationship to create new business opportunities

Strategy 8: Retain revenue stream

A company in this cell differs from the previous one in that its technology is only of medium-strength and the market is one of low attractiveness. This company could adopt a strategy for maintaining their revenue stream with lower operational costs. This can be achieved by means of minimising investment in the technology and in the market and concentrating efforts in customer segments, which are still profitable. Minimisation of investments, however, runs the risk of further erosion of the technological base. This may have negative consequences in the long run. Indeed the unattractive market may force some firms to exit. The ones that will survive will have the opportunity to operate in a different competitive environment and retain their revenue stream.

Furthermore, the unattractive character of the market suggests that firms with medium technological strength should explore the option of utilising their technological expertise in other more attractive markets. Clearly the market identification and positioning problem requires marketing technology in addition to strength in product or process technologies. This can be achieved by means of collaborative arrangements with firms knowledgeable about market conditions elsewhere. The decision whether to remain in the current market or gradually withdraw with an intention to look for other applications of the technology elsewhere will depend on the results of the customer attractiveness ratings. Where existing or prospective customers do not show signs of future recovery, a phased withdrawal should be considered.

Action Points

✓ Minimise investment
✓ Maintain low-cost operations to serve low-profit market
✓ Consider second generation and intermediate technology applications to other markets
✓ Consider combinations with other technologies
✓ Consider collaboration with firm possessing market knowledge of other more attractive markets.

Strategy 9: Divest

In the case of a firm with a low technological basis operating in an unattractive market it is most likely that the long-run problems will overwhelm any prospect of profits. In such a situation the appropriate strategy entails planned exit from this market, divesting the technology and channelling the firm's efforts and resources elsewhere. Normally, investments are minimised in this situation although selective low-cost, low-risk moves can extend the life of the technology briefly and enhance possible selling prices. Also, the requirements of existing and other potential customers should be carefully evaluated in an attempt to determine how the technology should be eliminated and whether it could be re-introduced as a 'special' to serve the needs of customers elsewhere (e.g. developing countries). Such moves may allow the firm to retain a steady, albeit poor, revenue stream and divert resources to more attractive technologies, products, markets and customer segments.

Action Points

✓ Sell when possible to maximise cash value
✓ Cut fixed costs and avoid further investments
✓ Consider other countries and overseas second generation applications
✓ Maintain low-cost operations to serve low-profit market

GUIDELINES FOR USE OF THE FRAMEWORK

It is important to recognise that these strategies outlined above provide generic options for managing the technology assets of the organisation. The array of generic market-technology strategies offered by the matrix serves primarily as a framework within which management can identify and evaluate the strategic possibilities for their business units. However, the feasibility of the specific options in each situation is dictated by a number of factors such as the macro-environment of the business and the needs of its internal and external stakeholders.

Although the choice of a strategy will depend on the positioning of the business unit in the market-technology matrix, it should be noted that in some 'borderline' cases the analysis might recommend a 'combination' of strategies to fit the specifics of the situation faced by the firm in different technological spaces and market arenas. Furthermore, the implementation of any one of these strategies requires the further development of detailed action steps, resource deployments and viability of operations in that individual situation. This particular stage is highly creative and requires decisiveness and reflection. The methods and concepts described in the various parts of this chapter can facilitate this process.

Applying this framework for technology analysis in several firms has produced other benefits beyond the development of the strategy itself. These include:

1 The analysis leads to the identification of key success factors regarding the products, markets, customers and technologies under review.
2 It identifies the business's strengths and weaknesses in these factors.
3 The framework provides a common language that all members of the management team can use to describe both the current situation they face and the options that should be considered for strategic action.
4 The process promotes a dialogue and exchange between managers, engineers, R&D staff and other personnel in the various functions who are required to be involved in assessing the various aspects of the business that are outlined in the methodology in this chapter.
5 The framework amalgamates diverse functional and disciplinary views within the business regarding its technological position and the strategic options it faces.

Example
Formulating technology strategy in
Electrosonic Co.

Company Background[4]

This is a medium-sized research-based firm that was set up by two entrepreneurs in the 1960s as a spin-off from a major electronics group and a university research laboratory. When the founders pulled out in the early 1990s it was subsequently taken over in a management buy-out and is now owned by the main directors two of whom are non-executive. The firm is now organised in three divisions. One conducts contract R&D in military (70 per cent) and civilian (30 per cent) applications of primarily electronics, vibration analysis and ultrasonic technologies with 38 employees; a second develops and manufactures a range of equipment and precision instruments, utilising technologies that were internally and externally acquired, for the aerospace, marine, petrochemical, mining and telecommunications industries (47 staff). The third grouping is a small technical consultancy arm with five staff.

The company was both technologically and commercially successful, with a turnover of £18m in 1999. It had, however, reached the stage where the management team were concerned that several market opportunities were being overlooked by the very nature of the technical, research-driven nature of its key actors (i.e. themselves!). The technical developments tended to be driven by a combination of key customer requirements and contracts and 'R&D momentum'. The Technical Director expressed this as follows, 'Once a project starts it is hard to stop unless the prospects of completion are far off and it is eating money hand over fist, or another more pressing call on researchers' time comes into play'. Although technical networks and knowledge was excellent in existing and potential emergent fields, it was felt that market knowledge beyond existing sectors and customers was negligible. Growth areas and new applications of existing products and techniques were not being developed or even considered in many cases. Indeed the company was only aware that opportunities existed either when customers came to them or they saw competitors' developments taking shape in new markets/ applications where the company had an obvious capability.

The aim of the analysis in this case is help the company to develop a technology strategy that is coherent, integrated and pro-active. This contrasts with the *ad hoc*, technically driven, but successful direction which had been the pattern in the past.

The Process

It is possible to begin the analysis process either from the starting point of a specific market, a specific product or a specific tech-nology. In this case we start with a product offering or offering group, then the technol-ogies supporting that product are identified and similarly the markets served by the product. Alternatively, if we commence with a technology, the products that it sup-ports are identified first and then the markets served by them. Wherever the process begins, eventually it builds up to create an overview map, of all the company's signifi-cant technologies, products and markets.

Although the extrapolation of this exer-cise to cover all the customers, technologies and products of even such a medium-sized firm may appear a daunting and exhaustive exercise, in practice most technology-based firms or business units of this scale will not have more than six or eight key product groups which will account for the majority of sales. Equally, the significant technol-ogies on which companies like this depend and those that are distinctive will be small in number. Such firms are comparatively specialised and offer value through the exploitation of a relatively small number of technologies in narrow applications. In addition, we have found that once this process has been conducted for one area (market, product offering or technology)

the managers and engineers involved rapidly learn how to carry out the analysis for other areas and thus the process speeds up. Usually the analysis involves a group such as the technology/engineering manager/ technical director; the marketing director/ manager; a senior manager with knowledge of specific operations, technology and sales and the managing director/chief executive/ head of the business unit particularly in the early stages.

All four categories of staff carried out the analysis described here, within the con-straints of their expertise. After this stage they met to compare their respective scores for each of the sections on product, market, customers and technologies and to agree composite scores for each question. As well as resulting in an agreed (or at least composite) score, the discussion itself pro-duced useful ideas and sharing of views across disciplinary functions. Even though the managers disagreed, they found the dia-logue productive and informative. Such meeting can rarely occur beyond the first round and therefore with self-completion rounds the scores are averaged.

The Assessment Scores

In the case of Electrosonic Co. here, the basic steps in the analysis are building up to the identification of the strategic alterna-tives appropriate for one key product and its supporting technologies and its market pos-sibilities. The results shown here are the composite scores for one product which managers in the firm chose to analyse, its associated technologies, customers and markets. The product consists of an 'anti-noise' system, based on acoustics technol-ogy, which had been developed elsewhere for military application. The key equipment was bought in by the company, based on the supplier's technology and adapted by Electrosonic's engineers for installation in civilian passenger aircraft.

For each of the four sections covering product strength, market attractiveness, customer attractiveness and technology strength each respondent gave two ratings on a score from 1–10 to each factor listed (prior to this they are asked to add any other factors to each list if they consider them relevant). This is shown in Table 11.5 below

The first 'weighting' column shows how important each factor is considered to be by the managers for succcss in that product, that technology or that market in *general*. For example, in any market for this product, the importance of its size for attractiveness is rated '3' and its profitability is rated '10'. This suggests that when assessing potential market application for the AntiNoise product Electrosonic's managers consider that it is better to have a small profitable market than one with large potential scale. The second column shows the rating for this factor for this particular product, market, technology, etc. So the chosen market selected here, aircraft construction and design, scores '5' for size and '8' for profitability.

The third column shows the total composite strength rating for each factor by multiplying $W \times R$ on a scale of 1–100. The rationale for distinguishing W from R is that some factors are comparatively much more important for, say, customer attractiveness, than others. A high rating in this case in customer innovativeness (W5) would be considered a much less important customer feature than a high level of relationship maturity (W10). The totals for column 3 for each section are translated to and averaged out of 10 for the factors in that section, e.g. overall product strength is 6.72; market attractiveness 6.72, customer attractiveness 8.54; technology strength 5.88. These points

are then plotted on the positioning matrices. (See Fig. 11.4)

Identifying the Appropriate Strategic Option

The strategy indicated by the combination of scores on the overall market-technology positioning matrix is strategy 2 – Invest to Build. (See Fig. 11.4) Here the firm operates in an attractive market, but growth is limited by a medium-strength technology. Fleshing out this strategic option for Electrosonic Co. involved a more detailed examination of the factor scores in order to reveal key strengths and weaknesses in the technology, product, market and customer areas.

The market attractiveness index is only just in the high category with a score of 6.7. Its strengths are partially offset by lower than average potential and relative lack of ability to enforce barriers to competitors. The position on this dimension is stronger than this score suggests because within this market sector the customer base to which the company's technologies are applied in this case is very attractive because of much higher long-term prospects and excellent collaboration, resulting in a high overall score of 8.5. Therefore, while the customer base should be defended and carefully developed, the emphasis on the investment-to-build must be on improving the technology strengths.

For the technology, there were strengths in the number of customers and products it supported and in its compatibility with other technologies required for this application. The key weakness was the fact that the technology was basic and external to the company, rather than internal and distinctive. The technology was embodied in an ultrasonic kit, which was manufactured elsewhere using acoustics-based technologies

Table 11.5 Electrosonic Co. Ratings

	Factor	Weighting	Rating	Total
Product Strength	Product	AntiNoise		
	Cost effectiveness	10	8	80
	Product diversity	10	9	90
	Price competition	7	5	35
	Product quality	10	8	80
	Additional product features	7	8	56
	Stage of development/maturity	4	7	28
	Product flexibility	5	5	25
	Vary capacity	8	4	32
	Research and development	10	6	60
	Modern, well located facilities	7	5	35
	Product support service	10	8	80
	Company image	8	8	64
	Advertising/promotion	5	7	35
	Past experience	10	8	80
	Delivery timescales	7	1	7
	Product entry/launch	3	8	24
	Risk	9	8	72
	Through life costs	4	7	28
	Knowledge of customer requirements	10	7	70
	Track record	10	6	60
	ROI	10	5	50
	Ease of use	9	8	72
	Average	*7.9*	*6.6*	*52.9*
	Total for matrix			*6.7*
Market Attractiveness	Market	Aircraft Construction/design		
	Market size	Medium		
	Market size	3	5	15
	Market profitability	10	8	80
	Economic trends	7	4	28
	Political and legal factors	5	1	5
	Stage of development/maturity	Mature		
	Maturity	7	4	28
	Competitive structure	10	7	70
	Long term potential	10	7	70
	Market stability	8	6	48
	Competitors	Few		
	Barriers to entry	8	10	80
	Innovation	6	7	42
	Ability to enforce barriers	10	6	60
	Market presence	10	8	80
	Knowledge of the market	7	8	56
	Ability to evaluate the market	8	6	48
	OEM potential	10	9	90
	Average	*7.9*	*6.4*	*53.3*
	Total for matrix			*6.7*

Table 11.5 Continued

	Factor	Weighting	Rating	Total
Customer Attractiveness	Customer	AeroCo		
	Profit contribution/margins	10	8	80
	Quality/maturity of relationship	10	8	80
	Innovative	5	7	35
	Additional market contacts	8	10	80
	Further orders/long term prospects	10	10	100
	Likely growth	6	6	36
	Demand on resources	8	9	72
	Stability	7	8	56
	Personal relationships	8	8	64
	Collaboration	6	10	60
	Financial reliability/order history	7	9	63
	Size	8	8	64
	Operational philosophy	8	8	64
	Geographical location	5	5	25
	International spread of customers	10	3	30
	Average	7.7	7.8	60.6
	Total for matrix			8.54
Technology Strength Analysis	Technology	Acoustics technology		
	Type	Product		
	Application	Anti-noise		
	Origin	Externally acquired		
	Life cycle	Technology application		
	Cost	High		
	Category	10	1	10
	Standing (this application)	4	4	16
	Standing (other applications)	4	2	8
	Standing (overall)	4	3	12
	Newness	4	4	16
	Number of products	10	9	90
	Number of customers	8	10	80
	Strategic technology area	3	10	30
	Copied by competitors	1	3	3
	Dependence on the technology	10	8	80
	Directly supports the customer	8	7	56
	Performance in acquiring	8	8	64
	Performance in exploiting	8	5	40
	Performance in managing	8	3	24
	Quality assurance	10	3	30
	Compatibility	10	10	100
	Through life costs	8	8	64
	Average	6.9	5.8	42.5
	Total for matrix			5.88

that Electrosonic Co. did not possess. This may go some way to explain why they also had a very poor performance in quality assurance despite its critical requirement for the key market, aircraft manufacture. Therefore the strategy to improve their position should concentrate on overcoming these weaknesses by other means. These could include attempts to find other means of acquiring internal distinctive technology in acoustics, such as by internal R&D. Alternatively the company could invest to improve its quality levels, perhaps employing engineers with experience of aerospace quality control techniques (a supporting process technology). The company could also try to improve its exploitation and management of the technology in this application, however it was acquired. Perhaps also, the company could consider joint ventures with firms with more expertise in acoustics. These would help the company to improve its standing in the technology in the long term. It would be unlikely, and probably unneccessary, for the company to start from this position and achieve technology leadership, given the strengths in the customer base.

NOTES

1 Technology Auditing, Portfolio Analysis and Strategy (TAPAS), a technology decision support tool, jointly developed by Professor M Saren and Dr N Tzokas of the University of Strathclyde with OTM Consulting Ltd., Guildford.
2 For the sake of simplicity we will assume throughout that the analysis is being carried out on a product technology. It is equally applicable to other types of technology.
3 Ford, D., Gadde, L.E., Hakansson, H., Lundgren, A., Snehota, I., Turnbull, P., and Wilson D., *Managing Business Relationships*, Chichester, John Wiley, 1998.
4 The case example described here to illustrate the application of the technology analysis in this chapter is based on an anonymous firm, a fictitious technology and a hypothetical product. The methodology, analysis and strategic options are, however, real.

Index

Page numbers appearing in **bold** refer to figures; those in *italic* refer to tables.